Object-Oriented Design Knowledge:
Principles, Heuristics and Best Practices

Javier Garzás
Oficina de Cooperación Universitaria (OCU) S.A., Spain

Mario Piattini
University of Castilla - La Mancha, Spain

IDEA GROUP PUBLISHING
Hershey • London • Melbourne • Singapore

Acquisitions Editor: Michelle Potter
Development Editor: Kristin Roth
Senior Managing Editor: Jennifer Neidig
Managing Editor: Sara Reed
Copy Editor: April Schmidt
Typesetter: Marko Primorac
Cover Design: Lisa Tosheff
Printed at: Yurchak Printing Inc.

Published in the United States of America by
        Idea Group Publishing (an imprint of Idea Group Inc.)
        701 E. Chocolate Avenue
        Hershey PA 17033
        Tel: 717-533-8845
        Fax: 717-533-8661
        E-mail: cust@idea-group.com
        Web site: http://www.idea-group.com

and in the United Kingdom by
        Idea Group Publishing (an imprint of Idea Group Inc.)
        3 Henrietta Street
        Covent Garden
        London WC2E 8LU
        Tel: 44 20 7240 0856
        Fax: 44 20 7379 0609
        Web site: http://www.eurospanonline.com

Library of Congress Cataloging-in-Publication Data
Library of Congress Cataloging-in-Publication Data

Object-oriented design knowledge : principles, heuristics, and best practices / Javier Garzas and Mario Piattini, editors.
        p. cm.
 Summary: "The software engineering community has advanced greatly in recent years and we currently have numerous defined items of knowledge, such as standards, methodologies, methods, metrics, techniques, languages, patterns, knowledge related to processes, concepts, etc. The main objective of this book is to give a unified and global vision about Micro-Architectural Design Knowledge, analyzing the main techniques, experiences and methods"--Provided by publisher.
 ISBN 1-59140-896-2 (hardcover) -- ISBN 1-59140-897-0 (softcover) -- ISBN 1-59140-898-9 (ebook)
 1. Object-oriented methods (Computer science) 2. Object-oriented programming (Computer science) I. Garzas, Javier, 1975- II. Piattini, Mario, 1966-
  QA76.9.O35.O244 2006
  005.1'17--dc22
                                2006010089

British Cataloguing in Publication Data
A Cataloguing in Publication record for this book is available from the British Library.

All work contributed to this book is new, previously-unpublished material. The views expressed in this book are those of the authors, but not necessarily of the publisher.

Object-Oriented Design Knowledge:
Principles, Heuristics and Best Practices

Table of Contents

Preface

In order to establish itself as a branch of engineering, a profession must understand its accumulated knowledge. In addition, software engineering as a branch of engineering must take several basic steps in order to become an established profession, highlighting understanding of the nature of its knowledge.

Software engineering experts always have used proven ideas. Concretely, in the object-oriented (OO) design knowledge field, the practical experience of it has been crucial to software engineers, and it is in the last years when these ideas, materialized in items such as patterns or refactorings have reached their biggest popularity and diffusion. And in this regard, the software engineering community has advanced greatly and we currently have numerous and defined chunks of knowledge, including standards, methodologies, methods, metrics, techniques, languages, patterns, knowledge related to processes, concepts, and so forth. Although these different areas of knowledge relate to the construction of an OO system, there is a lot of work still to be done in order to systematize and offer this knowledge to designers in such a way that it can be easily used in practical cases.

A software architecture is a description of the subsystems and components of a software system and relationships between then.[1] Usually, the software architecture is subdivided into macro and micro architecture. Whereas macro architecture describes the metamodel of design, this that provides the high-level organization, the micro architecture describes details of a design at a lower level.

OO design is a software design technique, which is expressed in terms of objects and relationships between those; at the level of micro architecture it includes elements such as classes, its relationships, responsibilities, refactorings, and so on.

OO micro architectural knowledge is built upon design experiences, such as problem solving, or lessons learned. Therefore, the OO micro architectural design knowledge has grown with time and the increasing complexity of software. This knowledge expands and accumulates when it is stored in books and other media for the use of designers.

In addition, the major part of OO design knowledge is difficult to identify and use. The experience has demonstrated that design often omits common principles, heuristics, and so on, with a consequent major loss of experience. Consequently, actually, serious difficulties are still encountered when we tackle the construction of OO systems. Although designers have accumulated a body of knowledge that they apply during these processes, this is very implicit. Fortunately, it is now being specified and popularized in different forms: principles, heuristics, patterns, and more recently, refactoring techniques. However, today, the difference between these concepts is generally unclear and not all of them have received the same amount of attention or have reached the same degree of maturity. In addition, a strong knowledge does not exist on items such as design principles, best practices, or heuristics. The problem confronting the designer is how to articulate all this explicit knowledge and to apply it in an orderly and efficient way in the OODA, in such a way that it is really of use to him or her. In fact, in practice, even such advanced subjects like OO patterns have this problem

Design knowledge and best practices are stored in individual expert minds, or implicitly encoded and documented in local organisational processes. It has always been true that a significant part of design knowledge resides in the minds of the experts that make it up. However, communities and companies are beginning to find that it is easy to lose a vital element of their intellectual property: corporate design knowledge. Therefore, we can say that the major part of the design knowledge today is tacit knowledge: it in the form of project experiences, heuristics, or human competencies that are difficult to be captured and externalised.

The effective management of this knowledge is today a significant challenge. For knowledge management to be effective, this knowledge should be organized and classified. In addition, with this purpose, developing unified catalogues of knowledge, ontologies, empirical studies, and so on, books and studies such as those we present here, are very important issues to improve the use of OO design knowledge.

Therefore, in this context, we present this book whose main objective is to give a global vision of micro-architectural design knowledge, exposing the main techniques and methods, and analyzing several aspects related to it.

The subject matter in this book is divided into ten chapters. The chapters seek to provide a critical survey of the fundamental themes, problems, arguments, theories, and methodologies in the field of OO micro architectural design knowledge. Each chapter has been planned as a self-standing introduction to its subject.

Therefore, in **Chapter I** Javier Garzás and Mario Piattini present an introduction to "The Object-Oriented Design Knowledge," where they show the main issues and problems of the field. In OO micro-architectural design knowledge, design patterns are the most popular example of accumulated knowledge, but other elements of knowledge exist such as principles, heuristics, best practices, bad smells, refactorings, and so forth, which are not clearly differentiated; indeed, many are synonymous and others are just vague concepts.

An essential issue to building an OO design knowledge discipline is organizing this knowledge. In **Chapter II**, titled "The Object-Oriented Design Knowledge Ontology," Javier Garzás and Mario Piattini show an ontology that organize and relation the OO knowledge. The authors propose an ontology in order to structure and unify such knowledge. The ontology includes rules (principles, heuristic, bad smells, etc.), patterns, and refactorings. They divide the knowledge on rules, patterns, and refactorings and they show the implications among these. Moreover, they show an empirical validation of the proposed conclusions.

Chapter III, "Using Linguistic Patterns to Model Interactions," by Isabel Díaz, Oscar Pastor Lidia Moreno, and Alfredo Matteo, is a pivotal chapter that changes the focus of the book to more technical information systems issues. This chapter shows an elegant example of how highly relevant clinical questions can be addressed in a scientific manner. In this chapter, heuristic-oriented techniques and linguistics-oriented techniques proposed by several authors to model interactions are analyzed. In addition, a framework to facilitate and to improve the interaction modeling is described. This framework was conceived to be integrated into automatic software production environments. It uses linguistic patterns to recognize interactions from use case models. The validation process used and the main results are also presented.

In **Chapter IV**, Manoli Albert, Marta Ruiz, Javier Muñoz and Vicente Pelechano show "A Framework Based on Design Patterns: Implementing UML Association, Aggregation and Composition Relationships in the Context of Model-Driven Code Generation." The chapter proposes a framework based on design patterns to implement UML (Unified Modeling Language) association, aggregation, and composition relationships, and for it they propose a semantic interpretation of these concepts that avoids the ambiguities introduced by UML.

Therefore, in "Design Patterns as Laws of Quality" Yann-Gaël Guéhéneuc, Jean-Yves Guyomarc'h, Khashayar Khosravi, and Houari Sahraoui, **Chapter V**, show how design patterns can be used as facts to devise a quality model and they describe the processes of building and of applying such a quality model.

The chapter highlights the need for principles in software engineering, where these can be laws or theories formalizing and explaining observations realized on software.

For the sake of completeness in this book, automatic verification of design knowledge is addressed in **Chapter VI**. Andres Flores, Alejandra Cechich, and Rodrigo Ruiz present "Automatic Verification of OOD Pattern Applications."

Chapter VII, "From Bad Smells to Refactoring: Metrics Smoothing the Way", is authored by Yania Crespo, Carlos López, María Esperanza Manso Martínez, and Raúl Marticorena. This chapter discusses one of the current trends in refactorings: when and where we must refactor. From the bad smell concept, it is possible to discover their existence from an objective viewpoint, using metrics. The chapter presents a study on the relation of refactorings, bad smells and metrics, including a case study on the use of metrics in bad smells detection. The chapter leads to the determination where refactoring is the basis of heuristics and metrics, which is likely to be the single most important factor at the moment of use refactorings in the maintenance phase.

Therefore, in **Chapter VIII**, "Heuristics and Metrics for OO Refactoring: A Consolidation and Appraisal of Current Issues," Steve Counsell, Youssef Hassoun, and Deepak Advani cover this topic in great depth. They look at some of the issues which determine when to refactor (i.e., the heuristics of refactoring) and, from a metrics perspective, open issues with measuring the refactoring process. They thus point to emerging trends in the refactoring arena, some of the problems, controversies, and future challenges the refactoring community faces.

A key point to building a OO design knowledge field is to understand the several contributions to it. Since several OO metrics suites have been proposed to measure OO properties, such as encapsulation, cohesion, coupling, and abstraction, both in designs and in code, in **Chapter IX**, titled "A Survey of Object-Oriented Design Quality Improvement," Juan José Olmedilla reviews the literature to find out to which high level quality properties are mapped and if an OO design evaluation model has been formally proposed or even is possible. The chapter is an excellent example of how performing a systematic review of the estate of art.

At last, in **Chapter X**, "A Catalog of OOD Knowledge Rules for OO Micro-Architecture," by Javier Garzás and Mario Piattini, several types of knowledge such as principles, heuristics, bad smells, and so on, are unified in a rules catalog.

In summary, these chapters constitute an evidence of the importance of micro-architectural design knowledge, representing important ideas in different software design areas. These are intended to be useful to a wide audience, including software engineers, designers, project managers, software architects, IS/IT managers, CIOs, CTOs, consultants, and software students.

We hope that the practical vision, scientific evidence and experience presented in this book will enable the reader to use the design knowledge within the field of software engineering and to help the field of software engineering answer how software engineers might acquire its rich and essential accumulated knowledge.

Javier Garzás and Mario Piattini, Editors
Ciudad Real, Spain
January 2006

Endnote

[1]   Buschmann, F., Meunier, R., Rohnert, H., Sommerlad, P., & Stal, M. (1996). *A system of patterns: Pattern-oriented software architecture*. Addison-Wesley.

Acknowledgments

We would like to thank all the authors, because without their contribution this book would not have been possible. We would also like to thank Kristin Roth, our development editor, for her help and encouragement.

Chapter I

The Object-Oriented Design Knowledge

Javier Garzás, Oficina de Cooperación Universitaria (OCU) S.A., Spain

Mario Piattini, University of Castilla - La Mancha, Spain

Abstract

In order to establish itself as a branch of engineering, a profession must understand its accumulated knowledge. In this regard, software engineering has advanced greatly in recent years, but it still suffers from the lack of a structured classification of its knowledge. In this sense, in the field of object-oriented micro-architectural design designers have accumulated a large body of knowledge and it is still have not organized or unified. Therefore, items such as design patterns are the most popular example of accumulated knowledge, but other elements of knowledge exist such as principles, heuristics, best practices, bad smells, refactorings, and so on, which are not clearly differentiated; indeed, many are synonymous and others are just vague concepts.

Introduction

"Chaos is order waiting to be deciphered"

~ José Saramago

Twenty years ago, Redwine (1984) commented that "an expert in a field must know about 50,000 chunks of information, where a chunk is any cluster of knowledge sufficiently familiar that it can be remembered rather than derived," adding that in mature areas it usually takes about 10 years to acquire this knowledge. Since then, many authors (Shaw, 1990) have commented on the need for defined chunks of knowledge in the software engineering field. In this regard, the software engineering community has advanced greatly in recent years, and we currently have numerous and defined chunks of knowledge, including standards, methodologies, methods, metrics, techniques, languages, patterns, knowledge related to processes, concepts, and so on.

Nevertheless, the field of software engineering is still beset by a lack of structured and classified chunks of knowledge (McConnell, 2003) and not all knowledge is transmitted, accessible or studied in the same way. For example, what and where is the enormous amount of practical knowledge regarding object-oriented micro-architectural design? We mean *knowledge* that has been accumulated from the experience of working with the inherent properties of software, knowledge which normally comes under what is generally accepted or "practices which are applicable to most projects, about which there is a widespread consensus regarding value and usefulness" (Bourque & Dupuis, 2004, p. A-10). Such knowledge may take the form of a source code, components, frameworks, and so on, but these are no mechanisms for obtaining designs throughout the software life cycle.

At this point, many will have already identified one of the essential items of knowledge based on experience with object-oriented micro-architectural design: design patterns. These are just the tip of the iceberg. Let us simplify matters and suppose that we want to specialize as software engineers in object-oriented design. By means of projects like SWEBOK, we can now ascertain what "design" is, how it is subdivided, find the main bibliographical references, and so on, and quite easily acquire a sound theoretical knowledge. If indeed we concentrate part of our professional activity on design, we find that we need to study the practical experience of other experts in the area, and at that moment, the concept of *pattern* occurs to us. Yet, after examining the main pattern references in object-oriented design, we still feel that something is missing. Missing elements for the formulation of a good micro-architectural design include principles, heuristics, best practices, bad smells, refactorings, and so on. Table 1 gives an example of each of these.

Table 1. Examples of OO design knowledge

PRINCIPLES
The Dependency Inversion Principle (DIP) "Depend upon Abstractions. Do not depend upon concretions" (Martin, 1996).
HEURISTICS
"If two or more classes only share common interface (i.e., messages, not methods), then they should inherit from a common base class only if they will be used polymorphically" (Riel, 1996).
BEST PRACTICES
"See objects as bundles of behavior, not bundles of data" (Venners, 2004).
BAD SMELLS
Refused bequest Subclasses that do not use what they inherit (Fowler, Beck, Brant, Opdyke, & Roberts, 2000).
REFACTORINGS
Extract Interface "Several clients use the same subset of a class's interface, or two classes have part of their interfaces in common. Extract the subset into an interface. [...]" (Fowler et al., 2000).
PATTERNS
Observer "Intent: Define a one-to-many dependency between objects so that when one object changes state, all its dependents are notified and updated automatically" (Gamma, Helm, Johnson, & Vlissides, 1995).

Considerable progress has been made in the accumulation of experience-based knowledge of OO micro-architectural design, but we have advanced considerably less in its exploitation and classification. This could be seen as a case of the "Feigenbaum Bottleneck": "as domain complexity grows, it becomes very difficult for human experts to formulate their knowledge as practical strategies" (Pescio, 1997).

First, in the following section, we will analyze the maintenance and design patterns and relationship with analyzability and changeability in more detail. Later, we will show a measurement of the impact of the patterns used. In the last sections, we present acknowledgments, our conclusions and future projects, and references.

The Object-Oriented Design Knowledge

Serious difficulties are still encountered when we tackle the construction of OO systems, especially in the transition between the analysis processes and the OO design, an aspect which is very vague in this type of paradigm (Henderson, Seller & Eduards, 1990). In practice, designers have accumulated a body of knowledge that they apply during these processes. Up until a few years ago, this knowledge was very implicit but fortunately, it is now being specified and popularized in different forms: principles, heuristics, patterns and more recently, refactoring, and so on. The difference between these concepts is generally unclear and not all of them have received the same amount of attention or have reached the same degree of maturity.

In fact, OO design principles are often confused and few formalized. In this regard, there are few works about it, with the exception of the contributions of a few (Gamma et al., 1995; Liskov & Zilles, 1974; Martin, 1995, 1996; Meyer, 1997).

Regarding OO design heuristics the main works to which we can refer are those of Riel (1996) and Booch (1996).

Patterns, however, are without doubt one of the elements that have undergone the greatest evolution and proof of this is the existence of numerous publications on the theme. The application of patterns in OO began at the beginning of this decade (Coad, 1992) and was consolidated by the work of Gamma et al. (1995), Buschmann, Meunier, Rohnert, Sommerlad, and Stal (1996), Fowler (1996), and Rising (1998). Amongst the different types of patterns, we can distinguish, mainly, although other categories exist (antipatterns, specific domains, etc.):

- **Architectural:** These focus on the structure of the system, the definition of subsystems, their responsibilities and rules.
- **Object-oriented analysis/design (OOAD):** To support the refining of the subsystems and components as well as the relationships between them.
- **Idioms:** They help us to implement particular aspects of the design in a specific programming language.

As we already know, the use of patterns means that we can avoid constant reinvention, thus reducing costs and saving time. Gamma et al., 1995 point out that one thing that expert designers do not do is resolve each problem from the beginning. When they find a good solution, they use it repeatedly. This experience is what makes them experts. However, at the present time, when patterns are used, several types of problems can occur (Schmidt, 1995; Wendorff, 2001): difficult application, difficult learning, temptation to recast everything as a pattern, pattern overload, ignorance, deficiencies in catalogs, and so forth.

Refactoring techniques are characterized by their immaturity, although it is true to say that this topic is rapidly gaining acceptance, the main works in this area are Kent Beck and Fowler's (2000), Tokuda and Batory (2001), and Opdyke (1992).

The problem confronting the designer is how to articulate all this explicit knowledge and to apply it in an orderly and efficient fashion in the OODA, in such a way that it is really of use to him or her. In fact, in practice, even such advanced subjects like patterns have this problem. Ralph Johnson comments in this sense that "for one thing, the large number of patterns that have been discovered so far need to be organized. Many of them are competitors; we need to experiment and find which are best to use. ... Analyzing existing patterns, or making tools that use patterns, or determining the effectiveness of patterns, could all be good topics" (Johnson, 2000, personal communication). These problems could give rise to incorrect applications of the patterns (Wendorff, 2001).

The differences between these elements are not clear. Many concern a single concept with different names, while others on occasions do not contain knowledge gained from experience, and still others are simply vague concepts. This confusion leads to a less efficient use of knowledge, so concepts such as principles or heuristics are still unknown to some software engineers, few of whom understand completely their goals or relationships. This problem has been brought up at several major congresses, for example the OOPSLA 2001 Workshop: "Beyond Design: Patterns (mis)used," where such authors as Schwanninger (2001) say "We got more and more aware that a good description of the proposed solution is necessary, but useless for the reader if the problem and the forces that drive the relationship between problem and solution are not covered properly."

Conclusion

Expert designers have always used proven ideas. It is in recent years when these ideas, materialized mainly into the pattern concept, have reached their greatest popularity and diffusion. However, more knowledge exists apart from that related to patterns, although it would be true to say that this other knowledge is frequently "hidden." We should consider that OO micro architectural design knowledge is associated with the pattern concept, but other elements exist, such as principles, heuristics, best practices, bad smells, and so forth. These other elements show a confused description, unification, definition, and so on.

Therefore, few studies systematize and offer the OO design knowledge to designers in such a way that it can be easily used in practical cases. In addition, the different studies published show the elements related to design knowledge in a disconnected way. There has not been much effort made on empirical studies about OO design knowledge, and the few works we have found are mainly focused on design patterns.

As Shaw (1990) states, a branch of engineering must take several basic steps in order to become an established profession, highlighting understanding of the nature of knowledge. We as a discipline must ask how software engineers might acquire this knowledge.

References

Abran, A., Moore, J. W., Bourque, P., & Dupuis, R. (Eds.). (2004). *Guide to the software engineering body of knowledge: SWEBOK*. Los Alamos, CA: IEEE CS Press.

Booch, G. (1996). *Object solutions. Managing the object-oriented project*. Redwood City, CA: Addison-Wesley.

Buschmann, F., Meunier, R., Rohnert, H., Sommerlad, P., & Stal, M. (1996). *A system of patterns: Pattern-oriented software architecture*. New York: John Wiley & Sons.

Coad, P. (1992). Object-oriented patterns. *Communications of the ACM, 35*(9), 152-159.

Fowler, M. (1996). *Analysis patterns: Reusable object models*. Boston, MA: Addison-Wesley.

Fowler, M., Beck, K., Brant, J., Opdyke, W., & Roberts, D. (2000). *Refactoring: Improving the design of existing code* (1st ed.). Boston: Addison-Wesley Professional.

Gamma, E., Helm, R., Johnson, R., & Vlissides, J. (1995). *Design patterns*. Reading, MA: Addison-Wesley Professional.

Henderson Seller, B., & Eduards, J. M. (1990). The object-oriented system life cycle. *Communications of the ACM, 33*(9), 142-159.

Liskov, B. H., & Zilles, S. N. (1974). Programming with abstract data types. *SIGPLAN Notices, 9*(4), 50-59.

Martin, R. C. (1995). Object-oriented design quality metrics: An analysis of dependencies. *ROAD, 2*(3).

Martin, R. C. (1996). The dependency inversion principle. *C++ Report, 8*(6), 61-66.

McConnell, S. (2003). *Professional software development*. Boston: Addison-Wesley.

Meyer, B. (1997). *Object-oriented software construction* (2nd ed.). Upper Saddle River, NJ: Prentice Hall.

Opdyke, W. (1992). *Refactoring Object Oriented Frameworks.* Illinois, Urbana-Champain.

Pescio, C. (1997). Principles versus patterns. *Computer, 30*(9), 130-131.

Redwine, S. T. (1984). *DOD-related software technology requirements, practices, and prospects for the future* (Tech. Rep. No. P-1788). Alexandria, VA: Institute of Defense Analyses.

Riel, A. J. (1996). *Object-oriented design heuristics.* Boston: Addison-Wesley Professional.

Rising, L. (1998). *The patterns handbook: Techniques, strategies, and applications.* Cambridge: Cambridge University Press.

Schmidt, D. C. (1995). Experience using design patterns to develop reusable object-oriented communication software. *Communications of the ACM, 38*(10), 65-74.

Schwanninger, C. (2001). *Patterns as problem indicators.* Paper presented at the Workshop on Beyond Design Patterns (mis)Used. OOPSLA, Tampa Bay, FL.

Shaw, M. (1990). Prospects for an engineering discipline of software. *IEEE Software, 7*(6), 15-24.

Tokuda, L., & Batory, D. (2001). Evolving object-oriented designs with refactoring. *Automated Software Engineering, 8*(1), 89-120.

Venners, B. (2004). *Interface design best practices in object-oriented API design in Java.* Retrieved March 25, 2006, from http://www.artima.com/interfacedesign/contents.html

Wendorff, P. (2001). *Assessment of design patterns during software reengineering: Lessons learned from a large commercial project.* Paper presented at the Proceedings of the 5th European Conference on Software Maintenance and Reeingineering (CSMR).

Chapter II

The Object-Oriented Design Knowledge Ontology

Javier Garzás, Oficina de Cooperación Universitaria (OCU) S.A., Spain

Mario Piattini, University of Castilla - La Mancha, Spain

Abstract

It has been a long time since the object-oriented (OO) paradigm appeared. From that moment, designers have accumulated much knowledge in design and construction of OO systems. Patterns are the most refined OO design knowledge. However, there are many others kinds of knowledge than are not yet classified and formalized. Therefore, we feel it necessary to define ontology in order to structure and unify such knowledge; a good understanding of practical experience is crucial to software engineers. Therefore, this chapter proposes an ontology for object-oriented design knowledge.

Introduction

Since Simula 67 up until the present day, knowledge related to the construction of object-oriented (OO) systems has evolved significantly. Nowadays, due to experience acquired during years of investigation and development of OO systems, numerous techniques and methods that facilitate their design are available to us.

By the middle of the 1990s the first catalogue of patterns was published by Gamma, Helm, Johnson, and Vlissides (1995). The application of patterns in OO design was consolidated, among others, by the work of Coad (1992), Gamma et al. (1995), Buschmann, Meunier, Rohnert, Sommerlad, and Stal (1996), Fowler (1996), and Rising (1998).

However, more knowledge exists apart from that related to patterns, and this other knowledge is frequently "hidden." Moreover, now the exclusive use of patterns is not sufficient to guide a design, and the designer's experience is necessary to avoid overload, non-application or the wrong use of patterns due to unawareness, or any other problems that may give rise to faulty and counteractive use of the patterns. In summary, when patterns are used, several types of problems may occur (Wendorff, 2001): difficult application, difficult learning, temptation to recast everything as a pattern, pattern overload, deficiencies in catalogues (search and complex application, high dependence of the programming language, and comparatives), and so on.

In this sense, we need others' chunks of knowledge such as principles, heuristic, patterns, best practices, bad smells, refactorings, and so on. Nevertheless, there is much uncertainty with the previous elements, and these elements have never been studied as a whole. Its compatibility has been studied nor does a method based in this knowledge exist.

In order to improve OO designs, using all OO design knowledge in a more systematic and effective way, we have defined an ontology, which unifies principles, heuristics, best practices, and so on, under the term of "rule"; the ontology show the relationship among these "rules" and patterns and refactorings. We have also defined an improved OOD process, which takes into account this ontology and the OOD knowledge.

Moreover, we present in this chapter an empirical evaluation of this approach. The empirical validation is based on Prechelt, Unger, Philippsen, and Tichy (1997); Prechelt, Unger, Tichy, Bössler, and Votta (2001); and Wohlin, Runeson, Höst, Ohlson, Regnell, and Wesslen (2000). This controlled experiment is ascertain if the usage of the ontology for OOD knowledge really improves the OOD process, helping in the detection of defects (rules violated) and solutions (patterns).

Ontology

An ontology describes knowledge of a domain in a generic way and provides an agreed understanding of it.

Ontologies have a number of advantages: structuring and unifying accumulated knowledge, benefits for communication, teaching concepts and their relationships, sharing of knowledge and resolving terminological incompatibilities. It would therefore be beneficial to define an ontology for the structuring and unifying of OO micro-architectural design knowledge (see Figure 2).

Before describing the ontology, we shall explain its field and scope. To this end and to avoid ambiguity, we start by referring to the SWEBOK (Abran, 2004) to ascertain where an ontology for OO micro-architectural design knowledge could fit in, to find that it falls under "software design" (see Figure 1). What is not so clear, however, is which of the five sub-areas of software design it belongs to (see Figure 1), although we do find places for two elements of knowledge: principles within "basic concepts" ("enabling techniques" in the SWEBOK text) and design patterns in "structure and architecture." However, the place of such other concepts as refactorings is not so obvious (it is only briefly touched on in the maintenance section). As our ontology concentrates on micro-architectures, after examining the other areas, we consider the best place to be "structure and architecture," as this is what the strategies of architectural design are focused on. Our proposition (see Figure 1) is to include a more generic area within

Figure 1. Context and situation of the ontology of OO micro-architectural design knowledge according to the SWEBOK

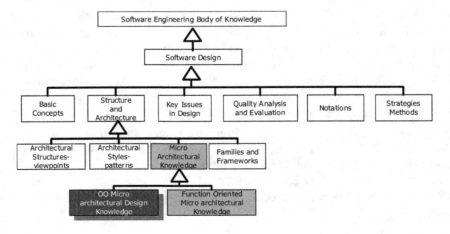

"structure and architecture" called "micro-architectural knowledge" and divide it into OO and functional micro-architectural knowledge. Our ontology structures the OO part.

Entities

When we start to describe the elements of the ontology, as we mentioned before, we find many terms related with essential knowledge gained from experience with object-oriented micro-architectural design, together with others arousing confusion as to whether they constitute knowledge or not. In order to clarify the situation, we have grouped the terms in question into two initial groups:

- **Declarative knowledge:** Concepts describing what to do with a problem: Heuristics, patterns, bad smells, best practices, and so forth.

- **Operative knowledge:** Where there is a body of accumulated knowledge concerning operations or processes for carrying out changes in software (i.e., parameterized transformation of a program preserving its functionality (Opdyke, 1992) including such concepts as refactoring.) Here we should stress that we mean design refactoring, not code refactoring, which is more common. Although we consider it important to group together all knowledge related to OO micro-architectural design, we are naturally aware that

Figure 2. OO Micro-architectural design knowledge ontology

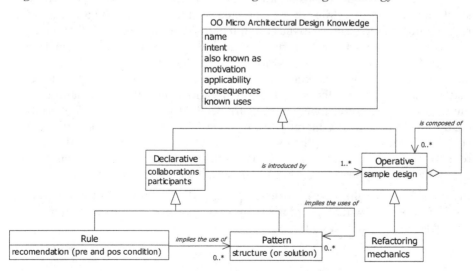

refactoring could be placed under the maintenance category in the SWEBOK.

We can thus establish an initial classification of essential experience-based knowledge of software design with two parts: declarative (what) and operative (how). The former tells us what to do and the latter how, in both cases according to experience (see Figure 2, where a UML class diagram is used to express the ontology).

Considering "declarative knowledge" alone without regard to design patterns, we have observed that principles, heuristics, bad smells, and so forth, have the same common structure, there being no substantial difference between them, as they all have the structure and form of a rule — they posit a condition and offer a recommendation. It should be stressed that the "recommendation" is not a solution like that of the pattern. Patterns are more formalized than rules and pattern descriptions are always broader. They propose solutions to problems, while rules are recommendations which a design should fulfill. Unlike patterns, rules are greatly based on using natural language, which can be more ambiguous (Pescio, 1997).

Lastly, in order to complete the description of the entities, we will concentrate on their attributes. We based our determination of these on the terms used in Gamma et al. (1995) to describe a design pattern: name, intent, also known as motivation, structure, applicability, participants, collaborations, consequences, implementation, sample code, known uses, and related patterns. It will be observed that many of these items are common to other elements of knowledge and these common attributes are located in the top entity (see Figure 2). As to the other attributes under consideration, the structure attribute is a synonym for solution in a pattern, while we have created the recommendation attribute for rules, which would be close to the solution of the pattern (Pescio, 1997) and the mechanics attribute for refactorings, our choice of name being taken from Fowler, Beck, Brant, Opdyke, and Roberts' (2000) refactoring catalogue. The attributes participants (the classes and/or objects participating in the design pattern and their responsibilities) and collaborations (how the participants carry out their responsibilities together) concern declarative knowledge. The sample design attribute concerns operative knowledge. The implementation attribute is substituted for mechanics (this is in refactoring, as we are dealing with design refactoring, not code refactoring). The related patterns attribute has been generalized and appears in each of the relationships between entities.

In line with our ontology we have developed a unified catalog of rules, which we see in Chapter X, where in order to improve the detection of rules, these are named according to their condition.

Relationships

We shall now concentrate on the relationships between entities (see Figure 2):

- "To apply a rule implies the use of a pattern." Often, when we introduce a rule, we obtain a new design, which needs a pattern. One example of this situation is the application of the "dependency inversion" rule, a principle (Martin, 1996) which introduces an abstract class or an interface, which in turn necessitates a creational pattern (Gamma et al., 1995) to create instances and associate objects in the new situation. Observe that this does not always happen (cardinality 0 to n), not all the rules imply the introduction of a pattern, a clear example of this being when we apply rules which work only inside a module, for example the "long method" rule, a bad smell according to Fowler et al. (2000).

- "To apply a pattern implies the use of another pattern." This relationship is quite obvious, since it has been featured in catalogs and pattern languages for some time. An example of this is the map of relationships between patterns presented in (Gamma et al., 1995). Observe that in this case, cardinality is from 0 to n (we can see in Gamma et al. (1995) how adapter, proxy and bridge patterns are isolated).

- "The declarative knowledge is introduced by operative knowledge." This relationship expresses that all declarative knowledge (rules and patterns) is introduced in the design by an element of operative knowledge (a refactoring); note that cardinality is from 1 to n. This is quite obvious since it does not make sense for an element of declarative knowledge to exist if it cannot be introduced.

- The relationship between patterns and refactorings can be observed in an implicit way by reading some of the refactoring catalogues which concentrate on the design level, a good example of this being the Fowler et al. (2000) catalog. Gamma et al. (1995) state that "design patterns provide the refactorings with objectives," and there is a natural relationship between patterns and refactorings, where the patterns can be the objective and the refactorings the way of achieving them. In fact, as Fowler et al. (2000) say, there should be catalogs of refactorings which contemplate all design patterns. In this way, refactorings, such as "replace type code with state/strategy" or "form template method," concentrate on introducing patterns within a system (again to emphasize that these are design refactorings, not code refactorings).

- The relationship between rules and refactorings has not been studied as much as that between patterns and refactorings. Generally, we observe that rules are introduced in the design, just like patterns, by means of the refactorings. And in the light of what has been said previously, it becomes clearer how refactorings store knowledge about how to introduce elements in designs in a controlled way. Continuing with the example of the "dependency inversion" rule we see that in order to resolve the violation of this rule we insert an abstract entity into the design, which would be carried out with the refactorings.

- "An element of operative knowledge is composed of others." Examples of this composition can be found in refactoring catalogs such as Fowler et al. (2000) where, for example, the refactoring "extract method" is not composed but it is used by others (cardinality 0 to n).

Lastly, we shall explain why other relationships are not included.

- **Relationship:** "A pattern implies the use of a rule." The introduction of a pattern must not allow a rule to be violated (applying a pattern should never reduce design quality).

- **Relationship:** "A rule implies the use of a rule." In a similar way to the previous case, the introduction of one rule must not allow another rule to be violated (applying a rule should never reduce design quality).

- **Relationship:** "An operative knowledge implies a declarative knowledge." A refactoring does not know what rule or pattern it uses.

An Empirical Validation

In this section, we will present a description of the process followed to carry out the empirical validation, which is based on Wohlin et al. (2000); Prechelt and Unger (1998); Prechelt et al. (1997); Prechelt et al. (2001); Kitchenham, Pfleeger, Pickard, Jones, Hoaglin, El Eman, et al. (2002); and (Kitchenham, Dybå, and Jorgensen, 2004). The main intention of this controlled experiment was to compare the effectiveness and efficiency of "traditional" OO design vs. the use of OO design knowledge. Moreover, we aimed at analyzing if disposing of a rules catalog that unifies design knowledge as principles, best practices, heuristics, and so on, and their relations with patterns has influence on the effectiveness and efficiency in the improving of the quality of OO micro architectures.

Based on the GQM (goal question metrics) template, the goal definition of our experiment can be summarized as shown in Table 1.

Table 1. Definition of experiment

Analyze	The improvement method based on the rules catalog
for the purpose of	evaluating
with respect to	effectiveness and efficiency
from the point of view of	software engineers
in the context of	software companies in Spain

Planning

The experiment is specific since it is focused on one technique applied to one domain; the ability to generalize from this specific context is further elaborated below when discussing threats to the experiment. The experiment addresses a real problem, which is whether the method presented is more effective and efficient to be used in OO micro architectural quality improvement.

Eighteen professionals of two companies carried out the experiment. The selected subjects were professionals having extensive experience in OO design. We classified the subjects into two groups according to their professional experience. The subjects were asked to fill a questionnaire out about their expertise, and taking into consideration the collected responses, we formed two groups of subjects, trying to have the same number of subjects with good marks and bad marks in each group. Both groups had a patterns catalog (Gamma et al., 1995), but only one of them had the rules catalog (see Chapter X). In addition to this, in a previous 30 minutes session, we explained to this group some notions about rules and their relationships to patterns and how to apply the rules catalog. For each subject, we had prepared a folder with the experimental material. Each folder contained one micro-architectural diagram and a questionnaire for answers.

We had to consider what independent variables or factors were likely to have an impact on the results. These are OO micro-architecture.

We considered two dependent variables (Thelin, Runeson, Wholin, Olsson, & Andersson, 2004):

- **Effectiveness:** Number of defects found/total number of defects. This is the percentage of the true improvements found by a designer with respect to the total number of defects.
- **Efficiency:** Number of defects found/inspection time, where inspection time is related to the time that subjects spent on inspecting the micro architecture; it is measured in minutes.

Hypotheses Formulation

Our purpose was to test two groups of hypotheses, one for each dependent variable.

Effectiveness hypotheses:

- $H_{0,1}$. There is no difference regarding effectiveness of subjects in detecting the violation of rules using a rules catalog and their relationship with patterns as compared to subjects without using the rules catalog. // $H_{1,1} : \neg H_{0,1}$

- $H_{0,2}$. There is no difference regarding effectiveness of subjects in detecting the application of patterns implicated by rules using a rules catalog s and their relationship with patterns as compared to subjects without using the rules catalog. // $H_{1,2} : \neg H_{0,2}$

- $H_{0,3}$. There is no difference regarding effectiveness of subjects in detecting the application of patterns not implicated by rules using a rules catalog and their relationship with patterns as compared to subjects without using the rules catalog. // $H_{1,3} : \neg H_{0,3}$

Efficiency hypotheses:

- $H_{0,4}$. There is no difference regarding efficiency of subjects in detecting the violation of rules using a rules catalog and their relationship with patterns as compared to subjects without using the rules catalog. // $H_{1,4} : \neg H_{0,4}$

- $H_{0,5}$. There is no difference regarding efficiency of subjects in detecting the application of patterns implicated by rules using a rules catalog and their relationship with patterns as compared to subjects without using the rules catalog. // $H_{1,5} : \neg H_{0,5}$

- $H_{0,6}$. There is no difference regarding efficiency of subjects in detecting the application of patterns not implicated by rules using a rules catalog and their relationship with patterns as compared to subjects without using the rules catalog. // $H_{1,6} : \neg H_{0,6}$

Operation

In this section, we will describe the preparation, execution, and data validation of the experiment. Before the day of the experiment execution, we gave a seminar to the subjects of the group that would use the rules catalog. In this seminar, we explained to the subjects how to apply the rules catalog. The subjects had to manually fulfill their proposed solution, writing down the start and end time of the activity. We collected the forms filled out by the subjects, checking if they were complete.

Analysis and Interpretation

Figure 3 shows the averages obtained from the experiment. Outliers have not been identified. In order to decide how to test the validity of the hypotheses, we evaluated if the data followed a normal distribution. The result was normal; we decided to perform a t-Student test. In Table 2 the results obtained by means of t-Student are shown. The first column represents the t-stat and the second column shows the t critical two-tail.

We have obtained the following results. Firstly, it was confirmed by the t-Student test that the group with the rules catalog obtained better results in "efficacy and efficiency in detection of rules" and "efficacy and efficiency in detection of patterns implicated by rules." In the second place, the t-Student test could not confirm that the group with the rules catalog obtained better results in "efficiency in detection of patterns not implicated by rules." However, this group obtained better averages; we have to highlight that "efficiency in detection of patterns not implicated by rules" is not influenced by the rules catalog, since these patterns are not in the catalog because they are not implicated by rules, and the application of these patterns will result in the detection of design problems more than design recommendations. Lastly, in a similar way, we could not confirm by using the t-Student test that the group without the rules catalog obtained better results in "efficacy in detection of patterns not implicated by rules"; however, again, this result is not influenced by the rules catalog.

Figure 3. Averages obtained from the experiment

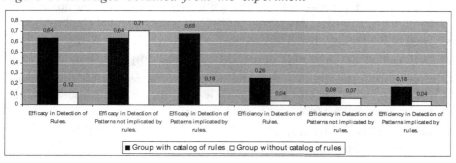

Table 2. Results obtained by means of t-Student

	t stat	t Critical two-tail
Efficacy in Detection of Rules.	5.38887	2.26215
Efficacy in Detection of Patterns not implicated by rules.	-0.22360	2.20098
Efficacy in Detection of Patterns implicated by rules.	3.36269	2.20098
Efficiency in Detection of Rules.	7.03868	2.26215
Efficiency in Detection of Patterns not implicated by rules	0.22269	2.26215
Efficiency in Detection of Patterns implicated by rules	4.35678	2.17881

Threats to Validity

A list of issues that threatens the validity of the empirical study is identified below.

Conclusion Validity

The results confirmed by means of the t-Student test that there was a significant difference between the two groups, and that the new approach seems to be more effective and efficient for carrying out the OO micro architectural quality improvement. The statistical assumptions of each test were verified, so that the conclusion validity was fulfilled.

Internal Validity

- **Differences among subjects:** We formed two groups, and the subjects were apportioned between these two groups according to their expertise and skills. For this reason, the subjects were asked to fill out a questionnaire about their expertise, and taking into account the collected responses, we formed the two groups of subjects.
- **Differences among OOD diagrams:** We used only one OOD diagram.
- **Precision in the time values:** The subjects were responsible for recording the start and finish times of each test, so they could introduce some imprecision but we think it is not very significant.
- **Fatigue effects:** The average time for carrying out the experiment was 20 minutes, so fatigue effects were minor.

- **Persistence effects:** Persistence effects are not present because the subjects had never participated in a similar experiment.
- **Subject motivation:** The subjects were very motivated.
- **Other factors:** For instance, plagiarism and influence among subjects were controlled.

External Validity

Two threats to validity have been identified which limit the possibility of applying any such generalization:

- **Subjects:** We are aware that more experiments with professionals must be carried out in order to be able to generalize these results. However, the subjects could be considered "common" OO designers at least in the context of Spanish software companies.
- **Material used:** We believe that the documents used might not be representative of an industrial problem, so more experiments with larger diagrams are needed.

Works Related with Empirical Studies About OO Knowledge

There are few empirical studies and related work about this topic. The recent interest in empirical studies about patterns, mainly, or any other kind of knowledge has focused on how these factors impact on the software maintenance process. In this regard, the main and more important studies are Prechelt's works that are the best example of empirical investigation about patterns.

The Prechelt et al. (1997) empirical study affirms that depending on the particular program, change task, and personnel, pattern documentation in a program may considerably reduce the time required for a program change and may also help improve the quality of the change; and recommends that design patterns are always explicitly documented in source code.

In Prechelt and Unger (1998), the experiments showed that carefully documenting patterns usage is highly recommendable because it works well during maintenance and that design patterns can be beneficial even when an alternative solution appears to be simpler but that unsuitable application can also be harmful in other situations. The resulting practical advice calls to apply common sense when using design patterns instead of using them in a cookbook fashion. Prechelt et al. (2001) state that it is not always useful to apply design patterns if there are simpler alternatives; they recommend using common sense to find the exceptions where a simpler solution should be preferred and even where this common sense suggests that using a patterns might not be a good idea.

On the other hand, there are very few works related to empirical studies about design knowledge different to patterns. In this sense, we can highlight (Deligiannis, Shepperd, Roumeliotis, & Stamelos, 2003) work, which investigated the effects of a single design heuristics (god class) on system design documents (with respect to understanding and maintainability), where the results showed that design heuristics can affect maintainability, where designs with heuristics are easier to understand and modify. According to this study, a design initially structured under heuristics has a higher probability of continuing to evolve in a resilient and flexible manner; if heuristics are violated, the probability of maintenance changes leading to poorer designs increases.

Acknowledgments

This research is partially supported by the ENIGMAS (*Entorno Inteligente para la Gestión del Mantenimiento Avanzado del Software*) project, supported by the Department of Education and Science of the *Junta de Comunidades de Castilla - La Mancha* (Regional Government of Castile - La Mancha) (PBI-05-058).

Conclusion

The motivation of the authors of the first catalog of patterns and of the community that investigates patterns has been to transfer the OODK accumulated during years of experience. Since then, designers have been reading and using patterns, reaping benefit from this experience. Nevertheless, more knowledge exits apart from patterns. We need to characterize the OO design knowledge, and we created an OODK ontology for it. An ontology describes domain knowledge in a generic way and provides agreed understanding of a domain. As Gruber (1991) said, "I use the term ontology to mean a specification of a conceptualization. That is, an ontology is a description of the concepts and relationships that can exist".

On the other hand, there are few empirical studies related to OO design knowledge. We presented a description of the process followed to carry out an empirical validation, which is based on the use of OO design knowledge. The main objective of this controlled experiment was to compare the effectiveness and efficiency of a "traditional" OOD process with the new OOD approach. Eighteen professionals (selected for convenience) of four Spanish companies (divided in two groups) carried out the experiment. In a previous session of 30 minutes we trained one group in the using of the new approach. For each participant, we had prepared a folder with one OO class diagram and one questionnaire, and for the members of the "new approach" group we included the OOD ontology with the main OOD "knowledge" (rules, patterns, etc.). The results confirmed by means of t-Student test that there was a significant difference between the two groups, and that the new approach seems to be more effective and efficient for carry out the OOD Process.

References

Abran, A. (Ed.). (2004). *Guide to the software engineering body of knowledge: SWEBOK*. Los Alamos, CA: IEEE CS Press.

Buschmann, F., Meunier, R., Rohnert, H., Sommerlad, P., & Stal, M. (1996). *A system of patterns: Pattern-oriented software architecture*. Addison-Wesley.

Coad, P. (1992). Object-oriented patterns. *Communications of the ACM, 35*(9), 152-159.

Deligiannis, I., Shepperd, M., Roumeliotis, M., & Stamelos, I. (2003). An empirical investigation of an object-oriented design heuristic for maintainability. *Journal of Systems and Software, 65*(2), 127-139.

Fowler, M. (1996). *Analysis patterns: Reusable object models*. Boston: Addison-Wesley.

Fowler, M., Beck, K., Brant, J., Opdyke, W., & Roberts, D. (2000). *Refactoring: Improving the design of existing code*. Boston: Addison-Wesley Professional.

Gamma, E., Helm, R., Johnson, R., & Vlissides, J. (1995). *Design patterns*. Reading, MA: Addison-Wesley Professional.

Gruber, T. (1991). *The role of a common ontology in achieving sharable, reusable knowledge bases*. Paper presented at the Second International Conference on Principles of Knowledge Representation and Reasoning, Cambridge.

Jurisica, I., Mylopoulos, J., & Yu, E. (1999, October). *Using ontologies for knowledge management: An information systems perspective knowledge: Creation, organization and use.* Paper presented at the 62nd Annual Meeting of the American Society for Information Science (ASIS 99), Washington, DC.

Kitchenham, B. A., Dybå, T., & Jorgensen, M. (2004). *Evidence-based software engineering.* Paper presented at the International Conference on Software Engineering (ICSE), Edinburgh, Scotland, UK.

Kitchenham, B. A., Pfleeger, S. L., Pickard, L., Jones, P., Hoaglin, D., El Eman, K., et al. (2002). Preliminary guidelines for empirical research in software engineering. *IEEE Transactions on Software Engineering, 28*(8), 721-734.

Martin, R. C. (1996). The dependency inversion principle. *C++ Report, 8*(6), 61-66.

Opdyke, W. (1992). *Refactoring object-oriented frameworks.* Thesis, Computer Science, Urbana-Champain, IL.

Pescio, C. (1997). Principles versus patterns. *Computer, 30*(9), 130-131.

Prechelt, L., & Unger, B. (1998). *A series of controlled experiments on design patterns: Methodology and results.* Paper presented at the Softwaretechnik 1998 GI Conference (Softwaretechnik-Trends), Paderborn.

Prechelt, L., Unger, B., Philippsen, M., & Tichy, W. (1997). Two controlled experiments assessing the usefulness of design pattern information during program maintenance. *IEEE Transactions on Software Engineering, 28*(6), 595-606.

Prechelt, L., Unger, B., Tichy, W., Bössler, P., & Votta, G. (2001). A controlled experiment in maintenance comparing design patterns to simpler solutions. *IEEE Transactions on Software Engineering, 27*(12), 1134-1144.

Rising, L. (1998). *The patterns handbook: Techniques, strategies, and applications.* Cambridge: Cambridge University Press.

Thelin, T., Runeson, P., Wholin, C., Olsson, T., & Andersson, C. (2004). Evaluation of usage based reading conclusions after three experiments. *Empirical Software Engineering, 9*(1-2), 77-110.

Wendorff, P. (2001). *Assessment of design patterns during software reengineering: Lessons learned from a large commercial project.* Paper presented at the Proceedings of the 5th European Conference on Software Maintenance and Reeingineering (CSMR), Lisbon, Portugal.

Wohlin, C., Runeson, P., Höst, M., Ohlson, M., Regnell, B., & Wesslen, A. (2000). *Experimentation in software engineering: An introduction.* Kluwer Academic Publishers.

Chapter III

Using Linguistic Patterns to Model Interactions

Isabel Díaz, Central University of Venezuela, Venezuela

Oscar Pastor, Technical University of Valencia, Spain

Lidia Moreno, Technical University of Valencia, Spain

Alfredo Matteo, Central University of Venezuela, Venezuela

Abstract

The dynamic behavior of a system is elicited, specified, and analyzed by means of interaction modelling. This activity is important for object-oriented software development because it provides the information that is required to construct the system conceptual model. Several interaction modelling techniques have been proposed. However, this activity continues to be a complex and tedious task for the modellers. These problems arise from the intrinsic difficulties of interaction modelling and the lack of effective techniques and tools to support to the modellers. In this chapter, heuristic-oriented techniques and linguistics-oriented techniques proposed by several authors to model interactions are analyzed. In addition, a framework to facilitate and to improve the interaction modelling is described. This framework was conceived to be integrated into automatic software production environments. It uses linguistic patterns to recognize interactions from use case models. The patterns were validated with expert modellers. The validation process carried out and the main results are also presented.

Introduction

Dynamic models fulfil an important role in the development of object-oriented software systems. These describe the behavior of a system in terms of: (1) the state change of an object, which is due to an event or the execution of an operation (intraobject dynamic perspective); and (2) how the objects should interact to provide the system with a determined behavior (inter-object dynamic perspective). This chapter is based on the study of the interobject dynamic perspective and, in particular, on the construction process of the object interaction models in order to describe the behavior of a system.

The modelling of interactions is one of the most frequently overlooked practices in software development. While the structural model is considered to be fundamental for the analysis and design of the systems, the dynamic model is considered to be optional (Larman, 2004; Rosenberg & Scott, 1999). Nevertheless, both models contribute two complementary views of the system design that, taken separately, would be insufficient. Our experience, which coincides with that reported by other authors, has led us to believe that this problem may have originated in the high level of difficulty of interaction modelling, especially for inexperienced modellers (Larman, 2004; Rosenberg & Scott, 1999; Song, 2001). On the one hand, modelling is an inherently complex activity that, in any case, depends on the experience and the domain knowledge of the modeller. On the other hand, the difficulty of constructing interaction models is also determined by other circumstances that are explained below.

The result of a thorough review of the literature has indicated that software development approaches that describe a technique for interaction modelling are scarce. The aids offered to the modeller to facilitate the task of identifying and specifying interactions are very few when compared to the extensive descriptions that are made of the modelling language. The nature of the diagrams that are used to graphically represent the interaction models, generally sequence diagrams (SDs) or message sequence charts (MSCs), also constitutes an obstacle for modelling (ITU, 2000; OMG, 2003). The amount of time that must be spent on elaborating and troubleshooting these diagrams makes them tedious activities, which many modellers attempt to avoid. Model editing tools available on the market, such as Rational or Visio, are not very flexible and do not offer mechanisms that adapt to specific graphical needs. The complexity of interaction modelling is even greater when the difficulty of maintaining consistency between this model and other structural and dynamic models of the system is added.

The purpose of this chapter is to establish the basis that a generic framework created to facilitate interaction modelling and to promote this activity during system development must have. The strengths and weaknesses of the interaction modelling techniques that are commonly applied are analyzed in order to determine the requirements that this framework must fulfil. Thus, the framework is defined in the context of the contributions that other approaches have made to interaction modelling.

The goal of this framework (hereafter called metamorphosis) is to provide support to modellers in the interaction model construction during the first stages of the development of a system. However, its use can be extended to the complete life cycle of the software (OMG, 2003; Van Lamsweer, 2000). Metamorphosis assumes that the system *behavior specification* is expressed through use case models (Nuseibeh & Easterbrook, 2000; OMG, 2003). A use case is a document written in natural language that describes part of the system functionality from the perspective of its users (Jacobson, Christerson, Jonsson, & Övergaard, 1992). The *analysis or interpretation* of the use cases shows how the system components exchange information so that the system has the behavior specified by the analysts (OMG, 2003; Van Lamsweer, 2000). The result of this analysis is represented using interaction models.

In metamorphosis, the analysis process lies in the automatic generation of the interaction diagrams from the use cases in order to guarantee the following: (1) *consistency* of the interaction model itself, as well as its consistency with the corresponding use case model; (2) *ease of use* promoting the automatic generation of the interaction diagrams, so that the modeller can spend more time on more important tasks such as the resolution of conflicts originated by the ambiguity inherent in the use of natural language, the incorporation of supplementary information into the interaction diagrams (restrictions, comments, etc.), or the validation of the model obtained; (3) *traceability* to establish links that can be documented, controlled, and maintained, so that the modeller can determine the part of the use case text from which an interaction was generated and vice-versa; and (4) *representation richness* to incorporate relevant semantic information beyond the basic elements of an interaction (i.e., synchronous/asynchronous messages, concurrence specification, repetition, or conditioning of interactions, parameter identification, consultations/updating, etc.).

The metamorphosis framework must reconcile contributions from both computational linguistics and software engineering to be able to fulfil the requirements described above. Computational linguistics provides metamorphosis with the natural language processing techniques and tools to recognize the elements participating in an interaction model from the use case text. Software engineering provides metamorphosis with a system development orientation that is focused on the construction and the successive transformation of these models. Thus, text analysis of the use cases is defined at a high level of abstraction, making it independent from the domain of the system under development and from specific implementation considerations. In addition, it is convenient to use patterns to describe the analysis solutions. A pattern can specify the generic solution to a recurrent problem of use case analysis. The patterns are suitable resources for storing the knowledge about these solutions so that it can be reused, shared and communicated whenever this knowledge is necessary (Gamma, Helm, Johnson, & Vlissides, 1992).

This chapter has been structured in five sections. The next section presents an overall view of the most representative approaches about interaction modelling as well as their advantages and disadvantages. The second section explains how metamorphosis interprets the interaction concept and describes the properties of the interaction model. The third section explains the process of extracting information from the use cases, and the strategy followed to transform them into interactions. It also presents an example of the application of the transformation framework. The fourth section describes an experiment performed to validate the transformation patterns as well as some of the results obtained. The last section presents the lessons learned and future directions.

Interaction Modelling Techniques: An Overview

In general, approaches that propose interaction modelling as a resource to develop systems emphasize the description of the syntax and semantics of its elements; however, they barely explain how this model can be constructed. Some approaches have attempted to answer this question by formulating procedures to aid modellers in their work. In this study, the procedures set forth by these approaches will be referred to by the generic name of *interaction modelling techniques* regardless of the scope, formality or level of complexity (Rumbaugh, 1995; Wieringa, 1998). Interaction modelling techniques can be characterized as being based on: (1) a heuristic application, using a step-by-step guide in the construction of interaction models (*heuristic-oriented techniques*); or (2) the use of linguistic information, as a way to identify and to specify interactions (*linguistics-oriented techniques*). The purpose of this type of classification is to simplify the analysis and to determine the strengths and weaknesses of these techniques.

Heuristic-Oriented Techniques

One of the pioneers in the use of interaction models to describe the behavior of a system was Jacobson, whose object-oriented software engineering (OOSE) method introduces object interaction diagrams (Jacobson et al., 1992). These diagrams are prepared for each use case after preparing their robustness diagrams. A robustness diagram shows the entity classes, interface (or boundary) classes, and control classes of each use case, and the possible dynamic relations between these object classes, including the participation of the actors. To construct the object interaction diagrams, the OOSE method suggests going through the following steps: (1) partitioning the use case text, and placing these fragments on the left side of the diagram; (2) placing the use case actors; (3) adding the interface and control objects identified in the robustness diagram; (4) adding the entity objects of the use case identified in the robustness diagram; and, (5) identifying the messages exchanged by the classes for each piece of text of the use case (each piece of text is located on the left side of the diagram, near the identified messages). The OOSE method transfers the complexity of elaborating interaction diagrams to the robustness diagrams. However, the method does not offer further help to construct the robustness and interaction diagrams; therefore, the identification of the interactions (step 5) remains unresolved. Furthermore, the interaction diagrams are troublesome to prepare due to the use of different types of classes and the incorporation of the pieces of text of the use cases.

Rosenberg and Scott basically follow the same procedure described by the OOSE method for modelling interactions (Rosenberg & Scott, 1999). In an attempt to facilitate the recognition of messages, they suggest the use of class-responsibility-collaboration (CRC) cards (Wirfs-Brock, Wilkerson, & Wiener, 1990). This strategy helps in determining the operations of a class, but it is not performed in the context of message exchange. Thus, the CRC cards cannot guarantee the identification of all the necessary operations for the system to adopt certain behavior.

Another process that proposes the construction of SD as part of the analysis and design activity of the system use cases is the rational unified process (RUP) (Jacobson, Booch, & Rumbaugh, 1999). The procedure set forth in the RUP offers no substantial differences with respect to the techniques described previously. The Ambler technique formulated to facilitate SD construction is similar to the RUP technique (Ambler, 2004).

A similar process is carried out during the requirements analysis phase of the OO method (object-oriented method) (Insfrán, Pastor & Wieringa, 2002; Pastor, Gómez, Insfrán, & Pelechano, 2001). The main activity of this phase is the elaboration of SD, which is based on a characterization of the information contained in the system use cases. The paths of the use cases describe actor/ system communication actions (actions performed by the actor or the system to exchange information) or system response actions (system actions that are potentially capable of changing the system state). The SD of the OO method uses the Unified Modelling Language (UML) and distinguishes the types of object classes introduced by Jacobson: entity, boundary and control classes (Jacobson et al., 1992; Rosenberg & Scott, 1999). The steps that the modeller must perform are the following: (1) to prepare a SD for each of the use case paths (one for the basic path and one for each alternate path); (2) the use case actors participate as classes in the SD; (3) each actor/system communication action of the use case is represented through one or more messages between an actor class and a boundary class (which is usually called *system*); (4) each use case action of the system response type is represented in the SD by one or more messages between the boundary class and the entity classes, or by one or more messages between entity classes. As in the above-mentioned approaches, the OO method provides no further help to recognize the entity classes or the messages that they exchange.

The technique proposed by Larman uses *system sequence diagrams* to represent the use case scenarios (Larman, 2004). These diagrams show the interaction between the actor and a generic entity called *system*. This entity acts as a black box that hides the system internal structure. Each identified interaction must later be analyzed using patterns. A pattern explains in detail how this interaction can be broken down into one or more messages between system objects. The SD uses the UML and does not distinguish the types of objects in an explicit way. Larman's idea based on patterns is novel and seems effective. Nevertheless, it lacks both a systematic process to be able to apply conveniently these patterns and a catalog containing the patterns corresponding to the most representative interactions.

Song sets forth the application of the ten-step heuristic on sequence diagram development (Song, 2001). The application of this technique requires the prior preparation of the system object model and the use case model (diagrams and textual specification). It uses the UML to represent the SD in which the types of objects (entity, control, and boundary) are distinguished. The steps of this technique can be summarized as follows: (1) the message initiating the flow of events is sent by the actor to the system; (2) a primary boundary object and a primary control object are defined for each use case; if needed, secondary objects (boundary or control) are created; (3) a secondary control object is defined for each use case that is included or extended; (4) the problem-solving operations (creation/destruction, association forming, or attribute modification) are identified in the use case; and (5) each message is named and supplied with optional parameters. To identify the types of problem-solving operations, Song suggests highlighting the verbs in the use case text and selecting those that indicate actions that were formulated to solve the problem. These verbs can be considered as names of potential problem-solving operations. This technique can be considered a step forward with respect to other techniques, because it is more thorough in identifying instances and in recognizing messages (through the problem-solving operations). However, Song's technique leaves two questions unresolved: how to identify the sending and receiving classes of these messages and how to deduce an interaction composed by more than one message from a single verb.

Hilsbos and Song have improved their initial proposal with the tabular analysis method (TAM) (Hilsbos & Song, 2004). The introduction of this method attempts to answer the two preceding questions. The TAM lies in applying heuristics to complete a seven-column table before constructing the SD of each use case. Each column respectively indicates the number of each step of the use case, the action described in that step, the name of the message, its parameters, its restrictions, its sender, and its receiver. Initially, messages that are always sent and received by the actor or the system are obtained from the table. Then, this information is refined by breaking down each of the messages in terms of other messages that have been established between the primary control object and entity objects, or between two or more entity objects. To support the task of identifying these messages, the guidelines that recognise the problem-solving operations presented in Song should be followed (Song, 2001). The TAM facilitates the organization of the information obtained from the use cases. However, it supplies no further help for the modeller to recognize this information. The graphic representation of the SD can be carried out with the information contained in the table.

Linguistics-Oriented Techniques

In recent decades, many approaches have relied on natural language processing techniques to facilitate the development of software systems (Boyd, 1999; Chen, 1976; Métais, 2002; Rumbaugh, Blaha, Premerlani, Eddy, & Lorensen, 1991). In this section, we refer to those approaches that are based on the linguistic properties of a text to obtain information and that allow the automatic construction of models (Burg & van de Riet, 1996; Juristo, Moreno, & López, 2000; Overmyer, Lavoie & Rambow, 2001). More specifically, we study the approaches that allow dynamic models to be obtained from system behavioral specifications written in unrestricted natural language (Burg & van de Riet, 1995; Flield, Kop, Mayerthaler, Mayr, & Winkler, 2000). To facilitate this review, we distinguish two groups. The first group includes first-generation proposals that do not set forth a procedure to directly derive the system interaction model. The proposals representing this group are: Color-X (Burg & van de Riet, 1995; Dehne, Steuten, & van de Riet, 2001), NIBA (Kop & Mayr, 2002), and the behavior model presented in Juristo et al. (2000). These works are very interesting from the perspective of natural language processing; however, they are not studied in this chapter, as these approaches do not allow the direct deduction of complete interaction models. They use intermediate models to give information to the modellers so that they can later obtain the interaction models.

The second group of linguistic-oriented techniques includes second-generation proposals. They have been especially created to deduce interactions from use cases, such as the works of Feijs and Li, which can be considered referential for our research (Feijs, 2000; Li, 2000). Feijs establishes correspondences between some types of sentences written in natural language and MSC (ITU, 2000). A use case is considered as a sequence of sentences, each of which is associated to a semantically equivalent type of MSC. A sentence has a specific syntactic structure that contributes information about active and passive objects, values, instance identities, properties (attributes), methods, and events. This information has a counterpart in its corresponding MSC.

Sentences are classified as information, action, or state. They describe information exchange, object handling, or state, respectively. A context-free grammar is defined, and a set of correspondence rules is proposed between the syntactic components of each sentence and the elements of an MSC. It assumes the preexistence of a domain object model to ensure the terminological consistency of the use cases. The proposal does not address the identification of message arguments, nor does it study conditional sentences, iterations, or relationships between use cases (extension and inclusion) and their respective equivalents in an MSC.

Li also sets forth a semiautomatic process for deriving SD from the textual descriptions of the use cases. The text of the use case is normalized. The description can only use sentences with a single subject and a single predicate or action. The translation partially generates a set of instances and some of the messages that are exchanged. The SD must then be completed manually by the analyst. This proposal takes into account conditional sentences and iterations, but it does not address the relationships between use cases (extension and inclusion).

An Outline of Interaction Modelling Techniques

Each of the techniques studied reveals the trends followed in areas such as software engineering, which serves as the framework for heuristic-oriented techniques.

Therefore, the predominant aspect of the heuristic-oriented techniques is the use of models that are especially created to both specify and analyze system dynamic behavior. The information used to generate the interaction diagrams is obtained from an initial model that describes the system domain. The semantic richness of the modelling language acquires importance. Thus, most heuristic-oriented techniques coincide in the following:

1. To differentiate the instances that participate in these diagrams, using Jacobson's classification on control, boundary, and entity objects (Jacobson et al., 1992).

2. To establish close semantic relationships between some of the model abstractions from which information is extracted and the abstractions of the obtained model (i.e., the actor in the use case model is an element in the interaction model having the same meaning).

3. To derive the interactions using information from the use case model. A use case is considered as an analysis unit to derive interaction diagrams.

4. To use the object model to facilitate the identification of the instances that participate in a SD and to ensure the consistency of the models.

5. To establish structural correspondences between the elements that describe both the use case model and the interaction model (i.e., a control object is created for each use case included or extended).

6. To set up heuristics or rules to obtain the interaction model. The application of these rules depends exclusively on the modeller's criterion, personal experience, and domain knowledge.

7. To facilitate the graphical representation of the interaction models with the aid of tools. The tools do not support the automatic generation of these representations or the handling of the model consistency.

Computational linguistics has served as the basis for linguistics-oriented techniques. In particular, the second-generation outline of these techniques has been adjusted to the most important characteristics of the heuristic-oriented techniques. Thus, second-generation linguistics-oriented techniques synthesize the properties of all the other techniques, overcoming many of their weaknesses. They have adopted a model-oriented approach, both to describe the information extraction source and the interaction representation. Syntactic analysis has been considered as a fundamental resource for generating the interaction model. The main characteristics of second-generation linguistics-oriented techniques are the following:

1. The use case model is used to extract information. This model is widely known and has been developed to specify system behaviors.

2. The dynamic model generated is based on the basic primitives for interaction representation (instances, messages, and parameters).

3. In addition to the information provided by the syntactic analysis of the use case sentences, the interaction deduction process uses the system structural information.

4. The second-generation linguistics-oriented techniques presume the support of a tool that allows the (semi)automatic generation of the interaction diagrams. The modeller's participation is then limited to completing the generated diagrams and validating them.

New Alternatives

In spite of the contributions of the interaction modelling techniques, they have some weaknesses that should be eliminated in order to improve this activity. The creation of the metamorphosis framework attempts to fulfil this goal. Therefore, the metamorphosis definition must: (1) overcome the limitations of the interaction modelling techniques that have been proposed until now; (2) take into account the strengths that these techniques have demonstrated; and (3) utilize the current proposals in software engineering and computational linguistics to enrich the interaction modelling techniques. These three factors have contributed to determinate an outline for the metamorphosis framework. This outline has the following characteristics.

Model-centered transformation architecture. Until now, use case information extraction and interaction diagram generation have been described through a set of rules that apply the techniques. The information source and the form that it takes later on are not treated as models when specifying the deduction process. This produces some inconveniences that affect the efficiency of the systems that provide support to these techniques; this not only makes maintenance difficult, but it also makes the code evolution and generation tasks more complex. Great interest in model-driven approaches that are based on the automatic transformation of models has recently emerged. In this software development paradigm, the models and their transformations are specified at a high abstraction level, separating the system structure and behavior from its implementation and supporting evolution, refinement, and code generation (Kleppe, Warmer, & Bast, 2003). Following this approach, metamorphosis proposes the automatic generation of a target model (the interaction model) from a source model (the use case model). The model definition is abstract at the metamodel level so that the transformation does not depend on the technological aspects nor on a specific domain.

Linguistic orientation. Metamorphosis uses natural language processing to support information extraction from the text of a use case (Boyd, 1999). Currently, natural language processing is a mature area of computer science that provides techniques and tools to perform this task efficiently (Métais, 2002; Mich, Franch, & Inverardi, 2004).

Based on patterns. Metamorphosis attempts to capture the transformation knowledge by means of patterns (Gamma et al., 1992). These patterns are going to describe how each sentence of a use case is transformed into interactions. In metamorphosis, a pattern is a reusable and generic specification that can be implemented using any programming language and integrated into several automatic software production environments.

Role-driven. Metamorphosis provides special meaning to the modelling elements by means of role definition. The roles contribute to the recognition of these elements at model-time and facilitate the understanding of the patterns (France, Kim, Ghosh, & Song, 2004; Gildea & Jurafsky, 2002).

Flexible normalization. The normalization process requires use cases to be written using only a previously known set of syntactic structures. Imposing such a restriction facilitates the information extraction process and allows the elimination of the potential ambiguities generated by the use of natural language (Ben-Achour, Rolland, Maiden, & Souveyet, 1999; Berry & Kamsties, 2004; Rolland & Ben-Achour, 1998). Nevertheless, the advantages achieved by imposing this normalization on the language reduce the expressive capability of the system specification. Therefore, establishing restrictions could only be justified as a means to ensure the quality of the use cases, in terms of their completeness and correctness. Furthermore, this quality could be ensured through using other resources without overloading the modeller with this responsibility. Metamorphosis proposes to make the normalization process of use cases flexible by means of: (a) a tool guiding the modeller in the use case editing process; or (b) automatically identifying text ambiguities (structural or semantic) and resolving them (i.e., transforming it; marking it with information to clarify its semantics; classifying doubtful text; etc.).

UML compliant. Metamorphosis uses UML because this language allows us to specify models and transformations that can be comprehended and applied by many modellers and tools. The UML semantics and syntax is currently a de-facto standard due to its widespread use (OMG, 2003). Furthermore, the UML 2.0 version thoroughly describes the interaction concept taking into account the necessary semantics and notation to represent both the SD and the MSC. Interactions in the UML 2.0 version can be represented graphically using: *sequence diagrams* (that synthesize the properties of the MSCs), *communication diagrams*, or *interaction overview diagrams* (OMG, 2003). For simplicity, in this chapter, we use the generic terms *sequence* or *interaction diagram* to refer to the graphic representation of the interactions.

Bidirectional transformation. Interaction modelling techniques describe how to obtain interaction diagrams from use cases. However, nothing has been said about how use cases can be deduced from interaction diagrams. This would be useful to determine how use cases change when modifications on interaction diagrams are performed. Metamorphosis leans towards the bidirectionality of the transformation in order to ensure the consistency of the models and to facilitate the tasks of reengineering, maintenance, refinement, validation, and verification of the system functional requirements.

Simultaneous deduction of the object model. Almost all interaction modelling techniques assume the prior existence of the system object model. The use of this representation attempts to guarantee its consistency and that of the interaction model. However, this model is not always available, and when it is available, it may not be sufficiently developed. Metamorphosis takes into account the simultaneous and iterative deduction of both models while maintaining the linguistic orientation. Thus, the information of one of the models is complemented by the information of the other model, which keeps the consistency of both models in a natural way. This also contributes to reducing the gap between the analysis and the design of the system and to promoting its development based on the succeeding refinement of models.

Empirical validation of the technique. It is necessary to demonstrate the way in which the technique responds to quality indicators. Metamorphosis must establish a validation strategy that allows it to continually improve itself.

Metamorphic Interactions

Metamorphosis is a conceptual framework conceived to facilitate the interaction modelling of an object-oriented system in an automatic software production environment. This section explains how metamorphosis understands interaction modelling. First, some definitions about dynamic behavior of the systems are established. Second, the models used by metamorphosis to represent this dynamic behavior are described. These models were defined in order to facilitate information deduction from the use cases.

Dynamic Behavior

A system consists of a set of components interacting with one another to achieve one or more goals (Blanchard & Fabrycky, 1990). The way in which these elements interact over time determines the system's complete behavior. To facilitate its specification, this behavior is broken down into units so that each of these units responds to a goal that the system wants to achieve. A *behavior unit* is a specific group of interactions that take place between certain system components in order to achieve a specific goal (Wieringa, 1998). An *interaction* shows the data exchange established between the system and the elements in its environment (*external perspective* or *interaction communication*), or between the different components that integrate the system (*internal perspective* or *interaction structure*).

The specification and analysis of the system behavior are two of the most important activities in software development. In the first phases of their life cycle, these activities are determinant in understanding the system functionality. *Behavior specification* allows the description of the functional requirements, according to the needs of the system potential users, emphasizing the external perspective or interaction communication. Since Jacobson introduced the use case concept, most object-oriented software development methods are based on the use case model to specify the system behavior (Jacobson et al., 1992; OMG, 2003). *Behavior analysis* emphasizes the internal perspective or interaction structure. The output of this activity is expressed in an interaction model showing how the system components must exchange data so that it can behave as previously specified (ITU, 2000; Rosenberg & Scott, 1999).

Like many of the object-oriented software development methods, Metamorphosis uses the use case model and the interaction model as the principal artifacts to study behavior. The construction of these models relies on the semantics and syntax given to its elements by the UML. Using the extension mechanisms that this language provides, the UML metamodel has been enriched with the information needed to establish connections between its elements. This facilitates the automatic derivation of some elements from other elements (OMG, 2003).

Behavior Specification

In metamorphosis, each *use case* is considered as a behavior unit that is described by a text written in natural language. The use case model is the fundamental input to deduce the interaction model. A use case shows the complete and organized sequence of actions that the system must perform, when interacting with the actors, to fulfil a certain goal. The complete sequence of actions make up the basic path of a use case. Some use cases can have one or more alternative paths that describe optional or exceptional sequences of actions.

The metamorphosis use case model is based on the UML usecases package concepts (OMG, 2003). To guarantee the recognition of the linguistic properties of the use case text, the elements in this package have been extended and described in the metamorphosis use case linguistic profile (Díaz, Moreno, Pastor, & Matteo, 2005; Rolland & Ben-Achour, 1998). This profile was developed based on the action concept, which is a fundamental element in the description of use cases. The action of a use case is studied from three perspectives, which are orthogonal but supplementary to each other: the conceptual, the syntactic, and the semantic perspectives. Figure 1 shows the structural relationships established between some elements of the use case linguistic profile of metamorphosis. These elements have been grouped according to the perspective that they describe. This is explained in the following subsections.

The Conceptual Perspective

The conceptual perspective describes the meaning of a use case action. An *action* can express: (1) a *communication* that is established between the actor and the system to exchange information; (2) an internal *behavior* of the system, which responds to the communication established with the actor. *Special* actions can also be distinguished to allow conditioning, restricting, adding, or repeating communication/internal actions or groups of these. Figure 1 represents the kinds of actions by means of a generalization relationship. Each action belongs to a use case path. A path is an action group of a use case that fulfils a specific goal.

Figure 1. Use case linguistic profile (partial view)

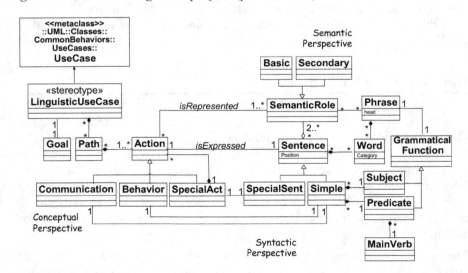

Figure 2. Unidirectional action

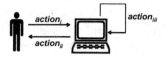

An action represents an *interaction fragment* of the system behavior if it complies with the unidirectional and atomicity properties. An *action is unidirectional* if the interaction described refers to one, and only one, of the following three situations: (1) an actor communicates with the system by sending information; (2) the system communicates with the actor by providing information; (3) the system executes an action on itself. Figure 2 shows all the possible directions of an action.

An *action is atomic* if it cannot be broken down in two or more unidirectional actions. Thus, a complex action contains two or more unidirectional actions. An interaction fragment describes a single atomic action that is performed by the actor or the system and that has meaning in the context of one of the action's three possible situations. For example, the following action: *"The customer introduces her password and the system verifies the identification data"* is complex because it can be broken down into two unidirectional atomic actions: *"The customer introduces her password"* and *"The system verifies the identification data."*

The Syntactic Perspective

From the syntactic or grammatical perspective, an action is expressed by means of a use case sentence (see Figure 1). A use case is a text that consists of a sequence of sentences that can be either simple or special (Díaz, Losavio, Matteo & Pastor, 2004). A *simple sentence* represents a unidirectional atomic action, which is of the communication or behavior type. Each sentence is described as a set of words, which can be associated to a syntactic category (i.e., adjective, noun, verb, etc.). These words can also form groups, according to the grammatical function that they fulfil in the sentence, configuring phrase structures (i.e., noun phrase, prepositional phrase, etc.). *Special sentences* are distinguished by having a predefined format that uses key words (for example: INCLUDE, EXTEND, and REPEAT).

In metamorphosis, the *syntactic normalization* of the use cases has a different implication to that commonly given in other approaches. The purpose of this process is to ensure that the use case text is specified in a correct and complete way (Ben-Achour, 1998; Rolland & Ben-Achour, 1998). Some authors have proposed applying style and content guidelines indicating how to write a use case and what type of information it supplies (Ben-Achour, 1998; Cockburn, 2001). Some experiments have proven the effectiveness of these guidelines to improve the use case documentation (Ben-Achour et al., 1999). However, because they are based on the reduction of the syntactic possibilities of the simple sentences, they also diminish their expressive capability for modelling effects. To achieve a reasonable balance between documentation and expressiveness, the metamorphosis translation strategy assumes the application of only those style and content guidelines that are mandatory to ensure that the use cases fulfil their purpose in the system development. These guidelines are the following: (1) sentences must be edited in a declarative, affirmative, and active way; (2) each sentence must have a single subject and a single main verb; and (3) the main verb of the sentence must be transitive, ensuring the presence of a direct object in the sentence. The following structure describes the components that a sentence can have:

<subject><main-verb>{<direct-object>{<preposi-phrase>[connector]}*}+|<subor di-clause>

Based on these elemental guidelines, it is deduced that the function of the subject of a simple sentence can only be performed by the nominal phrase designating the actor or the system being developed. The predicate is an expression that contains the verb action. In general, the predicate function is fulfilled by nominal and prepositional phrases. For example, the syntactic structure of the sentence *"The system registers the information in the accident report and in the insurance police"* is:

"{ *The (system)*$_{head}$ }$_{noun-phrase/subject}$
{ *(registers)*$_{main-verb}$ [*the (information)*$_{head}$]$_{noun-phrase/direct-object}$
[*in the (accident report)*$_{head}$]$_{place-prepositional-phrase}$ *(and)*$_{conjunction-connector}$
[*in the (insurance policy)*$_{head}$]$_{place- prepositional-phrase}$ }$_{predicate}$"

The Semantic Perspective

From the semantic perspective, a use case action can be represented as a relationship that is established between one or more *semantic* or *thematic roles* (see Figure 1). A sentence can be characterized by the semantic roles that it contains. Each one of these roles denotes an abstract function that is performed by an element participating in an action. This abstract function is defined independently from the syntactic structure that it can have in a sentence. These semantic role properties allow metamorphosis to represent interactions in a generic way; this is done independently from the language that is used to write the use cases and from the various grammatical resources that a language offers to express the same interaction.

Many types of roles have been defined with different grades of specificity (Guildea & Jurasfsky, 2002). In metamorphosis, roles proposed by different authors have been selected. The selection was based on the following criteria: (1) *generality* or *abstraction* so that the roles do not depend on a specific verb or domain; and (2) *applicability* so that they can be useful in recognizing and treating the interaction fragments. The roles used by metamorphosis can be: (1) *basic roles* if they always participate in a transitive sentence such as *agent* (what/who performs an action) and *object* (what/who undergoes an action); and (2) *secondary roles* if they are not required by the verbal action and always appear linked to a basic role. Some secondary roles are: *destination* (receiver/beneficiary of the action), *owner* (what/who possesses), *owned* (possessed entity), *instrument* (the means used to execute an action), *state* (entity status/condition), *location* (where an action takes place), *cause* (entity that causes something) and *time* (when the action occurs). The identification of roles is illustrated in the following sentence: "[*The salesman*]$_{agent}$ registers [*the identification*]$_{object/owner}$ [*of the buyer*]$_{owned.}$"

A *semantic context* allows the definition of a family of sentence types in terms of semantic roles as well as relationships that are established among them. A semantic context (SC) is specified using a logic formula SC=<a, m, y>, where a and m are sets of variables and constants, respectively, and y is a set of functions that are applicable to SC terms. The main objective of this formula is to determine which semantic roles participate in a sentence.

Table 1 shows a formula that describes the Shared Action Semantic Context, which has the following characteristics: (1) actions that have an active entity that initiates or controls the action (the *agent*), and a passive entity on which such action falls (the *object*); (2) the number clause operation determines the number of clauses in the sentence (in Metamorphosis, a clause represents a unidirectional atomic action that is obtained from a complex action); (3) the sentence can be decomposed into two or more clauses with the same *agent*, the same *mainverb* and the same *object*; each clause is associated to a different circumstance; (4) the *object state* may or may not change as a consequence of the action performed; (5) the *object* can have two or more *owner* entities at the same time; otherwise, (6) the *object* can be placed into two or more *locations* at the same time, or (7) the *object* can be sent to two or more *destinations*.

Table 1. Formula of a semantic context

Semantic Context: Shared Action

```
∀V,A,O,St,Or,L,D:
∃n>1 / NumberClause(Sentence)=n  ∧
( Action(verb:V,agent:A,object:O) ∧
   (State(object:O,state:St) ∨ State(object:O,state:?]) ) ∧
( ∀i=1..n  Ownership_i(owned:O,owner_i:Or) ∨
            Situate_i(agent:A,object:O,location_i:L) ∨
            Move_i(agent:A,object:O,destination_i:D) )  ;
```

For example, the sentence *"The system registers the information in the accident report and in the insurance police"* satisfies the formula of the Shared Action Semantic Context (see Table 1). The roles of this sentence are the following: "[*The system*]$_{agent}$ registers [*the information*]$_{object}$ [*in the accident report*]$_{location1}$ *and* [*in the insurance policy*]$_{location2}$." The sentence has a single *object* ("*the information*") and two clauses ("*The system registers the information in the accident report*" and "*The system registers the information in the insurance policy*"). The *object* ("*the information*") is registered by the *agent* ("*the system*") in two entities at the same time ("*accident report*" and "*insurance policy*"). The *object state* is not explicitly determined in the sentence.

Behavior Analysis

Interactions are the basic elements to express the results of a system behavior specification analysis. An *interaction* describes an information exchange that can be established between two or more instances to communicate with each other (OMG, 2003). In metamorphosis, these instances are considered to be *class objects* that describe the system internal composition. The information exchange or messages among these instances represent *operations* among these classes. The metamorphosis interaction structure profile describes the suitability of these concepts based on those presented in the UML interaction package (OMG, 2003). Figure 3 shows some elements of this profile. In this figure, the metaclasses distinguished as stereotypes were created by extension from base metaclasses that belong to the UML interaction package (OMG, 2003). These UML base metaclasses are: Interactions, LifeLine, and Message. The remaining metaclasses belong to the metamorphosis interaction structure

Figure 3. Metamorphosis interaction structure profile (partial view)

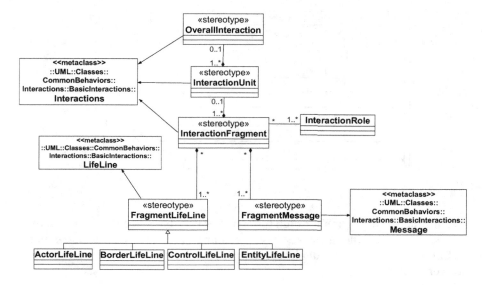

profile. One of the most important concepts in the metamorphosis interaction structure profile is the one that refers to the granularity of the interactions. Interaction granules depend on the specification granule that performs the system behavior analysis. If the analysis is performed based on a unidirectional and atomic action, the result is an *interaction fragment*. A fragment is an interaction that forms part of another interaction (OMG, 2003). It can be formed by one or more instances that interchange one or more messages (this is shown by means of the relationship multiplicity). Each lifeline of an instance is represented by the FragmentLifeLine, and each message is represented by a FragmentMessage, in Figure 3. In addition, the lifeline of an instance can be an actor class, a border class, a control class or an entity class. A fragment can contain one or more lifelines of several types.

If the complete set of use case actions is analyzed, an *interaction unit* is obtained. An interaction unit is the combination of all interaction fragments that are obtained from each of the use case actions. It is also possible to obtain more than one interaction unit from a use case: an interaction unit corresponds to the basic path of the use case and another interaction unit exists for each of its alternate paths. The combination of the fragments can be specified using the strict-sequence operator, which is defined by the UML (OMG, 2003). This operator joins the trace of one fragment with that of another, respecting the order

Figure 4. Generic structure of an interaction fragment (Fountain)

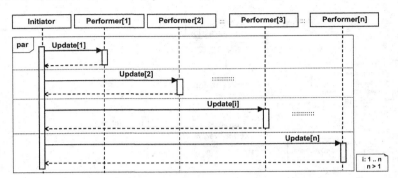

of occurrence of the action through time, just as they have been specified in the use case. When all the use cases have been analyzed, the system *Interaction Model* is obtained. This model integrates the information of all the interactions that were obtained.

In Metamorphosis, the interaction fragments are specified by means of a generic structure. This structure is described using roles to represent several action types and to add semantics to improve the comprehension of the interaction (France et al., 2004). Figure 4 presents the Fountain Interaction Fragment. This generic fragment has the following characteristics: (1) there are "*n*" lifelines; (2) the first lifeline plays the role of *initiator* (it is the sender of all the fragment messages); this lifeline can be represented by a boundary instance or a control instance; (3) the remaining lifelines play the role of *performers;* these lifelines are represented by entity instances (4) the messages sent by the *initiator* activate the *update* operations in *performer* (this operation type changes the object state); (5) the messages can be sent by the *initiator* simultaneously (this is allowed by the UML fragment operator *par*) (OMG, 2003).

In metamorphosis, the interaction fragments that are specified using roles are named *semantic fragments*. When these roles are expressed by means of syntactic structures, the interaction fragments are named *syntactic fragments*.

Interaction Linguistic Patterns

Metamorphosis conceives the interaction modelling as the automatic transformation of the actions of the use cases. An automatic transformation has two goals: (1) to extract relevant information of the use case sentences; and (2) to describe how the extracted information must be interpreted in order to obtain the interaction fragments. The modeller participation is limited to making design decisions, to resolving ambiguous situations, and to completing information about the interactions. Patterns specify the way that actions are transformed. These transformation patterns are based on linguistic information. This section explains the Metamorphosis transformation model, which is based on linguistic patterns, and how these patterns are specified and applied to the interaction modelling.

Action Transformation Model

The most important activity of the Metamorphosis framework is the transformation of an action. The complete transformation of a use case depends on the interactions obtained from each action that participates in the use case. Figure 5 describes the transformation model applied by Metamorphosis. This model has three levels: (1) the definition level; (2) the pattern specification level; and (3) the application level.

1. **The definition level:** The transformation definition of an action and the models that participate in this transformation are specified at metamodel level. In this level, the modelled elements that participate in the metamorphosis use case linguistic profile and in the metamorphosis interaction structure profile are related (see Figure 1 and Figure 3). Such relations are also defined.

2. **The pattern specification level:** This level describes how the semantic context of an action sentence is converted into a semantic fragment. At Model Level, the transformation patterns are specified. The roles are used to describe both the sentence and the fragment. The transformation rules explain how to obtain a semantic fragment from a semantic context. The specification of a transformation pattern is generic, domain-independent, and implementation-independent. The patterns are also independent of the

Figure 5. Transformation model of actions

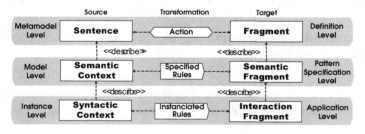

language used to write the sentences and their syntactic structures. The semantic fragments do not depend on the graphic representation styles. The next subsection describes the specification of a transformation pattern.

3.   **The pattern application level:** To obtain the desired interaction fragment, a transformation pattern must be applied. This application is carried out by the instantiation of a specified pattern. Thus, a particular sentence is transformed into a specific interaction fragment. This requires knowing the syntactic structure associated to the roles that participate in the sentence.

Transformation Patterns

The purpose of the transformation patterns is to capture transformation knowledge and to reuse them appropriately. Table 2 shows the specification of a transformation pattern. The description of the elements that were suppressed in this table can be found in previous sections. Each transformation pattern of Metamorphosis has been specified using the following elements:

1.   **Name.** It identifies the transformation pattern and distinguishes it from others.

2.   **Description.** It gives a concise explanation about the transformation pattern.

3.   **Semantic context.** It is a description of an action that is based on roles. A transformation pattern is only applicable to actions that fulfil the semantic context established by this pattern.

4.   **Transformation rules:** They describe how the participants of a semantic context are turned into elements of an interaction fragment. Each rule is expressed by means of a formula whose left side corresponds to the fragment elements. The right side of a rule indicates how to identify these elements. The transformation rules recognize roles in the semantic context to identify the interaction elements, using functions applied on the semantic roles.

5.   **Semantic fragment:** It is a description of an interaction structure that uses roles.

6.   **Observations:** They describe specific patterns, application examples, and/or several annotations.

Transformation rules are the key part of a pattern. Table 2 presents the rules that are applicable to sentences whose semantic context is described in Table 1. By

Table 2. Transformation pattern (simplified version): An example

Name	Shared Fountain
Description	This pattern can be applied to an action that represents an internal behavior of the system. The action is a simple sentence that can be decomposed into two or more clauses. These clauses have the same subject, the same main verb, and the same direct object. The only difference among these clauses is their prepositional-phrase. The obtained interaction contains one message for each sentence clause. The messages are sent from the same instance of concurrent form. The message order is irrelevant. They are received by different instances. The message tags are equals.
Semantic Context	Shared Action (see Table 1)
Transformation Rules	initiator $\leftarrow$ agent performer[i] $\leftarrow \forall i=1..n$ (<Head(owner$_i$)>^{Norm} $\vee$ <Head(location$_i$)>^{Norm} $\vee$ <Head(destination$_i$)>^{Norm}); Update[i] $\leftarrow \forall i=1..n$ (Sequence(verb,<object>^{Norm},state) $\vee$ Sequence(verb,<object>^{Norm}));
Semantic Fragment	Fountain (see Figure 4)
Observations	In general, the *initiator* role is played by a lifeline that represents a boundary instance. This instance is frequently named as the system in development. However, the *initiator* role can be played by a control instance, too.

applying these rules, a fragment is obtained that has the generic form shown in Figure 4. The rules given in the transformation pattern in Table 2 should be interpreted as follows: the lifeline of the *initiator* instance is identified by the *agent* of the sentence. Each lifeline of a *performer* instance is deduced from: (1) the *owner* contained in each clause of the use case sentence; or (2) the *location* contained in each clause of the use case sentence; or (3) the *destination* contained in each clause of the use case sentence.

The Head function extracts the most important constituent of the *owner*, *location*, or *destination*. The *normalization function* builds the canonical form of the role heads. The signature of the *update* operation is deduced by a *sequence function*. This function constructs a label with the *principal verb*, the *object*, and the *object state* of each sentence clause. All the messages received by each instance are equal.

Applying a Transformation Pattern

Before applying a transformation pattern, it must be instantiated. The instantiation process moves the action from the model level to the instance level (see Figure 5). This process assumes that: (1) the use case action is syntactically normalized;

and (2) the use case action contains the corresponding syntactic and semantic information (constituents/phrases and semantic roles). The instantiation process can be performed in fours steps:

First step: to recognize the semantic context. The semantic information of the action sentence to be analyzed is used to determine the semantic context of the action. The semantic context of each transformation pattern is evaluated using the semantic information of the sentence as was described earlier. The sentence: *"The system registers the information in the accident report and in the insurance policy,"* will be considered as an example for the instantiation process (see Table 1). This sentence satisfies the formula of the shared action semantic context.

Second step: to identify the transformation rules. This is immediate because each semantic context defines each action transformation pattern. The pattern that corresponds to the shared action semantic context has the transformation rules given in Table 2. When this transformation pattern is applied, a fountain interaction fragment is obtained.

Third step: to identify the syntactic structure of the sentence. To carry out the pattern instantiation, the syntactic structure of the roles that participate in the sentence must be known. The syntactic structure of the example sentence, has the following characteristics: (1) the *agent* and *object* roles are linked to noun-phrases; and (2) the *location* roles are expressed by place-prepositional-phrases. The syntactic and semantic information of the sentence is the following:

"{ *The (system)*$_{head}$ }$_{noun-phrase/subject(\textbf{agent})}$
{ *(registers)*$_{main-verb}$ [*the (information)*$_{head}$]$_{noun-phrase/direct-object(\textbf{object})}$
[*in the (accident report)*$_{head}$]$_{place-prepositional-phrase(\textbf{location1})}$ *(and)*$_{conjunction-connector}$
[*in the (insurance policy)*$_{head}$]$_{place- prepositional-phrase(\textbf{location1})}$ }$_{predicate}$ "

Fourth step: to apply the transformation rules. This consists of obtaining the interaction elements from the sentence. For example, when the transformation rules of the pattern given in Table 2 are applied to the example sentence, the elements identified are the following (Figure 6): (1) a border/control instance (*initiator*) whose name is extracted from the noun-phrase head of the *agent* (*"system"*); (2) two domain instances: *accident report* and *insurance policy*. These instances are recognized from the noun-phrase head of each place-prepositional-phrase (*location roles*). The canonical form of each head is verified; and (3) two synchronous and concurrent messages that are sent by the *system* instance. These messages are responsible for activating the operation execution identified as "register the information." The label of each message is obtained using the main-verb and the direct-object of the sentence.

Figure 6. An interaction fragment obtained by metamorphosis

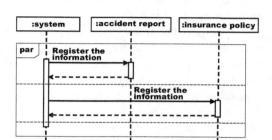

Transformation Strategy

The purpose of the transformation patterns is to recognize the basic elements that participate in an interaction fragment (i.e., lifelines/instances and messages). To identify other elements and to verify the consistency of the interaction model, it is necessary to analyze groups of actions or groups of use cases. The generated information of each transformed action must be integrated. An integration activity is, for example, to combine the interaction fragments that are deduced from each sentence of a use case until the interaction is completed. In addition, there is information that can only be deduced through either a partial or a complete analysis of the use case, such as to deduce the candidate parameters of each message. This information must also be incorporated into the obtained interactions.

Finally, the integration of the interactions deduced for each use case allows us to obtain the interaction model of the system. This task must resolve the possible conflicts that are generated when all partial representations are combined.

A Validation Experiment

An experiment to validate the transformation patterns was designed by OO method group researchers of the Technical University of Valencia, Spain (Díaz, Moreno, Fuentes, & Pastor, 2005). Until now, the experiment has been replicated four times to determine whether each pattern generates the expected interaction fragments from a use case action. The experiment was performed in four phases, which are outlined as follows:

Phase 1: design of the transformation patterns. This task consisted of discovering what correspondence could be established between a use case action and an interaction fragment. This activity was carried out by OOmethod group researchers, who specified the transformation patterns that would be validated. The steps followed to design these patterns were: (1) the identification of interaction fragments by means of the direct observation of a sample of sequence diagrams that had been deduced from use cases; this sample was extracted from the use case models and the interaction models of academic and commercial information systems; (2) the determination of correspondences between actions and fragments for each sentence; (3) the deduction of a generic interaction structure based on roles for each action and for each fragment; and (4) the definition of the corresponding transformation pattern. The transformation patterns identified were organized in an initial catalog to determine their validity.

Phase 2: manual deduction of interactions. Five experts in behavior modelling participated in this phase. They did not know the transformation patterns designed in Phase 1. These modellers had experience in the application of UML to develop use case models and sequence diagrams. To obtain the interactions, the modellers selected the modelling technique proposed by Song (2001). This technique was applied to construct the interaction model of the systems. The modellers also constructed the use case models. The use case models and the corresponding interaction models were extensively revised to reach a consensus on the results obtained manually.

Phase 3: automatic deduction of interactions. This process consisted of modelling interactions using the linguistic patterns specified during Phase 1. This task was performed with the same systems used in Phase 2. The automatic deduction was supported by a transformation tool that was developed for this purpose. This tool was integrated into the requirements engineering tool (RETO) (Insfrán et al., 2002). RETO supports the requirements specification and analysis activities of OO method, an automatic software production environment (Pastor et al., 2001). Figure 7 shows the components of the transformation tool and how this tool was integrated into RETO. It uses a parser to tag sentences with its constituents. These constituents are grouped in phrases according to a context-free grammar that had been previously constructed by OO method group researchers. This grammar allows us to know the syntactic structure of each use case sentence and to determine its semantic/syntactic context. Depending on the sentence context, the transformation tool applies a certain pattern. Later, the transformation tool combines the deduced fragments to obtain the corresponding SD.

Phase 4: interaction comparison. This task consisted of comparing the SD generated using the Metamorphosis transformer with the SD obtained manually. The purpose of this process was to determine the differences and similarities

Figure 7. The transformation tool architecture

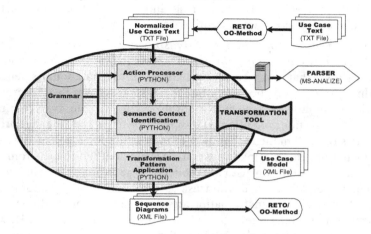

among the interaction fragments. This task was carried out by the modellers that participated in Phase 2. The manually obtained fragments were individually compared with the fragments generated automatically for each sentence of the use cases. The result of this comparison allowed us to determine whether both fragments were: (1) *equal*, when the two fragments were composed of the same instances and the same messages; (2) *equivalent*, if the two fragments represented the same interaction, even though the instances and messages were not the same; and (3) *different*, when the compared fragments were neither equal nor equivalent.

To date, this validation strategy has been applied to 280 use cases (3,112 simple sentences and 412 special sentences). Using the established criteria, 65% of the transformation patterns were equal, 28% were equivalent, and only 7% were categorized as different. This strategy allowed us to improve or to reject transformation patterns. It has also allowed us to identify new transformation patterns. Currently, the Metamorphosis catalog contains 25 transformation patterns that have been validated using this strategy.

Conclusion

This chapter has presented metamorphosis, a generic framework whose main purpose is facilitating the interaction modelling. This framework attempts to improve the offered possibilities of existing interaction modelling techniques.

However, there are still lines of research that continue open. In this sense, Metamorphosis can be considered as a mean and as a goal. The following issues describe some conclusions and potential areas of research.

The integration of the contributions from software engineering and computational linguistics can reinforce interaction modelling. The metamorphosis framework shows that some current proposals in computational science can support this activity. The strategic alliance between software engineering and computational linguistics is an important aspect to be able to overcome the limitations of interaction modelling. The application of natural language processing facilitates the automatic recognition of interaction model elements and the establishment of persistent links between these elements and those from which they are deduced. In addition, use case models can be enriched with information that is not only useful for the deduction task but also for improving documentation and comprehension. The transformation architecture based on models promotes the construction of robust interaction models from use case models. However, it is necessary to continue working with the purpose of strengthening bonds between these disciplines.

Interaction modelling can be an easier task and can produce better results. This can only be achieved with the support of a tool that performs tedious and troublesome tasks. The modeller can then concentrate on more important activities such as design decisions and validation of analysis results. A transformation tool based on metamorphosis was created for OO method, but its implementation depends on this application. It is necessary to design and to implement a tool that can be integrated in several automatic software production environments.

The use case normalization process can be flexible without causing a decrease in its quality. This can be achieved by establishing automatic controls that identify the possible problems of a use case text. These problems can then be solved using the convenient mechanisms according to the circumstances (i.e., natural language processing techniques, interaction with the modeller, the establishment of development-guided strategies, etc.). It is simply a matter of applying only the natural language restrictions that are strictly necessary and avoiding the reduction of its potential capability to express the system behavior. The current tools do not have use case editors in order to facilitate this task.

Pattern definition is a good, centralized way to record the action transformation knowledge. This resource enables the study of the correctness, completeness, and consistency of the designed transformations. In addition, it also facilitates the documentation, creation, understanding, application, and maintenance of this knowledge. However, in order to ensure their correct and consistent application, it is necessary to determine the best form to express the transformation patterns (formal/informal, graphic, etc.).

The definition of an architecture based on model transformation facilitates the description of the transition between the dynamic behavior specification and its analysis, at a high level of abstraction. This architecture must be independent of implementation considerations to facilitate their maintenance and extension. It also must control the complexity derived from the transformation strategy. This strategy can be defined using different levels interrelated by means of instantiation, integration, and refinement processes. Metamorphosis has proposed a transformation strategy. However, this must be reinforced and proved in order to determine its real reach.

It is possible to shorten the gap that traditionally exists between the specification and the analysis of a system dynamic behavior. This can be achieved through transformation patterns for which persistent links must be established between the elements of the use case model and the elements of the interaction model. These links must be documented, controlled, and maintained.

The transformation strategy must locate the dynamic model at the same level of priority as the system structural model. With this purpose, the dynamic model has to be independent on the information provided by the structural model. This strategy assumes that both models can be constructed simultaneously and iteratively in a complementary way. Extending the transformation patterns with structural information associated to the semantic context of an action is a pending task.

The use of semantic roles allows the specification of the transformation strategy to be independent from the language that is used to write the use cases. The semantic roles can be used to describe the actions of a use case without having to indicate its syntactic structure. Thus, the transformation patterns can be reused for texts in different languages. Within the same language, it is also possible to associate different types of syntactic structures to each role in order to establish variants of the language. The use of roles to define transformation patterns also facilitates their understanding and application. However, there is not a tool exclusively created to label the use cases with roles. A tool of this type should be designed in order to carry out this task efficiently.

The specification of interaction fragments based on roles provides a generic structure that is applicable to different transformation patterns. This is of special interest for the different types of actions of a use case that can be represented using the same type of interaction fragment. Furthermore, these generic structures facilitate the understanding of the interactions that derive from the analysis of an action and the definition of the transformation patterns. Research in this direction is being currently developed (see France et al., 2004).

Validation of transformation patterns can determine whether or not the interactions deduced are correct. We are currently carrying out more experiments to reinforce this assumption. We are also defining a strategy to ensure the continuous validation of the transformation pattern catalog not only in terms of its correctness but also in terms of its completeness and consistency.

References

Ambler, S. (2004). *The object primer: Agile model driven development with UML 2* (3rd ed.). Cambridge: Cambridge University Press.

Ben-Achour, C. (1998). Guiding use case authoring. In P. Chen & R. P. van de Riet (Eds.), *Proceedings of the Fourth IEEE International Symposium on Requirements Engineering (RE'98)* (pp. 36-43). Colorado Springs, CO: IEEE Computer Society.

Ben-Achour, C., Rolland, C., Maiden, N. A. M., & Souveyet, C. (1999). Guiding use case authoring: Results of an empirical study. In *Proceedings of the Fourth IEEE International Symposium on Requirements Engineering (RE'99)* (pp. 36-43). Limerick, Ireland. IEEE Computer Society.

Berry, D., & Kamsties, E. (2004). Ambiguity in requirements specification. In J. S. do Padro Leite & J. H. Doorn (Eds.), *Perspectives on software requirements* (pp. 7-44). Kluwer Academic Publishers.

Blanchard, B., & Fabrycky, W. (1990). *Systems engineering and analysis*. Englewood Cliffs, NJ: Prentice Hall.

Boyd, N. (1999). Using natural language in software development. *Journal of Object-oriented Programming, 11*(9), 45-55.

Burg, J. F. M., & van de Riet, R. P. (1995). Color-X: Linguistically-based event modeling. A general approach to dynamic modeling. In J. Iivari, K. Lyytinen, & M. Rossi (Eds.), *Advanced information systems engineering, 7th International Conference CAiSE'95, 932* (pp. 26-39). Berlin: Springer-Verlag.

Burg, J. F. M., & van de Riet, R. P. (1996). Analyzing informal requirements specifications: A first step towards conceptual modeling. In R. P. van de Riet, J. F. M. Burg, & A. J. van der Vos (Eds.), *Proceedings on applications of natural language to information systems (NLDB)*. Amsterdam, The Netherlands: IOS Press.

Chen, P. S. (1976). The entity-relationship model — Towards unified view of data. *ACM Transactions on Database Systems, 1*(1), 9-36.

Cockburn, A. (2001). *Writing effective use cases* (4th ed.). Addison-Wesley.

Dehne, F., Steuten, A., & van de Riet, R. P. (2001). WordNet++: A lexicon for the Color-X-Method. *Data & Knowledge, 38*, 3-29.

Díaz, I., Losavio, F., Matteo, A., & Pastor, O. (2004). A specification pattern for use cases. *Information & Management, 41*, 961-975.

Díaz, I., Moreno, L., Fuentes, I., & Pastor, O. (2005). Integrating natural language techniques in OO-Method. In A. Gelbukh (Ed.), *Computational linguistic and intelligent text processing, 6th International Conference, CICLing 2005* (pp. 560-572). Berlin: Springer-Verlag.

Díaz, I., Moreno, L., Pastor, O., & Matteo, A. (2005). Interaction transformation patterns based on semantic roles. In A. Montoyo, R. Muñoz, & E. Métais (Eds.), *Proceedings of the 10th International Conference of Applications of Natural Language to Information Systems, NLDB'05* (pp. 239-250). Berlin: Springer-Verlag.

Feijs, L. M. G. (2000). Natural language and message sequence chart representation of use cases. *Information and Software Technology, 42*, 633-647.

Flield, G., Kop, C., Mayerthaler, W., Mayr H., & Winkler, C. (2000). Linguistic aspects of dynamics in requirements specifications. *IEEE Proceedings of the 11th International Workshop on Databases and Expert Systems Applications (DEXA)* (pp. 83-90). London: IEEE Computer Society.

France, R., Kim, D.K., Ghosh, S., & Song, E. (2004). A UML-based pattern specification technique. *IEEE Transactions on Software Engineering, 30*, 193-206.

Gamma, E., Helm, R., Johnson, R., & Vlissides, J. (1992). *Design patterns. Elements of reusable object-oriented software.* Addison-Wesley Longman, Inc.

Guildea, D., & Jurafsky, D. (2002). Automatic labeling of semantic roles. *Computational Linguistics, 28*, 245-280.

Hilsbos, M., & Song, I.-Y. (2004). Use of tabular analysis method to construct UML sequence diagrams. In P. Atzeni, W. Chu, H. Lu, S. Zhou, & T. W. Ling (Eds.), *Proceedings of the 23rd International Conference on Conceptual Modeling, RE'04* (pp. 740-752). Berlin: Springer-Verlag.

Insfrán, E., Pastor, O., & Wieringa, R. (2002). Requirements engineering-based conceptual modeling. *Requirements Engineering, 7*, 61-72.

ITU: International Telecommunication Union. (2000). *International recommendation Z.120. Message Sequence Chart (MSC).* Geneva: ITU.

Jacobson, I., Booch, G., & Rumbaugh, J. (1999). *The unified software development process.* Addison Wesley Longman, Inc.

Jacobson, I., Christerson, M., Jonsson, P., & Övergaard, G. (1992). *Object-oriented software engineering. A use case driven approach.* Addison Wesley Longman, Inc.

Juristo, N., Moreno, A. M., & López, M. (2000). How to use linguistic instruments for object-oriented analysis. *IEEE Software, 17*(3), 80-89.

Kleppe, A., Warmer, J., & Bast, W. (2003). *MDA explained. The model driven architecture: Practice and promise.* Addison-Wesley.

Kop, C., & Mayr, H. (2002). Mapping functional requirements: From natural language to conceptual schemata. In *Proceedings of the 6th International Conference Software Engineering and Applications (SEA)*. Cambridge: IASTED.

Larman, C. (2004). *Applying UML and patterns: An introduction to object-oriented analysis and design and iterative development* (3rd ed.). Prentice Hall.

Li, L. (2000). Translating use cases to sequence diagrams. In *Proceedings of the Fifteenth IEEE International Conference on Automated Software Engineering ASE* (pp. 293-296), Grenoble, France. IEEE Computer Society.

Métais, E. (2002). Enhancing information systems management with natural language processing techniques. *Data & Knowledge Engineering, 41*, 247-272.

Mich, L., Franch, M., & Inverardi, N. (2004). Market research for requirements analysis using linguistic tools. *Requirements Engineering, 9*(1), 40-56.

Nuseibeh, B., & Easterbrook, S. (2000). Requirements engineering: A roadmap. In *Proceedings of the 22nd International Conference on Software Engineering: ICSE'2000* (pp. 37-46), Limerick, Ireland. ACM Press.

OMG: Object Management Group. (2003). *Unified modeling language: Superstructure specification. Version 2.0.* Retrieved April 10, 2006, from http://www.omg.org/uml

Overmyer, S., Lavoie, B., & Rambow, O. (2001). Conceptual modeling through linguistic analysis using LIDA. In *Proceedings of the Conference on Software Engineering, ICSE* (pp. 401-410), Toronto, Ontario, Canada. IEEE Computer Society.

Pastor, O., Gómez, J., Insfrán, E., & Pelechano, V. (2001). The OO-method approach for information systems modeling: From object-oriented conceptual modeling to automated programming. *Information Systems, 26*, 507-534.

Rolland, C., & Ben-Achour, C. (1998). Guiding the construction of textual use case specifications. *Data & Knowledge Engineering, 25*, 125-160.

Rosenberg, D., & Scott, K. (1999). *Use case driven object modeling with UML: A practical approach.* Addison-Wesley Longman, Inc.

Rumbaugh, J. (1995). What is a method? *Journal of Object-Oriented Programming, Modeling & Design Section, 8*(6), 10/16-26.

Rumbaugh, J., Blaha, M., Premerlani, W., Eddy, F., & Lorensen, W. (1991). *Object-oriented modeling and design*. Englewood Cliffs, NJ: Prentice Hall International Inc.

Song, I. Y. (2001). Developing sequence diagrams in UML. In A. R. Tawil, N. J. Fiddian, & W. A. Gray (Eds.), *Proceedings of the 20th International Conference on Conceptual Modeling: ER'2001* (pp. 368-382). Berlin: Springer-Verlag.

Van Lamsweerde, A. (2000). Requirements engineering in the year 2000: A research perspective. In *Proceedings of the 22nd International Conference on Software Engineering: ICSE'2000* (pp. 5-19). ACM Press.

Wieringa, R. (1998). A survey of structured and object-oriented software specification methods and techniques. *ACM Computing Surveys, 30*(4), 459-527.

Wirfs-Brock, R., Wilkerson, B., & Wiener, L. (1990). *Designing object-oriented software*. Englewood Cliffs, NJ: Prentice Hall International Inc.

Chapter IV

A Framework Based on Design Patterns:
Implementing UML Association, Aggregation and Composition Relationships in the Context of Model-Driven Code Generation

Manoli Albert, Universidad Politécnica de Valencia, Spain

Marta Ruiz, Universidad Politécnica de Valencia, Spain

Javier Muñoz, Universidad Politécnica de Valencia, Spain

Vincente Pelechano, Universidad Politécnica de Valencia, Spain

Abstract

This chapter proposes a framework based on design patterns to implement UML association, aggregation, and composition relationships. To build the framework, we propose a semantic interpretation of these concepts that avoids the ambiguities introduced by UML. This interpretation is achieved

by using a set of properties that allows us to characterize these kinds of relationships. Once the semantics of the relationships have been defined, we propose a framework based on design patterns for the systematic generation of a software representation. The framework is based on the properties that characterize the relationships. It provides a high-quality solution and introduces important benefits with regard to other existing implementation approaches. This work proposes an implementation strategy that defines a set of mappings between the conceptual abstractions and the proposed framework. This strategy enables the automatic instantiation of the framework. Finally, to validate the proposal, we present a C# implementation of a collaboration pattern. Collaboration patterns are analysis patterns constituted by two classes that are related by an association, an aggregation or a composition relationship.

Introduction

Current development methods and tools are focused on model-driven software development (MDSD) processes. In particular, the model-driven architecture (MDA) proposal of the object management group (OMG) constitutes an approach for the development of software systems that is based on a clear separation between the specification of the essential system functionalities and the implementation of this specification through the use of specific implementation platforms. MDA tries to raise the abstraction level in software development by giving more relevance to conceptual modeling. Models with a high level of abstraction (platform independent models, PIM) are translated into models that are expressed in terms of specific implementation technologies (platform specific models, PSM). The PSM can be used to generate automatically the application code. A practical application of MDA requires more mature techniques and tools than those that are currently available. In order to achieve the MDA goals, we consider that it is necessary to provide:

- **Conceptual modeling abstractions with a precise semantics:** The precision of the modeling abstractions is a key characteristic in building appropriate PIM. Rich conceptual models are needed to define transformations that guarantee that the generated code is functionally equivalent to the specification.

- **Implementation techniques:** Frameworks and design patterns facilitate the implementation of the modeling abstractions in target implementation languages, the definition of transformations, and the production of high-quality solutions.

The goal of this chapter is to provide solutions for these requirements, taking the association relationship as the target conceptual modeling abstraction. The association relationships include the aggregation and composition UML concepts.

The association relationship is one of the most widely used abstractions in OO conceptual modeling. Several authors (Civello, 1993; Guéhéneuc & Albin-Amiot, 2004; Henderson-Sellers & Barbier, 1999a, 1999b; Odell, 1994; Opdahl, Henderson-Sellers & Barbier, 2001; Saksena, France, & Larrondo-Petrie, 1998; Snoeck & Dedene, 2001; Wand, Storey, & Weber, 1999; Winston, Chan, & Herrmann, 1987) have studied the semantics of these relationships for many years. They have identified structural and behavioral properties that characterize this abstraction. Nevertheless, a consensus has not yet been achieved. UML does not provide a complete solution for this problem: The proposed semantics introduces many ambiguities, as recognized in Henderson-Sellers and Barbier (1999a); Genova, Llorens, and Palacios (2002); and Guéhéneuc and Albin-Amiot (2004). This lack of consensus leaves the association relationship without a precise and clear semantics. Modelers cannot use this relationship without ambiguities during the conceptual modeling step. Therefore, automatic code generation that takes the association relationship as input is very difficult.

With regard to design and implementation techniques, the current techniques for implementing association relationships (for object relation, see Graham, Bischof, & Henderson-Sellers, 1997; for metaclasses, see Dahchour, 2001; Klas & Schrefl, 1995; for genericity, see Kolp & Pirotte, 1997) only provide partial solutions. These solutions are either too difficult to apply (in the case of metaclasses and genericity due to the lack of support of the majority of programming languages) or too simple (references) to give support to the complex behavior of an association relationship. These drawbacks indicate the need for a high-quality implementation proposal. This proposal should enable the CASE tools that support model-driven development to provide code generation of the association relationship through a precise framework instantiation. This is the strategy that is recommended by the new development approach Software Factories (Greenfield, Short, Cook, & Kent, 2004).

The present chapter introduces four clear contributions:

- **To present an association model with a well-defined semantics:** This goal is achieved by providing a precise definition for the UML association, aggregation, and composition concepts, and removing the ambiguities introduced by the UML. This chapter proposes a semantic interpretation for these concepts. This interpretation is based on a conceptual framework that identifies a set of essential properties that allows the precise characterization of the association relationships.

- **To propose a framework based on a set of design patterns:** (Gamma, Helm, Johnson, & Vlissides, 1994) to improve the association relationship implementation. This framework provides a high-quality implementation of the association, aggregation, and composition relationships. This implementation is based on the properties that characterize the relationships.

- **To define a complete methodological approach for automatic code generation:** This chapter proposes an implementation strategy that defines a set of mappings between the conceptual abstraction and the proposed framework. The mappings permit the instantiation of the framework to obtain a fully operative association implementation. This implementation can be used to build industrial code generators. This approach improves the productivity and the quality of the final software product.

- **To validate our framework implementation proposal:** This chapter presents a C# implementation of the framework. We have used collaboration patterns (CP) (from Bolloju, 2004) to check the correctness of the implementation. The CP define the common association relationships identified in business applications. We have implemented these patterns using our framework. This chapter presents an instance of the implementation.

The rest of the chapter is structured as follows: the second section provides definitions and discussions of the topic and presents a review of the literature. The third section presents a conceptual framework that identifies a set of properties that characterize the UML association relationships. The framework is used to provide a precise interpretation for the semantics of the UML association, aggregation, and composition concepts. The fourth section presents a framework that is based on the Mediator, Decorator and Template Method design patterns. This framework provides a high-quality implementation for the association relationship within MDSD. The fifth section presents a code generation strategy that specifies how to instantiate the framework to implement the association relationship. This strategy defines how to obtain the structure and behavior of the classes that belong to the framework to give complete support to the implementation of the full functionality of the association relationship. To validate our proposal, the sixth section presents a C# implementation of a collaboration pattern. The seventh section presents further works, and the last section presents conclusions.

Background

Code generation is currently a leading topic in software engineering. The goal of code generation is to obtain automatic mechanisms to improve the quality and the productivity of the software production process. Several methods and tools have been developed to give support to these requirements. Tools like ArchStyler (www.arcstyler.com) or OptimalJ (www.compuware.com/products/optimalj) provide powerful code generation techniques.

One of the most recent contributions in the software engineering field is the MDA approach. The MDA proposal constitutes a suitable approach for carrying out the code generation process in a structured and documented way, following a strategy based on models. MDA promotes the separation between the specification of the essential functionalities of the system and the implementation of this functionality, thus allowing for the definition of transformations towards the implementation of the system independently of technological aspects. The main contribution of the MDA proposal is the emphasis on the use of conceptual models for code generation and the proposal of several OMG languages for performing that task.

Currently, the main efforts in the MDA are focused on the transformations between models. Some methods claim to give support to MDA, but actually there are few proposals that provide precise guidelines for the automatic transformation between models. Moreover, there does not exist a standardized way for specifying and applying model transformations. Currently, the OMG is working in the QVT (Object Management Group, 2002) standard for filling this important lack.

Following the MDA approach, we provide a precise definition for the association abstraction in an OO conceptual model. Once the association abstraction is precisely defined, we provide a framework that enables the definition of mappings for the translation of the conceptual model specification (PIM) into a platform specific model (PSM) based on a generic OO language. This proposal is being applied in OLIVA NOVA model execution (www.care-t.com), an industrial CASE tool that generates completely functional and executable software applications from models.

A recent trend in software engineering is to define and to use software patterns at several abstraction levels (requirements elicitation, analysis, design, etc.) during the development process. In this chapter, we use a set of design patterns for the construction of the proposed framework. Those design patterns enable the definition of mappings between the conceptual model and it software representation.

Association Relationships in Conceptual Models

The meaning of the association concept, central to and widely used in the OO paradigm, is problematic. The definitions provided in the literature for this construct are often imprecise and incomplete. Conceptual modeling languages and methods, such as Syntropy (Cook & Daniels, 1994), UML (Object Management Group, 2003), OML (Firesmith, Henderson-Sellers & Graham, 1997) or Catalysis (D'Souza, & Wills, 1998), include partial association definitions that do not achieve a consensus for an unified semantic definition. Several works have appeared highlighting the drawbacks of the proposals and answering many important questions regarding associations.

Henderson-Sellers has presented different works searching for answers to some relevant questions, such as the *directionality* of associations (Henderson-Sellers & Barbier, 1999), the special meaning of *aggregation* and *composition* (Henderson-Sellers & Barbier, 1999), and other interesting aspects. Genova presented a PhD thesis (Genova, 2001) which makes an intensive analysis of some problematic properties of associations: *multiplicity*, *navigability* and *visibility*. Other authors work specifically on the *aggregation* constructor. Saksena (Saksena et al., 1998) proposes a set of primary and secondary characteristics that allow determining when a relationship is an aggregation. In Henderson-Sellers and Barbier (1999), the authors refine Saksena's work, proposing different sets of primary and secondary characteristics. In Snoeck and Dedene (2001), the authors propose a single property, *existent dependency*, to characterize aggregation relationships (although these works do not focus on defining mappings to software representations, their studies are useful in the definition of the association concept). Guéhéneuc et al. in a recent work (Guéhéneuc & Albin-Amiot, 2004) try to bridge the gap between the conceptual specification of an association and its implementation. The authors identify four properties for characterizing associations and propose a set of detection algorithms to bring continuity between the implementation and the design. These algorithms are validated using reverse-engineering.

In summary, there are several proposals for the definition of association, but a consensus has not yet been reached. The analysis of the most relevant works can be used for the definition of a set of properties that allows the precise and complete definition of the association construct. In this chapter, we use this knowledge to build a conceptual framework that identifies a set of properties that can characterize the association relationships.

Implementation Techniques for Association Relationships

Most object-oriented programming languages do not provide a specific construct to deal with associations as first level constructs. Users of these languages should use reference attributes to implement associations between objects. Following this approach, an association is relegated to a second-class status. To improve this situation, several approaches have been proposed to implement association relationships (Dahchour, 2001).

- The most widely used approach implements associations as **references** (Graham et al., 1997; Rumbaugh, 1987). Participating classes hold references or pointers to their associated classes. The properties of the association are implemented in the participating classes. This approach provides a straightforward access to the relationship, but presents several limitations: Participating classes become more complex, the properties of the relationship are not implemented in a centralized way, and consistency must be maintained by hand within the business logic.

- Another well-known approach is the use of **relationship objects**. In this approach, association instances are represented by objects (relationship objects) with two references that are used to link two related objects. To support this approach, relationship classes are defined to describe the relationship objects. The properties of the association are implemented in the relationship classes. This approach permits the reuse of participating classes (no modifications to the data structure are required). Properties are implemented in a centralized way, and space is used only when relationships are needed. However, the problem of dangling references (during deleting operations) is an important limitation of this approach.

- A more complex technique is the use of **built-in primitives** (Díaz & Paton, 1994: Rumbaugh, 1987). The central idea of this approach is to supply a built-in primitive which helps to declare explicitly and specify a large variety of specific relationships. Based on these specifications, the underlying system automatically enforces and maintains the semantics of relationships. In this approach, properties are implemented in one class and relationships are reusable. However, some properties of the association cannot be captured by built-in primitives.

- The **genericity** approach (Kolp & Pirotte, 1997) is specifically used for implementing generic relationships (Pirotte, Zimanyi, & Dahchour, 1998). These relationships are implemented through parameterized classes. The genericity approach consists in defining one parameterized class that abstracts a set of specific relationships. One advantage of this approach is the reusability of the relationship; however a disadvantage is that it is not possible to deal with the class properties of the associations.

- **Metaclasses** (Dahchour, 2001; Klas & Schrefl, 1995) are also used to implement associations. This approach consists in defining the semantics of an association only once within a metaclass structure. This structure permits defining and querying the association at the class level. The related classes are instances of the metaclasses that represent the association. This approach permits the reusability of the associations, and facilitates the maintainability and the dynamicity of the associations. Nevertheless, it is a complex strategy, which is difficult to implement and which is not easily supported by most programming languages.

We conclude that implementing associations with current techniques may lead to reduced cohesion and increased coupling as well as difficulties with referential integrity. All the techniques have benefits and drawbacks; therefore, the context of use determines which of the presented strategies is selected.

Within the context of MDSD (and following an OO perspective), we provide an implementation for associations in OO languages. The implementation, based in the technique of relationship objects, is a high-quality mechanism for supporting the association properties while maintaining the most relevant quality factors of the software (reusability, maintainability, extensibility, complexity). Current techniques do not satisfy all these requirements, so we need a new proposal to achieve our goals.

We have found patterns in the design pattern literature that can be applied to implement association relationships (particularly the decorator, mediator, and template method presented in Gamma, Helm, Johnson & Vlissides, 1994). These design patterns provide quality and tested solutions. In this chapter, we use these design patterns to build a framework for the implementation of associations.

A Conceptual Framework for Characterizing UML Association Concepts

In the context of code generation, a precise semantics for the association concept must be defined to obtain a correct software representation. The definition of a precise semantics guarantees that the generated code is functionally equivalent to the specification.

To define a precise semantics for the association concept, we present a conceptual framework that identifies a set of properties that have been adapted from different OO modeling methods. These properties allow to characterize precisely association relationships in a conceptual model. The semantics proposed is based on the basic definitions of association, aggregation, and composition concepts in the UML.

The conceptual framework is based on a process in which we have studied several approaches that analyze the association relationships (the Olivé analysis in Olivé, 2001; the works of Henderson-Sellers et al. where the aggregation is analyzed: Opdahl, Henderson-Sellers, & Barbier (2001), and Henderson-Sellers & Barbier, 1999a, 1999b; Civello's proposal in Civello, 1993; Odell's composition study in Odell, 1994; Saksena et al. proposal for aggregations in Saksena, France & Larrondo-Petrie, 1998; Snoeck et al. arguments about existent dependency in Snoeck & Dedene, 2001; and Wand's ontological analysis in Wand et al., 1999).

We have selected some properties from these approaches taking into account a set of quality characteristics that are identified for evaluating the association properties. These quality characteristics are oriented to facilitate the construction of expressive conceptual models, taking into account that the goal of our models is to be transformed into design structures of an OO programming language. The quality characteristics that the properties must fulfil are *simplicity*, *precision* and *implementability* (influential on the software representation of the relationship). These characteristics allow us to select those properties of the association that help us to define an appropriate conceptual framework for the characterization of the associations. This framework should provide a well-balanced solution between expressiveness and implementability.

In the literature, we find some of the properties describing the association concept under different terms. For instance, the properties *delete propagation* and *multiplicity,* which are defined in this work, have an interpretation which is similar to the *existence dependency* from (Snoeck & Dedene, 2001). Also, the property *multiplicity* that we define (similar to the way in which the UML (object management group, 2003) defines it) is used to represent the semantics of the property *mandatory/optional* which appears in other approaches (Henderson-Sellers & Barbier, 1999a; Kolp & Pirotte, 1997).

The Association Relationship

To introduce the properties of the conceptual framework, we present some basic definitions that form the core semantics of an association relationship.

A commonly agreed upon categorization of relationships in OO conceptual modeling is the following (Dahchour, 2001):

- **Classification:** It associates a class with a set of objects that hold the same properties.

- **Specialization:** It allows the definition of new classes (subclasses) as a specialization of previously defined ones (superclasses).

- **Association/Aggregation:** It is a relationship between classes that defines structural or semantic connections between the instances of the classes.

In UML, an aggregation relationship is considered to be a special kind of the ordinary association, whereas in other models (as OML), an aggregation acquires its own status and comes with specific features. We use the term *association* to refer to the ordinary association, aggregation, and composition relationships. These relationships can be categorized using the proposed conceptual framework.

When the relationship is an *aggregation,* the class that plays the role of whole is the aggregate class, while the other class is the part class. If the relationship is a *composition,* the class that plays the role of whole is the composite class, and the other class is the component class.

Once the term association is introduced, we present the components of the conceptual model involved in an association:

- **Participating classes:** The domain classes that are connected through the association.

- **Association ends:** The endpoints of an association that connect the association to a class. We work only with binary associations; therefore, an association has two association ends. An association end is characterized by its own properties (such as the maximum number of objects of the class that can be connected to an object of the opposite end).

- **Relationship:** The connection between the classes. The relationship is characterized by its own properties (such as the possibility of connecting an object to itself).

A *link* is an instance of an association. It connects two participating objects.

Properties of the Conceptual Framework

This section presents the properties of the conceptual framework for characterizing association relationships. To present briefly the properties, we have created

Table 1. Properties of the conceptual framework

Temporal Behaviour	
Description	Specifies whether an instance of a class can be dynamically connected or disconnected (creating or destroying a link) with one or more instances of a related class (through an association relationship) throughout its life-time.
Type	Association End property
Values	• **Dynamic:** Connecting or disconnecting a link to an object of the opposite end is possible throughout the life of the object. • **Static:** Creating or destroying a link is not possible (it is only possible during its creation process).
UML	Attribute changeability of the association-end: *"specifies whether an instance of the Association may be modified by an instance of the class on the other end (the source end)."* (Object Management Group, 2003, p. 2-22)

Multiplicity (maximum and minimum)	
Description	Specifies the maximum/minimum number of objects of a class that must/can be connected to one object of its associated class.
Type	Association End property
Values	Nonnegative integers.
UML	Attribute multiplicity of the association-end: *"specifies the number of target instances that may be associated with a single source instance across the given Association."* (Object Management Group, 2003, p. 2-23)

Delete Propagation	
Description	Indicates which actions must be performed when an object is destroyed.
Type	Association End property
Values	• **Restrictive:** The object cannot be destroyed if it has links (an exception is raised if an attempt is made); otherwise it is destroyed. • **Cascade:** The links and the associated objects must also be deleted. • **Link:** The links must also be deleted (not the associated objects).
UML	Propagation semantics. *"A consequence of these rules is that a composite implies propagation semantics; that is, some of the dynamic semantics of the whole is propagated to its parts. For example, if the whole is copied or destroyed, then the parts so are (because a part may belong to at most one composite)."* (Object Management Group, 2003, p. 2-66)

Navigability	
Description	Specifies whether an object can be accessed only by its associated object/s.
Type	Association End property
Values	• **Navigable:** The objects of the opposite end can access the objects of the associated class. • **Not Navigable:** The access is not possible.
UML	Attribute navigability of the association-end: *"specifies the navigability of the association end from the viewpoint of the classifier on the other end."* (Object Management Group, 2003, p. 2-23)

Table 1. (continued)

Identity Projection	
Description	Specifies whether the objects of a participating class project their identity onto their associated objects. These objects are then identified by their attributes and by the attributes of their associated objects.
Type	Association End property
Values	• **Projected:** The class of the opposite end projects its identity. • **Not Projected:** The class of the opposite end does not project its identity.
UML	The identity projection of a composite: "*composite [...] projects its identity onto the parts in the relationship. In other words, each part in an object model can be identified with a unique composite object. It keeps its own identity as its primary identity. The point is that it can also be identified as being part of a unique composite.*" (Object Management Group, 2003, p. 3-81)

Reflexivity	
Description	Specifies whether an object can be connected to itself.
Type	Relationship property
Values	• **Reflexive:** The connection is possible • **Not Reflexive:** The connection is not possible.
UML	A characteristic of aggregation and composition relationships. "*[...] the instances form a directed, non-cyclic graph.*" (Object Management Group, 2003, p. 2-67).

Symmetry	
Description	Specifies whether a **b** object can be connected to a **a** object, when the **a** object is already connected to the **b** object.
Type	Relationship property
Values	• **Symmetric:** The connection is possible (not mandatory) • **Antisymmetric:** The connection is not possible.
UML	The antisymmetry property. "*Both kinds of aggregations define a transitive, antisymmetric relationship; that is, the instances form a directed, non-cyclic graph. Composition instances form a strict tree (or rather a forest).*" (Object Management Group, 2003, p. 2-67)

a table with four rows that contains: The intended semantics in an intuitive way; the property type, which identifies the element of the association that the property is applied to; the possible values of the property; and the UML attributes that have a semantics which is the closest to our proposed properties.

The presented properties are used in the next section to define a semantics of the association, aggregation, and composition relationships.

A Particular Semantic Interpretation

Due to the lack of a precise and clear semantics for the association relationship, we propose a specific semantic interpretation for the association, aggregation, and composition concepts. To define this semantics, we adopt only the basic definitions for the UML concepts, completing them with our own definitions. The following basic assertions have been adopted:

- **Association:** *An association declares a connection (link) between instances of the associated classifiers (classes).* (Object Management Group, 2003, p. 2-64)
- **Aggregation:** *A whole-part relationship. In this case, the association-end attached to the whole element is designated, and the other association-end of the association represents the parts of the aggregation.* (Object Management Group, 2003, p. 2-66)
- **Composition:** *Is a strong form of aggregation.* (Object Management Group, 2003, p. 2-66)

Although we adopt these assertions, we must fix the semantics of these concepts to avoid the ambiguities (Genova, Llorens, & Palacios, 2002; Henderson-Sellers & Barbier, 1999b) introduced by the UML. One way to define the precise semantics of these concepts is to determine the value of the properties of the conceptual framework for each concept.

The values of the properties for the association, aggregation, and composition concepts are presented in Table 2. For each concept (columns), this table shows the value of the proposed properties. We use the symbol [1] to show that a property can be set to any of its possible values:

Table 2. The values of the properties for the association, aggregation, and composition

Property/Concept	Association	Aggregation	Composition Composite, Component
Temporal Behaviour	*	*	Static, *
Multiplicity	*	*	(1,1) , (*,*)
Delete Propagation	*	*	*, Cascade
Navigability	*	*	Navigable, Not Navigable
Identification Projection	*	*	Not Projected, Projected
Reflexivity	*	Not Reflexive	Not Reflexive
Symmetry	*	Antisymmetric	Antisymmetric

- Association does not have fixed properties in our model because there are no constraints in the relationship between the related classes.
- Aggregation has two fixed properties because, in our model, it is:
  - ° *Not reflexive* (an object cannot be whole and part at the same time).
  - ° *Antisymmetric* (if an object is a part of a whole, then the whole cannot be part of its own part).
- Composition has a fixed value for each property. Traditionally, in the literature, the composition concept appears as a strong aggregation. We have fixed the values of the properties assuming that the composition concept implies that the components are totally subject to their composites:
  - ° The maximum and minimum multiplicities of the composite are *1* (a part must be included in one and only one composite).
  - ° The temporal behavior of the composite is *static* (a part cannot change its composite).
  - ° The delete propagation of the component is *cascade* (when a composite is destroyed, its parts are also destroyed).
  - ° The navigability of the composite is *not navigable* (a part cannot access its composite).
  - ° The identity projection of the composite is *projected* (a composite projects its identity onto its parts).
  - ° The reflexivity is *not reflexive* and thesymmetry is *antisymmetric* (composition is a type of aggregation, composition fulfils the constraints of aggregation).

Now that we have proposed a semantics for the association, aggregation, and composition concepts, we present a systematic method that obtains the software representation from an association relationship that is characterized by the framework properties.

Framework Definition

Our proposal for implementing associations provides a software framework that combines a set of design patterns. The instantiation of the framework allows the implementation of associations in an OO programming language, thereby obtaining software solution that implements all the properties identified in the conceptual framework. The use of design patterns in the construction of the framework, allows guaranteeing the high quality of the obtained implementation.

In this section, we present the design patterns that constitute the framework structure. To decide which design patterns should be selected, we first identify the software quality factors that our implementation must satisfy. Second, we present the design patterns that we have selected to implement the associations and to satisfy the identified quality factors.

Quality Factors

We have identified three quality factors (besides the traditional quality factors of the software, such as cohesion, modularity, maintainability, or complexity) that the final software implementation of the association must have:

- **Loose coupling:** An association constitutes a conceptual abstraction that adds some kind of knowledge to the participating classes of the conceptual model. Most of the implementation proposals introduce explicit dependencies (references, attributes, methods) whose result is a tight coupling between classes. In this sense, it is important for the implementation of the relationship and the implementation of the participating classes to be as independent (orthogonal) as possible.
- **Separation of concerns:** The objects of the participating classes could have additional behavior and structure to those specified in the domain class. It is important to implement this additional behavior and structure in an isolated and clear way. Following this strategy the maintenance degree of the software increases, since it is easy to identify which parts of the source code should be modified when a change has to be made.
- **Reusability and genericity:** Most of the association behavior and structure can be generalized. The genericity of code (for example, defining abstract classes, methods and common execution strategies for the creation and destruction of links) provide more reusable implementation solutions.

Design patterns for building the software framework are selected to give support to these quality factors.

Selected Design Patterns

The first step in applying design patterns to the construction of the framework is to select appropriate ones. These patterns must be applicable to the association abstraction, and the proposed solution must give support to the three quality factors. Taking the specification of an association in a conceptual model as an input, these design patterns propose a structure of design classes that implements the association. We have selected the following design patterns:

- **Mediator:** This pattern defines a mediator class that encapsulates the interaction of a set of objects of colleague classes. This pattern gives support to loose coupling by avoiding explicit references between colleague objects.

- **Decorator:** This pattern defines a decorator class that wraps/decorates another existing class. The application of this pattern extends the structure and behavior of objects by wrapping those objects with another object that provides an implementation of a new aspect. The application of this pattern gives support to the separation of concerns.

- **Template method:** This pattern defines template methods in abstract classes with execution strategies whose steps are implemented in subclasses. The application of this pattern provides support for the reuse of generic behavior.

The application of these three patterns also guarantees the reusability and the genericity of the implementation. This is due to the disciplined use of polymorphism, abstract classes, dynamic binding and method overriding.

Framework Structure

We combine the design patterns selected to obtain a more complex structure of design classes that implements an association relationship. Taking into account the association relationship and the participating classes, in this section, we present the design classes and the design patterns that are applied to build the framework.

First, we implement in a traditional way the domain classes that participate in an association. *For each participating class defined in the conceptual model, we define a design class* that implements the structure and the behavior specified in the conceptual model. We call these design classes **domain classes**.

The decorator pattern is applied to implement the association ends independently from the participating classes. *For each association end, we define a decorator design class* (called **decorator class**), which implements the additional structure and behavior of the participating objects as a result of participating in an association relationship. The *decorator* classes wrap/decorate the related domain classes, thus, the domain classes are totally independent from their associations.

The mediator pattern is applied to implement the relationship. The application of the mediator pattern implies the *definition of a mediator design class* (called **mediator class**), which implements the structure and behavior of the association relationship. The class connects the *decorator* classes (since the domain classes are independent from the association in which they participate). Following the nomenclature proposed by the pattern, we rename the d*ecorator* classes as **decorator colleague classes**.

Finally, we apply the Template Method pattern on the *mediator* and *decorator* classes. Then, we *define two abstract classes* that implement the common structure and behavior of associations, that is the structure and behavior of *generic* associations: (1) The superclass of the *mediator* class (called **abstract mediator class**), which declares the structure and behavior of a *generic association*. This class defines template methods for link creation and destruction and includes two references to the participating objects; and (2) the superclass of the *decorator* classes (called **abstract colleague decorator class**), which declares the structure and behavior of a *generic association end*. This class defines template methods for connecting and disconnecting links to/from the *decorator* objects. It also includes references to the decorated object

Figure 1. The structure of the design classes obtained by applying the selected patterns

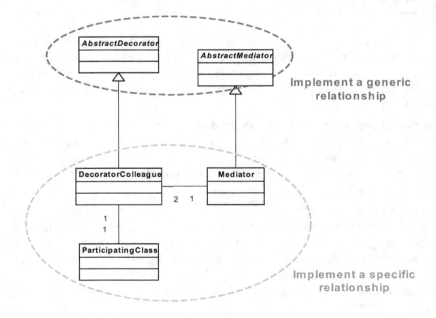

Figure 2. An example of associated objects through a WorkFor relationship

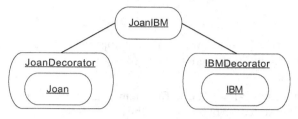

and to the *mediator* objects. Figure 1 shows the obtained structure of design classes.

The application of the Mediator and Decorator patterns allows the generation of a software solution that is characterized by the reusability of the participating classes and the improvement of its maintainability. This solution allows the implementation of:

- The properties and operations of the links in the *mediator* class;
- The properties and operations specific to participating objects (association ends) in the *decorator* classes; and
- The properties and operations inherent to the participating classes in their corresponding design classes.

The application of the Template Method pattern allows the definition of template methods that implement common execution strategies for all relationships.

Figure 2 shows an intuitive example of objects that were created following the proposed framework structure. Assume a *WorkFor* association between the Employer and Company classes. In the example, Joan, which is an object of the Employer class, is associated to the IBM object of the Company class through the JoanIBM link object. Joan and IBM objects are decorated by the *decorator* objects, JoanDecorator and IBMDecorator, which reference the JoanIBM object.

Mapping Association Relationships into Design Classes

Now that the framework is introduced, we define the mappings between the association abstraction and the framework. These mappings are the source of the association implementation.

The definition of the mappings can be divided into two sections depending on the implementation aspect that is affected:

- **The structural view:** We define mappings between the conceptual structures and the design classes (design classes, their attributes and relationships).
- **The behavioral view:** We define mappings between the properties that define the association behavior and the methods that implement the specific behavior of the association relationships.

Although most of the mappings can be generalized for all the associations, the final implementation is dependent on the values of the conceptual framework properties. These properties define functional and structural constraints that:

- allow or forbid the existence of attributes or methods in a design class, or
- imply checking or other actions when the functionality that affects the association is executed.

In the following sections, we present the mapping of conceptual structures into design classes (the structural view of the framework), and the mapping of properties into method implementations (the behavioral view of the framework).

The Structural View

This section presents the mappings between the elements of the association in the conceptual model and the elements of its software representation. The definition of the mappings makes it possible to obtain a structure of the design classes that represents an association from its specification in the conceptual model. To define the mappings, we specify (1) how the elements of an association construct (participant classes, association ends, etc.) are implemented and (2) how the properties of an association (multiplicity, reflexivity, etc.) are implemented into design attributes and methods.

Mapping Association Elements to Design Classes

The proposed model for associations distinguishes three basic elements in an association: the *participating classes*, the *relationship,* and the *association ends*. In Table 3, we present how these elements are represented through design

Table 3. The mapping of the components of an association to the elements of the software solution

Element	Design Class	Description
Participating Class	Domain Class	Implements the structure and behaviour of the associated class, independently from the association in which the class participates.
Association Relationship	Mediator class	This class is a *mediator* class of the *decorator* classes.
Association End	Decorator class	This class decorates a participating class and is a colleague class of the *mediator* class.

Figure 3. An example of an application of the framework to an association relationship

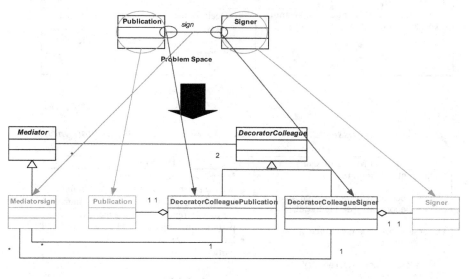

classes. These mappings are defined using the framework structure introduced in section.

Figure 3 shows an example of the mappings between the elements of an association in the conceptual model and the design classes of the implementation.

Table 4. An implementation of the design classes using the C# language

Domain/Participating Class	Description

public **DomainClassName**{
 	
...
 	
}
	• Implements the structure and behaviour of the associated classes independently from the association in which the class participates
	• Is accessible only by its *decorator* class (other client classes cannot access to it)

Abstract Decorator Class	Description

public abstract **DecoratorColleague**
{
   object DecoratedObject;
   MediatorCollection
         LinkCollection;
 	
   ...
 	
}
	• Defines a reference to the decorated object
	• Defines a reference to a link collection, which allows the *decorator* objects to access their links

Decorator Class	Description

public **DecoratorColleagueClassName**
  : Decoratorcolleague{
 	
   ...
 	
}
	• Declares the interface of the decorated class
	• Provides the public services of the decorated class

Table 5. Mapping association properties to design attributes and methods

Abstract Mediator Class	Description

public abstract **Mediator**{
 	
private DecoratorColleague source;
private DecoratorColleague target;
 	
DecoratorColleague getSource(){
   return source;
}
DecoratorColleague getTarget(){
   return target;
}
...
}
	• Defines a private reference to the *decorator* objects that participate in the link. We use the source and target names for the references to distinguish the two participating objects in a generic way.
	• Defines a *get* method for each participating object

Mediator Class	Description

public   **MediatorAssociationName** :
Mediator{
   ...
}
	• Is accessible only by its colleague classes, *decorator* classes (other client classes cannot access to it)

Mapping Association Properties to Design Attributes and Methods

In this section, we analyze the implication of the structural properties of the conceptual framework into the design of attributes and methods. We also propose a representation of this implication in the implementation.

Temporal behavior specifies whether an object of a class can be dynamically connected or disconnected (creating or destroying a link) with one or more objects of a related class (through an association relationship) during its life-time. The property values are:

- **Dynamic:** Links can be added or destroyed to or from the objects of the opposite end without any temporal restriction. This situation implies that methods for providing this functionality should be added to the design class that manages the links of the life cycle, which is the *decorator* class that implements the opposite end. The methods are the insertLink and deleteLink.

- **Static:** Links should not be modified after the creation of the object, so these methods are not included.

Example. Let us consider the example of a Professor class associated to a Department class through a *belongsTo* relationship. In this example, the Professor end is *dynamic* because a Department can hire or fire professors throughout its existence. Nevertheless, the Department end is *Static*, because a Professor must always be in the same department. In the definition of the Department *decorator* class, the following methods are implemented:

```
public DecoratorColleagueDepartment: DecoratorColleague{
    public Mediator insertLink(...){
    ...
    }
    public void deleteLink(...){
    ...
    }
}
```

The implementation of the insertLink and deleteLink methods is presented in following sections.

Identification projection specifies whether a participating class projects its identification mechanism to its associated class. The property values are:

- **Projected:** The design class that implements the opposite association end (a *decorator* class) adds the identification attributes of its associated class to identify its instances.
- **Not projected:** Nothing has to be added.

Example. Let us consider the example of a City class associated to a State class through a *belongsTo* relationship. In the example, the City class projects its identity to the State class (PI = *Projected*). In the definition of the State *decorator* class, the following attributes are implemented:

```
public DecoratorColleagueCity: DecoratorColleague
{
    private char[5] codCity;
    ....
    public getCodCity(){
        return codCity;
    }
}
```

```
public DecoratorColleagueState: DecoratorColleague
{
    private char[5] codState;
    private char[50] name;
    ....

    public getCodState(){
        return concat(getCodCity(), codState);
    }
}
```

Navigability specifies whether an object of a participating class can access its associated objects. The property values are:

- **Navigable:** The design class that represents the opposite association end (a *decorator* class) contains references to its links. The *mediator* class that represents the links must contain a reference to the participating object of the end (a *get* method allows access to this object). Thus, the participating object of the *opposite end* can access its associated objects through the link.

- **Not navigable:** The *decorator* class that represents the opposite end contains references to its links, but these do not provide access to the participating object of the end that is not navigable. In order to do this, the *get* method of the abstract *mediator* class, which returns the participating object of the *not navigable end*, does not have to be accessible. Overriding this method in the *mediator* subclass as a private method prevents objects of other classes from accessing it.

Example: Let us consider the example of an Employer class related to a Company class through a *WorksFor* association. In this example, the Company end is *Not Navigable*. Thus, in the *mediator* class, we have the following code (supposing the objects of the *not navigable end* are represented by the target reference):

```
public MediatorWorksFor: Mediator{
    override private DecoratorColleague getTarget(){
        return target;
    }
    ....
}
```

The Behavioral View

An association between two classes requires the implementation of additional functionality to the one provided by the participating classes. This additional functionality is the following:

- **Link creation and destruction:** This allows the creation and destruction of links between objects of the participating classes.
- **Associated object creation and destruction:** This allows the creation and destruction of objects of the participating classes.

Mapping association properties to design methods. Before presenting the implementation of the functionality, we analyze the implication of the behavioral properties in the design methods and propose a representation of this implication in the implementation.

Multiplicity is a constraint that must be satisfied by the association. The condition that the constraint establishes is defined over the LinkCollection attribute, which maintains the links of the *decorator* objects. The OCL condition is:

context od: DecoratorColleagueClassName inv:

Min ≤ od.LinkCollection.size() ≥ Max

Maximum multiplicity:

- If the maximum multiplicity is bounded, the system must ensure that the constraint is satisfied before creating a link.
- If it is not bounded, no checking is necessary, since the condition is always true.

Minimum multiplicity:

- If the minimum multiplicity is greater than zero, the system must ensure (1) that the object is associated to the minimum number of objects when it is created, and (2) that deleting a link does not violate the restriction.
- If it is not greater than 0, no checking is necessary, since the condition is always true.

In summary, since the *link creation* and *destruction* and the *associated object creation* update the LinkCollection attribute, the value of the attribute must be checked during the execution of these functionalities, carrying out the necessary actions to guarantee the fulfilment of the condition.

Reflexivity specifies whether or not a link between an object and itself is allowed.

- **Not Reflexive:** The reflexivity constraint is a condition that must be fulfilled by the system. The condition is defined over the source and target attributes of the links (that represent the participating objects). The OCL condition that must be satisfied is:

```
context e: MediatorAssociationName inv:
e.source <> e.target
```

- **Reflexive:** No testing needs to be done.

Since the *link creation* updates the source and target attributes, the value of the attributes must be checked during the execution of this functionality, carrying out the necessary actions to guarantee the fulfilment of the condition.

Symmetry specifies whether or not there can be a link between a and b if there already exist a link between b and a. The property values are:

- **Antysymmetric:** The constraint is a condition that must be fulfilled by the system. The OCL condition that must be satisfied is:

```
context e1,e2: MediatorAssociationName inv:
e1.source <> e2.target or
e2.source <> e1.target
```

- **Symmetric:** No testing needs to be done.

Since the *link creation* updates the source and target attributes, the value of the attributes must be checked during the execution of this functionality, carrying out the necessary actions to guarantee the fulfilment of the condition.

Delete Propagation specifies the actions that should be performed when an object is destroyed. The property values are:

- **Restrictive:** The object can only be destroyed if it does not have any link (if a link exists and exception is thrown).
- **Link:** All the links of the object must be deleted when it is destroyed.
- **Cascade:** Both the links of the objects and the related objects must be destroyed.

In summary, we can conclude that the delete propagation property determines the behavior of the *associated object destruction*.

Implementation Strategy

The following sections describe the details of the link creation and destruction as well as the associated object creation and destruction implementation. To clearly present how to implement this functionality, we provide the following strategy:

1. **Definition of the sequence of calls:** Since the framework provides several design classes that implement the functionality of the association relationship, for each specific functionality we should identify the classes, the methods and the sequence of method calls (interaction) among objects.

2. **Application of the Template Method pattern:** As presented above, the properties of reflexivity, symmetry and multiplicity are conditions/constraints that the association must fulfil every time a link is created or deleted. An implementation that provides complete support to the semantics of the association must check the fulfilment of these properties each time this functionality is required. The process of checking these properties defines a specific algorithm or execution strategy that can be implemented using the Template Method pattern. In this way, the abstract classes of the framework specify the steps (methods) of the execution strategy. The subclasses of these abstract classes implement the steps (methods). The responsibility of checking the properties is distributed among the classes of the framework depending on which elements of the association relationship are applied:

   a. **Properties of the relationship:** The Mediator classes are responsible for guaranteeing the fulfilment of the reflexivity and symmetry properties, since these classes implement the structure and behavior of the relationships.

   b. **Properties of the association end:** The Decorator classes are responsible for guarantying the fulfilment of the multiplicity and delete propagation properties, since these classes implement the structure and behavior of the association ends.

3. **Definition of the implementations that depend on the value properties:** The delete propagation and multiplicity properties determine the behavior of the associated object creation and destruction. Thus, the implementation of these functionalities depends on the value of the properties. The framework should provide an implementation for each meaningful value of the properties.

   To clearly introduce how to implement these functionalities, each one is documented as follows:

   a. **Goal:** Description of the behavior provided by the functionality.

b. **Affected properties:** The properties of the conceptual frame work that (1) should be checked to ensure that the execution of the functionality does not violate the constraints that the properties define or (2) determine the actions that should be performed to ensure that the execution of the functionality fulfils the property specification.

c. **Classes and methods:** Identification of both the classes and the methods of these classes that implement the functionality. The detailed implementation of each method is presented in the collaboration patterns implementation section.

d. **Interactions:** The sequence of method calls (represented by a UML sequence diagram) that is necessary to achieve the expected functionality.

Link Creation Implementation

Goal: To provide functionality for creating links between objects of associated classes. It implies the creation of the link object and the associated references (between the link and the objects and vice versa).

Affected properties: Reflexivity, symmetry, and multiplicity.

Classes and methods: The classes and methods that implement the link creation are the following:

- **Class:** DecoratorColleagueClassName
    - **Method:** insertLink starts the creation of a link from one of the participating objects. The method is overloaded, providing two kinds of link insertion:
        - **insertLink(DecoratorColleague):** connects the object to another object that is provided by the argument
        - **insertLink(DecoratorColleagueAttributeList):** connects the object to another object that is created using the attribute list provided by the argument
- **Class:** Mediator
    - **Method:**Mediator(DecoratorColleague, DecoratorColleague) Constructor method. It is a *template method*. Defines the strategy for creating a link. The method creates the link object and connects it to its participating objects. The strategy defines the steps necessary to guarantee that the *relationship properties* involved in the link creation (reflexivity and symmetry) are fulfilled.

- **Class:** DecoratorColleague:
  - ○ **Method:** connectLink(Mediator) It is a *template method*. Defines the strategy for connecting a link to a *decorator* object. The method connects the object that executes the method to the link argument. The strategy defines the steps necessary that guarantee that the *association end properties* involved in the link creation (maximum multiplicity) are fulfilled by the system.

Interactions: The interaction sequence is the following:

1. Call to the insertLink method of a *decorator* object.
2. The insertLink method calls to the constructor method of the *mediator* class.
3. The constructor method creates the link object and calls to the connectLink method of the participating objects.
4. The connectLink method connects a participating object to the new link.

Figure 4 shows an example of the interaction sequence that is produced when a link creation is required to connect the Joan employer to the IBM company.

Link Destruction Implementation

Goal: To provide functionality for destroying links between objects of associated classes. It implies the destruction of the link objects and the associated references.

Figure 4. The interaction sequence of a link creation

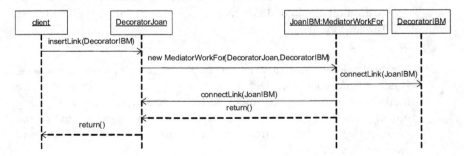

Affected properties: Multiplicity.

Classes and methods: The classes and methods that implement the link destruction are the following:

- **Class:** DecoratorColleagueClassName
  - ° **Method:** deleteLink triggers the link destruction from a participating object.
- **Class:** Mediator
  - ° **Method:** destroyLink(String). Destructor method. It is a *template method*. Defines the strategy for destroying a link object. It destroys a link object and the connections between the link and its participating objects. The method's argument indicates the origin of the method call to avoid an exception caused by the minimum multiplicity during the destruction of a participating object.
- **Class:** DecoratorColleague
  - ° **Method:** disconnectLink(Mediator, String). It is a *template method*. Defines the strategy for disconnecting a link from a *decorator* object. The method deletes the reference between the object that executes the method and the link object. The strategy defines the steps necessary to guarantee that the *association end properties* involved in the link destruction (minimum multiplicity) are fulfilled.

Interactions: The interaction sequence is the following:

1. Call to the deleteLink method of a *decorator* object.
2. The deleteLink method calls to the destroyLink method (destructor) of the *mediator* class.
3. The destroyLink method calls to the disconnectLink method of the participating objects.
4. The disconnectLink disconnects a participating object from the link.
5. The destroyLink method destroys the link object.

Figure 5 shows an example of the interaction sequence that is produced when a delete creation is required to disconnect the IBM company from the Joan employer.

Figure 5. The interaction sequence of a link destruction

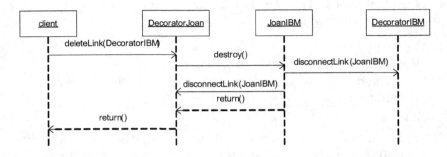

Associated Object Creation Implementation

Goal: To provide functionality for creating objects that participate in an association (associated objects). It implies the creation of an object of a participating class and the creation of its *decorator* object. The code for the creation of objects of participating classes is implemented in the participating classes, while the code for the creation of *decorator* objects is implemented in the *decorator* classes. It improves reusability and code maintainability.

Affected properties: Multiplicity

Classes and methods: The classes and methods that implement the associated object creation are the following:

- **Class:** DecoratorColleagueClassName:
  - **Method:** constructor builds a *decorator* object. The method is over-loaded, providing two kinds of object creation:
    - ➤ **When the minimum multiplicity is 0:** DecoratorColleagueClassName (AttributeList) creates the *decorator* object.
    - ➤ **When the minimum multiplicity is greater than 0:** Decorator ColleagueClassName(AttributeList, DecoratorColleagueClass NameCollection) creates the *decorator* object and associates it to the objects of the collection provided by the second argument.
- **Class:** DomainClassName:
  - **Method:** constructor builds an object of a participating class.

Interactions: The interaction sequence is the following:

- When the minimum multiplicity is 0:
  1. Call to the constructor method of the *decorator* class.
  2. The constructor method of the *decorator* class calls to the constructor method of its decorated class.

Figure 6 shows an example of the interaction sequence that is produced when an employer is created (without any connection).

- When the minimum multiplicity is greater than 0:
  1. Call to the constructor method of the *decorator* class.
  2. The constructor method of the *decorator* class calls to the constructor method of its decorated class.
  3. The constructor method of the *decorator* class calls to the constructor of the *mediator* class.

Figure 7 shows an example of the interaction sequence that is produced when an employer is created with an associated company (IBM).

Associated Object Destruction Implementation

Goal: To provide functionality for destroying objects that participate in a relationship. It implies the destruction of an object of a participating class and the destruction of its *decorator* object. In spite of the garbage collector provided by some languages, appropriate actions must be performed in order to guarantee the

Figure 6. The interaction sequence of an associated object creation when the minimum multiplicity is 0

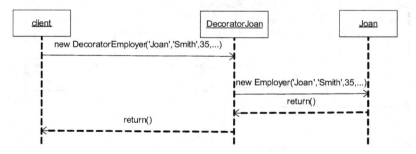

suitable destruction of associated objects. The code for the destruction of objects of the participating classes is implemented in the participating classes, while the code for the destruction of *decorator* objects is implemented in the *decorator* classes. It improves reusability and code maintainability.

Affected properties: Delete propagation

Classes and methods: The classes and methods that implement the associated object creation are the following:

- **Class:** DecoratorColleagueClassName:
    - ° **Method:** destroy destroys a *decorator* object.
- **Class:** DomainClassName:
    - ° **Method:** destroy destroys an object of a participating class.

Interactions: The interaction sequence is the following:

- When the delete propagation is *link*:
    1. Call to the destructor method of the *decorator* object.
    2. The destructor method of the *decorator* object calls to the deleteLink method of its links.
    3. The destructor method of the *decorator* object calls to the destructor method of its decorated object.

Figure 7. The interaction sequence of an associated object creation when the minimum multiplicity *is > 0*

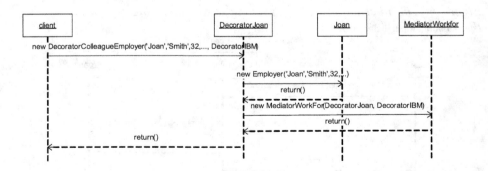

- When the delete propagation is *restrictive*:
  1. Call to the destructor method of the *decorator* object.
  2. The destructor method of the *decorator* object throws an exception if the *decorator* object has any link; Otherwise it callsto the destructor method of its decorated object.
- When the delete propagation is *cascade*:
  1. Call to the destructor method of the *decorator* object.
  2. The destructor method of the *decorator* object calls to the destructor method of its associated objects.
  3. The destructor method of the *decorator* object calls to the destructor method of its decorated object.

Figure 8, 9, and 10 show examples of interaction sequences that are produced when an employer is destroyed with the values for delete propagation: link, restrictive and cascade.

To illustrate how the operations of employers and companies are accessed, let us consider the example of Figure 11. Consider the employee class is the source and the company class the target.

Other classes of the system (clients) access the public operations of the Company and Employee classes through their decorator classes. For example, given a DecoratorIBM object of the DecoratorCompany class, and a DecoratorJoan object of the DecoratorEmployee class, these objects allow the accessing to the public operations of the Company and Employee class respectively:

DecoratorIBM.getName()

DecoratorJoan.sellUnit().

As the association ends are navigable, it is possible to access the public operations of the Company class through a *decorator employee;* and to the public operations of the Employee class through a *decorator company*. In this case, it is necessary to use the attribute LinkCollection of the decorator objects, indicating with a variable which link is referred:

DecoratorIBM.LinkCollection[i].source.updateSalary()

DecoratorJoan.Link Collection[i].target.getNumberEmployers()

Figure 8. The interaction sequence of an associated object destruction when delete propagation *is link*

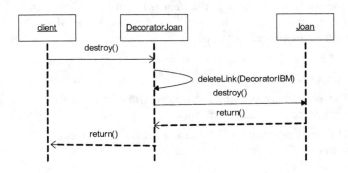

Figure 9. The interaction sequence of an associated object destruction when delete propagation *is restrictive*

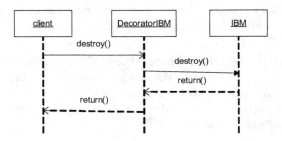

Figure 10. The interaction sequence of an associated object destruction when delete propagation *is cascade*

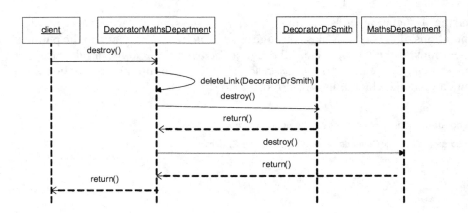

Figure 11. Example of operations in classes Employee *and* Company

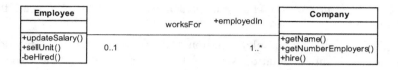

Employee		Company
+updateSalary() +sellUnit() -beHired()	worksFor +employedIn 0..1 1..*	+getName() +getNumberEmployers() +hire()

Validation of the Proposal

To validate the framework proposal, we have implemented the patterns presented by the Nicola et al. study (Bolloju, 2004). This work identifies 12 primary
analysis patterns that are mainly present in business applications. These patterns
are the *collaboration patterns (CP)*. The *CP* are constituted of two classes that
are related by an association, an aggregation, or a composition relationship. They
present different values in the properties of the relationship. The definition of
these patterns is based on the experience in consulting and development work for
business applications. The CP represent a set of irreducible patterns (which have
been identified in most business object models). All other patterns can be derived
from them. We have used these CP since they are useful for validating the
completeness of our framework proposal. If our framework can implement all
these patterns, it can be considered valid for implementing any relevant association relationship.

In this section, we present the implementation of only one of the twelve CP due to
the space constraints. Since our intention is to implement a *collaboration pattern*
using the proposed framework, we must first model the *collaboration pattern*
adapting it to our own model. Then, we can implement the modeled association by
instantiating the framework with the property values of the relationship.

The selected *collaboration pattern* models an association (there are also some
CP that model aggregations). We present an example for the pattern by
determining the value of the properties of the conceptual framework. Then, we
present a detailed implementation of the framework using the C# language. This
example completes the implementation proposed in the previous section. It
shows the implementation of all the methods introduced by the framework.

Following the nomenclature of Bolloju (2004), the pattern that we use is the T1
Pattern: Item - SpecificItem. We instantiate the framework with the following
example: a Video class is related to a VideoTape class through a *hasCopies*
relationship. The property values are presented in Table 3.

Figure 12 shows the design classes of the software representation.

Figure 13 and 14 show the implementation of the *abstract decorator* class and the *abstract mediator* class. The code presented is generic for the all the associations.

Figures 15 and 16 show the implementation of the participating classes, Video and VideoTape. The implementation is completely independent from the associations *hasCopies* in which they participate.

The implementation of the DecoratorColleagueVideo class is characterized by the value of the properties Multiplicity, Temporal Behavior, Identity Projection and Delete Propagation. Figure 17 shows the basic structure of the class. No attributes are

Table 3. The property values for the pattern example

Property	Video	VideoTape
Temporal Behaviour	*Static*	*Dynamic*
Multiplicity	*(1,1)*	*(0,*)*
Delete Propagation	*Link*	*Cascade*
Navigability	*Not Navigable*	*Navigable*
Identity Projection	*Not Projected*	*Projected*
Reflexivity	-	
Symmetry	-	

Figure 12. The design classes obtained by applying the framework on the pattern example

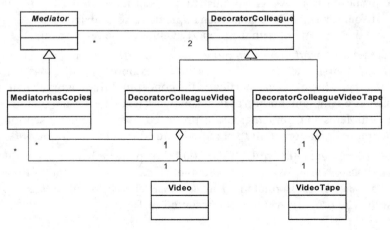

Figure 13. The implementation of the abstract decorator *class*

```
public abstract DecoratorColleague{
    object DecoratedObject;
    MediatorCollection  LinkCollection;

    public void connectLink(Mediator objLink) {
      checkMaximumMultiplicity();
      addLink(objLink);
    }
    public void disconnectLink(Mediator objLink, String org){
      checkMinimumMultiplicity(org);
      eliminateLink(objLink);
    }
}
```

Figure 14. The implementation of the abstract mediator *class*

```
public abstract Mediator{
    private DecoratorColleague source;
    private DecoratorColleague target;

    protected Mediator(DecoratorColleague objectSource,
DecoratorColleague objectTarget)
    {
      checkReflexivity(objectSource, objectTarget);
      checkSymmetry(objectSource, objectTarget);
      checkIdentity(objectSource, objectTarget);
      objectSource.connectLink(this);
      objectTarget.connectLink(this);
      source = objectSource;
      target = objectTarget;
    }

    DecoratorColleague getObject1(){
        return source;
    }

    DecoratorColleague getObject2(){
        return target;
    }

    public void destroyLink(String origin)
    {
        source.disconnectLink(this, origin);
        target.disconnectLink(this, origin);
    }
}
```

Figure 15. The implementation of the Video *class*

```
public Video {
    String title;
    int year;
    String summary;
    int time;
    ...
    //Video attributes
    public Video(String nTitle, int nYear, String nSum, int nTime){
        title = nTitle;
        year= nYear;
        summary = nSum;
        time = nTime;
    }
    ...
    //Video methods
}
```

Figure 16. The implementation of the VideoTape *class*

```
public VideoTape{
    String code;
    int year;
    ...
    //VideoTape attributes
    public VideoTape(String nCode, int nYear){
        code = nCode;
        year= nYear;
    }
    ...
    //VideoTape methods
}
```

Figure 17. The structure of the DecoratorColleagueVideo *class*

```
public DecoratorColleagueVideo : DecoratorColleague{
    ...
}
```

added to the *decorator* class since the Identity Projection is *Not Projected* in the Video end.

Figure 18 shows the implementation of the constructor method in the DecoratorColleagueVideo class. The implementation of the constructor in the

Figure 18. The implementation of the constructor method of the DecoratorColleagueVideo class

```
public DecoratorColleagueVideo(AttributeList AI){
        DecoratedObject = new Video(Al.title, Al.year,
                                    Al.summary, Al.time);
}
```

Figure 19. The implementation of the get methods of the DecoratorColleagueVideo class

```
public String getTitle(){
    return DecoratedObject.title;
}
public int getYear(){
    return DecoratedObject.year;
}
public int getSummary(){
    return DecoratedObject.summary;
}
public String getTime(){
    return DecoratedObject.time;
}
```

Figure 20. The implementation of the insertLink and deleteLink methods

```
public Mediator insertLink (DecoratorColleagueAttributeList DCaL){
    DecoratorColleagueVideoTape DCvT = new
                    DecoratorColleagueVideoTape(this, DCaL);
    int index = DCvT.findDecoratorColleague(this);
    return DCvT.linkCollection.item(index);
}

public void deleteLink(DecoratorCollegue DC){
        int index = findDecoratorColleague(DC);
        LinkCollection.Item(index).destroyLink(DEL)
}
```

decorator classes depends on the value of the Minimum Multiplicity. In the VideoTape end, the Minimum Multiplicity is 0, so the constructor only creates the decorated object.

Figure 19 shows the implementation of the get methods in the DecoratorColleagueVideo class. There is a get method for each attribute of the decorated domain class.

Figure 21. The implementation of the template methods in the DecoratorColleagueVideo *class*

```
public void checkMaximumMultiplicity(){
    //No testing
}
public void checkMinimumMultiplicity(){
    //No testing
}

public void addLink(Mediator objLink){
    LinkCollection.Add(objLink);
}
public void deleteLink(Mediator objLink){
    int index = findMediator(objLink);
    LinkCollection.Remove(index);
}
```

Figure 22. The implementation of the destroy *method in the* DecoratorColleagueVideo *class*

```
public void destroy(){
    for (int i=LinkCollection.Count; i>0; i--){
        LinkCollection.item(i).getTarget().destroy();
    }
    DecoratedObject.destroy();
}
```

Figure 23. The structure of the of the VideoTape *class*

```
public DecoratorColleagueVideoTape : DecoratorColleague{

    String title;
    int year;
    ...

}
```

The VideoTape end is *Dynamic*; this means that the *decorator* class of the opposite end, DecoratorColleagueVideo, must implement the insertLink and deleteLink methods. Figure 20 shows the implementation of these methods.

Figure 21 shows the implementation of the steps of the template methods of the *abstract decorator* class. The value of the Maximum Multiplicity in the VideoTape end is not bounded and the value of the Minimum Multiplicity is 0; therefore, no constrains have to be fulfilled.

Figure 22 shows the implementation of the destroy method in the DecoratorColleagueVideo class. The implementation is determined by the value of the Delete Propagation property; In the VideoTape end the value is *cascade*.

The implementation of the DecoratorColleagueVideoTape class is characterized by the value of the properties Multiplicity, Temporal Behavior, Identity Projection and Delete Propagation. Figure 23 shows the basic structure of the class. Since the Identity Projection is *Projected* in the VideoTape end, its *decorator* class adds the identification attributes of the Video class (title and year).

Figure 24 shows the implementation of the constructor method in the DecoratorColleagueVideoTape class. Since the Minimum Multiplicity is 1 in the Video end, the method must create the decorated object and connect the new object to the collection of objects of the second argument.

Figure 25 shows the *get* methods implemented in the DecoratorColleague VideoTape.

The insertLink and deleteLink methods are not implemented in the DecoratorColleagueVideoTape since the Video end is *static*.

Figure 26 shows the implementation of the methods that implement the steps of the template methods of the *abstract decorator* class. The value of the Maximum

Figure 24. The implementation of the constructor *in the* Decorator ColleagueVideo Tape *class*

```
public DecoratorColleagueVideoTape(AttributeList AI,
                DecoratorColleagueVideoCollection DCvC){
        DecoratedObject = new VideoTape(AI.code, AI.year);
        for (int i=0; i<DCvC.Count; i++)
            new MediatorhasCopies (DCvC.item(i), this);
}
```

Figure 25. The implementation of the get methods in the Decorator ColleagueVideoTape *class*

```
public String getCode(){
    return DecoratedObject.code;
}
public int getYear(){
    return DecoratedObject.year;
}
```

Figure 26. The implementation of the steps methods in the DecoratorColleagueVideoTape *class*

```
public void checkMaximumMultiplicity(){
    if ((LinkCollection.Count) == 1 )
        throws new Exception("Max Multiplicity Violation");
}
public void addLink(Mediator objLink){
    LinkCollection.add(objLink);
}
public void deleteLink(DecoratorCollegue DC){
    int index = findDecoratorColleague(DC);
    LinkCollection.item(index).destroyLink(DEL)
}
public void checkMinimumMultiplicity(){
    if ((LinkCollection.Count) == 1 )
        throws new Exception("Max Multiplicity Violation");
}
public void eliminateLink(Mediator objLink){
    int index = findMediator(objLink);
    LinkCollection.remove(index);
}
```

Figure 27. The implementation of the destroy *method of the* DecoratorColleagueVideoTape *class*

```
public void destroy(){
    for (int i=LinkCollection.Count; i>0; i--){
        LinkCollection.item(i).destroy();
    }
    DecoratedObject.destroy();
}
```

Figure 28. The structure of the MediatorhasCopies *class*

```
public MediatorhasCopies: Mediator{
    ...
}
```

Figure 29. The steps methods of the MediatorhasCopies *class*

```
public void checkReflexivity(DecoratorColleague objectSource,
                            DecoratorColleague objectTarget){
}
public void checkSymmetry(DecoratorColleague objectSource,
                            DecoratorColleague objectTarget){
}
public void checkUnicity(DecoratorColleague objectSource,
                            DecoratorColleague objectTarget){
    for (int i=0; i<objectSource.LinkCollection.Count;i++){
        MediatorhasCopies mhC =
            (MediatorhasCopies)objectSource.LinkCollection.item(i);

        DecoratorColleagueVideoTape DCvT =
            (DecoratorColleagueVideoTape)mhC.target;

        DecoratorColleagueVideoTape DCvT2 =
            (DecoratorColleagueVideoTape).objectTarget;

        if (DCvT.gsOid==(DCvT2.gsOid))
            throw new Exception("Existent Link");
    }
}
```

Figure 30. The overriding of the getTarget *method in the* MediatorhasCopies *subclass*

```
override private DecoratorColleague getTarget(){
    return target;
}
```

and Minimum Multiplicity in the Video end is 1; therefore, the methods verify that the association fulfils the conditions.

Figure 27 shows the implementation of the destroy method in the DecoratorColleagueVideoTape class. The implementation is determined by the value of the Delete Propagation property. In the Video end, the value is *link*.

The implementation of the MediatorhasCopies class is characterized by the value of the properties Navigability, Reflexivity and Symmetry. Figure 28 shows the basic structure of the class.

Figure 29 shows the implementation of the steps of the Template Methods of the *abstract mediator* class. The Reflexivity and Symmetry properties are not meaningful in this relationship; therefore, no testing is needed.

As the Navigability property is *Not Navigable* in the VideoTape end, the getTarget method must be overridden in order to avoid the access of objects of the opposite end to objects of the VideoTape class, as shown in Figure 30.

In this example, the framework has been instantiated by a collaboration pattern. Thus, an implementation for this pattern has been obtained. This implementation fulfils the identified quality factors and fulfils the specified requirements of the collaboration pattern. Then, the goals of the implementation proposal have been achieved.

Future Work

The proposed conceptual framework can be improved by capturing additional properties of the association relationship in the application domain (such as the mutability or transitivity properties). It could improve the expressiveness of the framework. Moreover, as this framework has allowed providing an interpretation for the association concept, it is possible to develop a wizard that helps the analyst in the specification of the association relationship during the modeling task. The wizard collects information through questions, which allows it to determine the kind of relationship (association, aggregation or composition) that is being modeled. These questions determine the value of the association properties. This future work is oriented to provide support to a methodology for the complete modeling of association relationships. Currently, it is necessary to propose methodological guides that help the analysts in the modeling task.

Regarding the implementation framework, an interesting work is the search for other design patterns to be used in the construction of the implementation framework. It could improve the quality of the generated software product. Patterns constitute a tool that has been recently taken into account in the Software Factories and MDA approaches. They provide a perfect mechanism to support the construction of transformation engines and they contribute in the production of high quality software in an automated way. Research in the area of model driven code generation that is based on design patterns and software frameworks can be considered a hot topic in which this work is positioned.

Following the MDA approach, this framework can also be applied in automatic code generators. We are currently specifying a graph grammar that implements the proposed mapping automatically (Muñoz, Ruiz, Albert, & Pelechano, 2004). This grammar transforms models that are built using our conceptual framework into models that extend and instantiate the design classes of the implementation framework. The investigation of techniques for the implementation of transformations between models is an actual trend in the MDA approach, where it is a great activity.

The proposal can be extended to n-ary associations. Currently, binary associations are the most typical ones. Moreover, modelers usually transform n-ary associations into binary associations. The extension to n-ary association does not require too much effort. One of these modifications is regarding graphical notation for the properties of the conceptual framework.

Conclusion

This work presents a framework for the implementation of association, aggregation, and composition relationships. We have presented a specific interpretation of the association, aggregation, and composition concepts introduced by UML. For the definition of these concepts, we have built a conceptual framework that is based on a study of the different approaches that deal with association constructs in conceptual modeling. The conceptual framework identifies the essential properties of associations and provides precise interpretations for the association, aggregation, and composition abstractions.

The selection of the properties is based on a set of quality characteristics that are identified for evaluating the association properties. These characteristics allow us to select those properties of the association that help us to define an appropriate conceptual framework for the characterization of the associations.

The interpretation provided for the association concepts (association, aggregation and composition) is based on most well-accepted notions that are present in different methodological approaches.

Once the semantics of these abstractions has been defined, we have proposed a framework that allows obtaining the implementation of an association. This framework determines the mappings between the specification of a relationship in the conceptual model and the software elements of its implementation. The framework is based on the use of design patterns for implementing these abstractions. We have selected three patterns that can be applied in the implementation of associations. The selected patterns provide an operational solution to the implementation of the association relationships and its properties. As we have commented in the chapter, those design patterns provide a framework with loose coupling, separation of concerns, and reusability. The application of design patterns during the software development provides interesting advantages since it allows the structuring of the code generation process and provides reusable and tested solutions that are abstract enough to be used in any programming language.

We have developed an example of a collaboration pattern to illustrate the instantiation of the framework. We have also implemented a set of automatic test cases using the csUnit testing tool to verify that the framework implementation gives support to the functionality that is required by the collaboration patterns. For reasons of brevity these test cases were not included.

The proposal presented has been extended for classes with n relationships. In this case the framework structure is the same, but some implementation details have been updated (for example some object attributes become to object collections). This chapter includes a reduced version of the proposal, since the main goal of the chapter is introducing the framework and the process for building it. The proposal of this chapter is being applied in an industrial CASE tool, OLIVA NOVA model execution.

The framework is centered in the business tier; the complete managing of the associations is made in this tier. We do not deal with the presentation and persistent tiers, where a basic management for associations should be proposed in order to provide a complete support for an application design.

Acknowledgment

This work has been developed with the support of MEC under the project DESTINO with reference TIN2004-03534 and co-financed by FEDER.

References

Bolloju, N. (2004, July). Improving the quality of business object models using collaboration patterns. *Communications of the ACM, 47*(7), 81-86.

Civello, F. (1993). Roles for composite objects in object-oriented analysis and design. In *Proceedings of The Conference on Object-Oriented Programming Systems, Languages, and Applications (OOPSLA'93)*, Washington, DC (pp. 376-393). ACM Press.

Cook, S., & Daniels, J. (1994). *Designing objects systems. Object-oriented modeling with syntropy.* Upper Saddle River, NJ: Prentice Hall.

Dahchour, M. (2001). *Integrating generic relationships into object models using metaclasses*. PhD thesis, Université Catholique de Louvain, Belgium, Department of Computing Science and Engineering.

D'Souza, D. F., & Wills, A. C. (1998). *Objects, components and frameworks with UML*. Boston: Addison-Wesley.

Díaz, O., & Paton, N. W. (1994). Extending ODBMSs using metaclasses. *IEEE Software, 11*(3), 40–47.

Firesmith, D. G., Henderson-Sellers, B., & Graham, I. (1997). *OPEN modeling language (OML) reference manual*. New York: SIGS Books.

Gamma, E., Helm, R., Johnson, R., & Vlissides, J. (1994). *Design patterns: Elements of reusable object-oriented software*. Boston: Addison-Wesley.

Genova, G. (2001). *Entrelazamiento de los aspectos estático y dinámico en las asociaciones UML*. PhD thesis, Department of Informática, Universidad Carlos III de Madrid, Spain.

Genova, G., Llorens, J., & Palacios, V. (2002). Sending messages in UML. *Journal of Object Technology, 2*(1), 99-115.

Graham, I., Bischof, J., & Henderson-Sellers, B. (1997). Associations considered a bad thing. *Journal of Object-oriented Programming, 9*(9), 41-48.

Greenfield, J., Short, K., Cook, S., & Kent, S. (2004). *Software factories*. Indianapolis, IN: Wiley Publishing.

Guéhéneuc, Y., & Albin-Amiot, H. (2004). Recovering binary class relationships: Putting icing on the UML cake. In *Proceedings of The Conference on Object-Oriented Programming Systems, Languages, and Applications (OOPSLA '04)*, Vancouver, B.C., Canada (pp. 301-314).

Henderson-Sellers, B., & Barbier, F. (1999a). What is this thing called aggregation? In A. C. Wills, J. Bosch, R. Mitchell, & B. Meyer (Eds.), *Proceedings of the Conference on Technology of Object-Oriented Languages and Systems (TOOLS 29)*, Nancy, France (pp. 216-230). IEEE Computer Society.

Henderson-Sellers, B., & Barbier, F. (1999b). Black and white diamonds. In R. France & B. Rumpe (Eds.), *Proceedings of UML '99. The Unified Modeling Language Beyond the Standard* (pp. 550-565). Fort Collins, CO: Springer-Verlag.

Klas, W., & Schrefl, M. (1995). *Metaclasses and their application: Data model tailoring and database integration*. New York: Springer-Verlag.

Kolp, M., & Pirotte, A. (1997). An aggregation model and its C++ implementation. In M. E. Orlowska & R. Zicari (Eds.), *Proceedings of The Interna-*

tional Conference on Object-Oriented Information Systems (OOIS'97), Brisbane, Australia (pp. 211–224).

Muñoz, J., Ruiz, M., Albert, M., & Pelechano, V. (2004). MDA aplicado: Una gramática de grafos para la transformación de relaciones de asociación. In *Proceedings of the IX Jornadas en Ingeniería Software y Bases de datos (JISBD'04)*, Malaga, Spain (pp. 539-546).

Object Management Group. (2002). *OMG MOF 2.0 query, views, transformations request for proposals*. Retrieved from http://www.omg.org

Object Management Group. (2003). *Unified Modeling Language, Version 1.5*.

Odell, J. J. (1994). Six different kinds of composition. *Journal of Object-Oriented Programming, 5*(8), 10-15.

Olivé, A. (2001). *Modelitzacio conceptual de sistemes de informacio. L'estructura*. Barcelona, Spain: Edicions UPC.

Opdahl, A. L., Henderson-Sellers, B., & Barbier, F. (2001). Ontological analysis of whole-part relationships in OO-models. *Information and Software Technology, 43*, 387-399.

Pirotte, A., Zimanyi, E., & Dahchour, M. (1998). *Generic relationships in information modeling* (Tech. Rep. No. YEROSS TR-98/09). Universite Catholique de Louvain, Belgium.

Rumbaugh, J. (1987). Relations as semantic constructs in an object-oriented language. In Meyrowitz. (Ed.), *ACM SIGPLAN Notices, 12*(22), 466-481.

Saksena, M., France, R. B., & Larrondo-Petrie, M. M. (1998). A characterization of aggregation. In C. Rolland & G. Grosz (Eds.), *Proceedings of 5th International Conference on Object-Oriented Information Systems (OOIS'98)*, Paris, France (pp. 11-19). Springer.

Snoeck, M., & Dedene, G. (2001). Core modeling concepts to define agreggation. *L'objet, 7*(3), 281-306.

Wand, Y., Storey, V. C., & Weber, R. (1999). An ontological analysis of the relationship construct in conceptual modeling. *ACM Transactions on Database Systems, 24*(4), 494-528.

Winston, M., Chan, R., & Herrmann, D. (1987). A taxonomy of part-whole relations. *Cognitive Science, 11*, 417-444.

Chapter V

Design Patterns as Laws of Quality

Yann-Gaël Guéhéneuc, University of Montreal, Canada

Jean-Yves Guyomarc'h, University of Montreal, Canada

Khashayar Khosravi, University of Montreal, Canada

Hourari Sahraoui, Unviersity of Montreal, Canada

Abstract

Software quality models link internal attributes of programs with external quality characteristics. They help in understanding relationships among internal attributes and between internal attributes and quality characteristics. Object-oriented software quality models usually use metrics on classes (such as number of methods) or on relationships between classes (for example coupling) to measure internal attributes of programs. However, the quality of object-oriented programs does not depend on classes solely: it depends on the organisation of classes also. We propose an approach to build quality models using patterns to consider program architectures. We justify the use of patterns to build quality models, describe the advantages and limitations of such an approach, and introduce a first case study in building and in applying a quality model using design patterns on the JHotDraw, JUnit, and Lexi programs. We conclude on the advantages of using patterns to build software quality models and on the difficulty of doing so.

Introduction

This chapter is a complete coverage of our current work on software quality models and on design pattern identification. In this chapter, we explore the idea of facts in science in relation with software quality models. We show how design patterns can be used as facts to devise a quality model and we describe the processes of building and of applying such a quality model.

In science, facts are the subject of observations by the scientists, who hypothesize laws to formalize recurring observations and theories to frame and to explain the laws. To the best of the authors' knowledge, many facts have been recorded and published but only few laws and theories have been developed (Endres & Rombach, 2003). This lack of laws and theories impedes the successful development of software and reduces our trust in software and in software science.

The lack of laws and theories is particularly visible in software quality. There do not yet exist general software quality models that could be applied to *any* software. It is indeed difficult to build quality models without concrete laws on software and software quality. Thus, existing quality models attempt to link internal attributes of classes and external quality characteristics with little regard for actual facts on software quality and without taking into account some dimensions of the evaluated software, such as its architecture.

In the following, we use design patterns (Gamma, Helm, Johnson, & Vlissides, 1994) as general laws to build a software quality model. We choose design patterns because they are now well-known constructs and have been studied extensively. Design patterns provide "good" solutions to recurring design problems. They define a problem in the form of an intent and motivations and provide a solution in the form of a design motif, a prototypical micro-architecture that developers use in their design to solve the problem. Design patterns are said to promote software elegancy through flexibility, reusability, and understandability (Gamma et al., 1994).

We assume that the design motifs provided by design patterns show flexibility, reusability, and understandability. Also, we assume that we can use design motifs as laws on software quality, as their authors intended, if not explicitly:

whenever developers use design motifs, they want to promote flexibility, reusability, and understandability in their design. Thus, whenever we find a micro-architecture similar to a design motif in a program architecture, we assume that this micro-architecture promotes (or was an attempt to promote) flexibility, reusability, and understandability.

We make the following parallels: a micro-architecture from a program architecture is a fact. That a micro-architecture displays flexibility, reusability, and understandability is an observation. A design motif defines some laws on the quality characteristics of the observed micro-architecture: it formalizes recurring micro-architectures that display flexibility, reusability, and understandability. We use these laws to assess the quality characteristics of software, that is, we use design motifs to build a software quality model to assess the quality of micro-architectures, identified in a program architecture.

Definition of the Problem

We want to build a quality model that considers quality characteristics covering software elegancy. Software elegancy is highly important during software maintenance to reduce the effort (time and cost) of maintainers. We need to choose external quality characteristics related to software elegancy and to find software metrics to fill the space between characteristics and software artifacts. We use design motifs as a basis to choose quality characteristics.

Existing quality models attempt to link internal attributes of classes and external quality characteristics with little regard for the actual architectures of the programs. Thus, these quality models can hardly distinguish between well-structured programs and programs with poor architectures. We use design motifs to assess programs' quality characteristics using both programs' internal attributes and their architectures as a mean to capture the quality of program architectures in a quality model.

Figure 1. A woman's profile: Cubist (left) and realist versions (right)

If we were in art rather than in informatics, we would say that identical quality models are used to compare a cubist painting, such as "Femme Profile" by Pablo Picasso (1939), with a realist picture, as shown in Figure 1. The two faces possess two eyes, one nose, two ears, and one mouth but with very different organizations, none being more beautiful, only more beautiful according to different laws.

Underlying Assumptions

In building a quality model using design motifs we make the following underlying assumptions.

Human factor. Some existing quality models can predict fault-proneness with reasonable accuracy in certain contexts. Other quality models attempt at evaluating several quality characteristics but fail at providing reasonable accuracy, from lack of data mainly.

We believe that quality models must evaluate high-level quality characteristics with great accuracy in terms well-known to maintainers to help these in assessing programs and thus in predicting maintenance effort.

Such quality models can also help developers in building better quality programs by exposing the relationships between internal attributes and external quality characteristics clearly.

We take a less "quantitative" approach than quality models counting, for example, numbers of errors per classes and linking these numbers with internal attributes. We favor a more "qualitative" approach linking quality characteristics related to the maintainers' perceptions and work directly.

Quality theory. Unfortunately, software engineering is known for its lack of laws and theories. Software engineers do not have theories to support their work on development, maintenance, and to explain quality yet.

Thus, it is important to gather as many facts and laws as possible. Design motifs are an interesting bridge between internal attributes of programs, external quality characteristics, and software engineers. We use motifs as laws to link internal attributes (concrete implementation of programs) on the one hand and subjective quality characteristics (subjective perceptions on programs) on the other hand.

Program architecture. Pair wise dependencies among classes and internal attributes of classes are not enough to evaluate the quality of a program: the organisations of classes, the program architectures, are important because they are the first things software engineers see and deal with.

A large body of work exists on program architecture, in particular on architectural drift or decay (Tran, Godfrey, Lee & Holt, 2000), which aims at analyzing, organizing, and tracking the modifications that architectures must undergo to keep them easy to understand and to modify, and thus to reduce maintenance effort (Kerievsky, 2004).

However, to the best of our knowledge, no work attempted to develop quality models using programs internal attributes while considering their architectures explicitly. We try to build such a quality model using design motifs as laws of architectural quality.

Process of Building a Quality Model

The general process of building a quality model decomposes in three main tasks:

- Choosing and organizing quality characteristics.
- Choosing internal attributes that are computable with metrics.
- Linking quality characteristics with internal attributes to produce evaluation rules.

The process of building a quality model decomposes in the following tasks when using design motifs to consider program architectures:

1. **Identifying the quality characteristics shared by a set of design motifs, which make programs more maintainable:** This task consists in identifying quality characteristics and subcharacteristics related to some motifs of interest. Among all possible characteristics, we focus on characteristics for program maintenance.

2. **Organizing the quality characteristics identified for the design motifs:** This task consists in organising quality characteristics and subcharacteristics hierarchically (Fenton & Pfleeger, 1997) to build a quality model, which can be linked with software artifacts using metrics.

3. **Choosing internal attributes relevant to design motifs and their quality characteristics:** This task consists of choosing internal attributes which can be measured with metrics. The internal attributes must relate to the quality model from Task 2, to link software artefacts with quality characteristics.

4. **Identifying programs implementing the design motifs:** This task consists in identifying a set of programs in which developers used the design motifs of interest. We name this set of base programs *BP*.

5. **Assessing the quality of design motifs using the quality model built in task 2:** This task consists in assessing the quality of design motifs in the set of base programs *BP* manually, with the characteristics and subcharacteristics of the quality model.

6. **Computing the metrics identified in task 3 on the design motifs in the base programs identified in task 4:** This task consists in computing metric values for the design motifs of interest identified in *BP*. If class-based metrics are used, then we can compute the metric values of the design motifs as the average or as the variance of the class-based metric values.

7. **Linking the metric values computed in task 6 and the evaluation of the quality subcharacteristics and characteristics performed in task 5:** This task consists in applying a machine learning technique to link internal attributes of programs measured with metric values computed in task 6 and the evaluation of the quality subcharacteristics and characteristics from task 5.

8. **Validating the obtained quality model on other well-known uses of design motifs:** This task consists in applying the evaluation rules from task 7 on other well-known programs to assess the evaluative power of the quality model. Using design motifs, we must apply our quality model on design motifs with known quality characteristics.

The result of the eight previous tasks is a quality model that can evaluate the quality characteristics of programs while considering the program architectures through the assessment of the quality of design motifs. The quality model decomposes in several rules for each quality subcharacteristics and characteristics. These rules depend on different metrics to assess quality.

Figure 2. Simplified process of building a quality model considering program architectures through design motifs

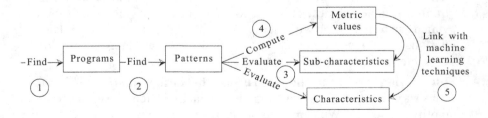

Figure 2 displays a simplified version of our process. First, we identify programs implementing design motifs. Second, we identify in these programs the design motifs used. Third, we evaluate the quality subcharacteristics and characteristics of the design motifs manually. Fourth, we compute metrics for each identified design motifs (by averaging class-based metrics, for example). Fifth, we use machine learning techniques to link metric values with the quality subcharacteristics and characteristics of design motifs.

Process of Applying a Quality Model

Once we built a quality model using design motifs to consider the quality of program architectures in addition to internal attributes of classes or couple thereof, applying such a quality model requires to consider micro-architectures in a program architecture and to apply the quality model on these micro-architectures to assess their quality.

Again, if we were in art, we could say that existing quality models assess the quality characteristics of paintings by looking at many tiny parts of the painting (for example, classes in program architectures) rather than by looking at larger pieces of the painting (micro-architectures in program architectures), such as sketched in Figure 3.

Thus, applying our quality model requires the four following tasks:

1. **Identifying micro-architectures similar to design motifs in the architecture of the program P under evaluation:** There are many techniques existing to identify design motifs in programs, for examples logic programming (Wuyts, 1998) or constraint programming (Guéhéneuc, Sahraoui, & Zaidi, 2004). In the following, we present our technique using explanation-based constraint programming.

Figure 3. Level of details considered in existing software quality model (left) vs. in quality models based on design motifs (right)

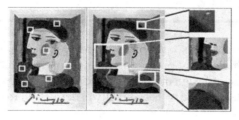

Figure 4. Adapting the rules of the quality model, ratio between minimum and maximum metric values of BP and P

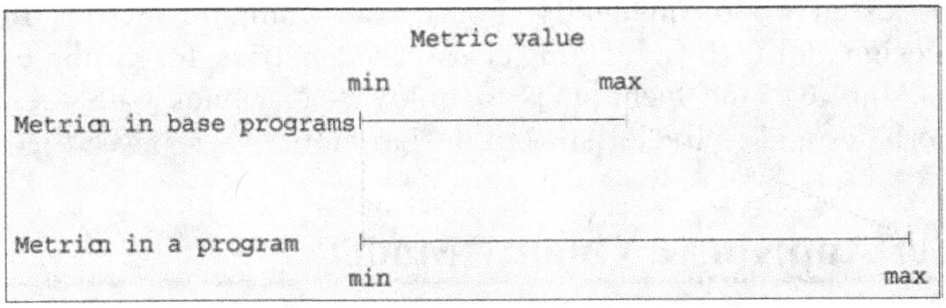

2. **Measuring the internal attributes of each class of the micro-architectures with metrics and averaging class-based metric values, if needed:** This task is straightforward, many tools existing to compute metrics from programs.

3. **Adapting the rules built from BP to P by computing the ratio between the metric values from BP and the metric values from P:** This task consists of adapting the rules associated with the quality model built from *BP*. Indeed, the rules are built from metric values with a certain minimum and maximum value depending on *BP*, these values differ from the minimum and maximum values for *P*. We compute the ratio between *minBP* and *maxBP*, on the one hand, and *minP* and *maxP*, on the other hand. Figure 4 illustrates rule adaptation.

   Yet again, if we were in art and we would like to compare the eyes in two different paintings, we would adapt the scales of the eyes before making any comparison.

4. **Applying our quality model on the identified micro-architectures:** This task consists in applying the rules adapted from the quality model on the metric values computed for the micro-architectures found in program *P*.

Discussion

The use of design motifs as laws of software quality brings an extra level of abstraction to the building of our quality model with respect to existing quality models. Indeed, we use design motifs for three purposes: first, we survey quality characteristics of design motifs theoretically to define and to organize the quality characteristics of our quality model; second, we validate our quality model on well-known uses of design motifs; third, we apply our quality model on micro-architectures similar to design motifs.

We can use our quality model on any micro-architecture, independently of their sizes and organizations, and thus potentially on complete program architectures. This use is similar to the use of existing quality models which are built using internal attributes and quality characteristics of given programs but applied on similar yet sometimes very differing programs.

The use of design motifs as a basis to build a quality model results in our choice to study qualitative quality characteristics over quantitative characteristics, such as fault-proneness. Thus, we want to build a quality model tailored for maintainers, evaluating "qualitative" characteristics with which maintainers can predict maintenance effort.

We choose design motifs and design patterns because developers always use patterns. Indeed, developers always use recurring solutions to solve design problems. Thus, design patterns are an integral part of any reasonably well-developed program (Gamma et al., 1994).

However, the use of design motifs is but a step towards quality models that can evaluate software quality while considering the architectures of programs. Indeed, a quality model built using design motifs assesses the quality of programs through larger *parts* than existing quality models because it uses micro-architectures instead of classes. Yet, it does not consider the overall architectures of the programs. It is similar in art to assessing the quality of a painting using parts rather than looking at the whole picture, such as in the right-hand side of Figure 3.

Background

Our work is at the conjunction of two fields of study: quality models on the one hand, design motif identification on the other hand. We present some major work in both fields of study. We show that none of the existing work attempts to build a quality model based on micro-architectures of the program architectures, using design motif identification.

Quality Models

Briand and Wüst (2002) present a detailed and extensive survey of quality models. They classify quality models in two categories: co-relational studies and experiments. Co-relational studies use univariate and multivariate analyzes, while experiments use, for examples, analysis of variance between groups (ANOVA). To the best of our knowledge, none of the presented quality models attempts to assess the architectural quality of programs directly. They all use class-based metrics or metrics on class couples.

Wood, Daly, Miller, and Roper (1999) study the structure of object-oriented C++ programs to assess the relation between program architectures and software maintenance. The authors use three different methods (structured interviews, survey, and controlled experiments) to conclude that the use of inheritance in object-oriented programs may inhibit software maintenance.

Harrison, Counsell, and Nithi (2000) investigate the structure of object-oriented programs to relate modifiability and understandability with levels of inheritance. Modifiability and understandability cover only partially the quality characteristics in which we are interested. Levels of inheritance are but one architectural characteristic of programs related to software maintenance.

Wydaeghe et al. (1998) assess the quality characteristics of the architecture of an OMT editor through the study of seven design patterns (bridge, chain of responsibility, facade, iterator, MVC, observer, and visitor). They conclude on flexibility, modularity, reusability, and understandability of the architecture and of the patterns. However, they do not link their assessment with any evaluative or predictive quality model.

Wendorff (2001) evaluates the use of design patterns in a large commercial software product. The author concludes that design patterns do not improve a program architecture necessarily. Indeed, architecture can be over-engineered (Kerievsky, 2004) and the cost of removing design patterns is high. The author does not link this study with any quality model.

Design Motif Identification

Most approaches to the identification of occurrences of design motifs are structural. They require a structural matching between a design motif and candidate micro-architectures. Different techniques have been used to perform the structural matching: rule inference and unification (Krämer & Prechelt, 1996; Wuyts, 1998), queries (Ciupke, 1999; Keller, Schauer, Robitaille, & Page, 1999), constraints resolution (Guéhéneuc & Albin-Amiot, 2001; Quilici, Yang, & Woods, 1997), and fuzzy reasoning (Jahnke & Zundorf, 1997).

Unification. Wuyts developed the SOUL environment in which design motifs are described as Prolog predicates and programs constituents as Prolog facts (classes, methods, fields, etc.) (Wuyts, 1998). A Prolog inference algorithm unifies predicates and facts to identify classes playing roles in design motifs. The main limitation of such a structural approach is the inherent combinatorial complexity of identifying subsets of all classes matching design motifs, which corresponds to a problem of subgraph isomorphism (Eppstein, 1995).

Constraint resolution. Quilici et al. (1997) used constraint programming to identify design motifs. Their approach consists in translating the problem of design motif identification in a problem of constraint satisfaction. Design motifs are described as constraint systems, which variables have for domain the entities (classes and interfaces) of a program. The resolution of a constraint system provides micro-architectures composed of entities respecting the constraints among the roles of a design motif. As with the unification approach, the combinatorial complexity of the resolution proves to be prohibitive.

Quantitative evaluation. Antoniol, Fiutem, and Cristoforetti (1998) used constraint programming extended with metrics to reduce the search space during design pattern identification. They designed a multi-stage filtering process to identify micro-architectures *identical* to design motifs. For each class of a program, they compute some metrics (for example, numbers of inheritance, of association, and of aggregation relationships) and they compare the metric values with expected values for a design motif to reduce search space. Then, they apply a constraint-based approach to identify micro-architectures. The expected values of metrics are derived from the theoretical descriptions of design motifs. The main limitation of their work lies in the assumption that implementation (micro-architectures) accurately reflects theory (design motifs), which is often not the case. Moreover, the theoretical characterization of roles, when possible, does not reduce the search space significantly.

Fuzzy reasoning. In an original work, Jahnke and Zundorf (1997) introduced fuzzy reasoning nets to identify design motifs. Design motifs are described as fuzzy reasoning nets, expressing rules of identification of micro-architectures similar but not identical to design motifs. They exemplify their approach with the identification of poor implementations of the Singleton design motif in legacy C++ code. They express identification rules with the formalism of fuzzy reasoning nets and then compute the certainty of a variable being a Singleton starting from a user's assumption. The main advantage of their approach is that fuzzy reasoning nets deal with inconsistent and incomplete knowledge. However, their approach requires description of all possible rules of approximation for a design motif and a user's assumption.

Building a Quality Model

We use design motifs from design patterns as a basis to build a quality model. Design patterns provide *good* solutions to architectural design problems, which maintainers can use in the assessment of the quality characteristics of program architectures naturally. Indeed, as Grady Booch says in his Foreword in *Design Patterns Elements of Reusable Object-Oriented Software*, "all well-structured object-oriented architectures are full of patterns" (Gamma et al., 1994). Also, design patterns provide a basis for choosing and for organizing external quality characteristics related to the maintenance effort.

Overview

The following general information offers a synthetic view on our quality model.

Dependent variables. The dependent variables in our quality model are quality characteristics. We choose these quality characteristics by studying the quality characteristics of the 23 design patterns in Gamma et al.'s (1994) book. We study the literature on design patterns and identify five quality characteristics which decompose in seven quality subcharacteristics, which we consider as external attributes.

Independent variables. The independent variables in our quality model are the internal attributes which we measure on programs. These internal attributes are similar to those in other quality models from the literature: size, filiation, cohesion, coupling, and complexity.

Analysis technique. We use a propositional rule learner algorithm, JRip. JRip is Weka — an open-source program collecting machine learning algorithms for data mining tasks (Witten & Frank, 1999) — implementation of the Ripper rule learner. It is a fast algorithm for learning "If — Then" rules. Like decision trees, rule learning algorithms are popular because the knowledge representation is easy to interpret.

Building a Quality Model

We perform the eight tasks identified previously to build a quality model considering program architectures based on design motifs.

1. **Identifying the quality characteristics:** We consider a hierarchical model, because such model is more understandable (Fenton & Pfleeger, 1997) and because most of standard models are hierarchical, for examples (ISO/IEC, 1991) and (McCall, 2001).
    *   Design patterns claim to bring reusability, understandability, flexibility, and modularity (Gamma et al., 1994). So, we add these quality

Figure 5. A quality model based on design motifs quality characteristics

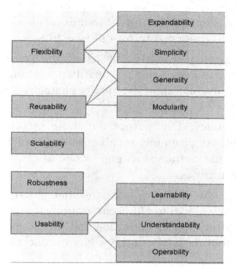

characteristics to our quality model. Also, through our past experience, we add robustness and scalability (which together define software elegancy (Ciupke, 1999) to our quality model.

2. **Organising the quality characteristics:** We organize the quality characteristics and decompose these in subcharacteristics using definitions from IEEE, ISO/IEC, and several other models (such as McCall, 2001; CBR Online, 2002; Smith & Williams, 2001; Firesmith, 2003; Khosravi & Guéhéneuc, 2004; Smith & Williams, 2001).

Figure 5 presents our quality model to evaluate software quality related to software maintenance based on design motifs.

3. **Choosing internal attributes:** We choose size, filiation, coupling, cohesion, and complexity as internal attributes. We use the metrics from Chidamber and Kemerer's (1993) study mainly to measure these internal attributes, with additions from other metrics by Briand, Devanbu, and Melo (1997a), by Hitz and Montazeri (1995), by Lorenz and Kidd (1994), and by Tegarden, Sheetz, and Monarchi (1995).

The complete list of metrics used to measure internal attributes is: ACAIC, ACMIC, AID, CBO, CLD, cohesionAttributes, connectivity, DCAEC, DCMEC, DIT, ICHClass, LCOM1, LCOM2, LCOM5, NCM, NMA, NMI, NMO, NOA, NOC, NOD, NOP, SIX, and WMC.

4. **Identifying programs with motifs:** We use the set of programs imple-
    menting design patterns from Kuchana's (2004) book. Each program in this
    set implements design patterns from Gamma et al.'s book (Gamma et al.,
    1994). This set of programs forms our base programs *BP*.

5. **Assessing the quality of motifs:** We assess the quality characteristics of
    design patterns manually, using our quality model and the set *BP*. Table 1
    summarizes our evaluation of the quality characteristics of the 23 design
    motifs.

6. **Computing metrics:** The metrics we chose in task 3 to measure the
    internal attributes of programs are all class-based metrics. Thus, we need
    first to compute the metric values and second to adapt the metric values to
    the micro-architectures.

    •   We analyze the base programs and their micro-architectures using
        PADL, a metamodel to represent programs. Then, we apply POM, a
        framework for metrics definition and computation based on PADL
        (Guéhéneuc et al., 2004), on the program models to compute the metric
        values.

    •   Then, we adapt the class-based metric values to the micro-architec-
        tures. For a given metric, we use the average of its values on all the
        classes forming a micro-architecture. However, average is not a good
        representative of the metric values for the micro-architecture. Indeed,
        we should compute and study the variance of the metric values to get
        a better understanding of the distribution of the metric values. Vari-
        ance indicates how much each of the metric values of the classes in
        the micro-architecture deviates from the mean. However, for the
        current exploratory study, we keep the average to allow a better
        analysis of the resulting rules.

7. **Linking internal attributes and quality characteristics:** We use a
    machine learning technique to infer rules linking the quality characteristics
    of the quality model and the metric values.

    •   We use the JRip algorithm to find the rules between quality character-
        istics and values of the metrics. The rule in Table 2 is the rule
        associated with the learnability quality characteristics, when applying
        JRip on the metric values and on the base programs from tasks 3, 4, and
        5. It shows that learnability is related to the NMI and NOP metrics
        more than to any other metrics.

    •   We do not introduce here all the rules found for the different quality
        subcharacteristics and characteristics in our model for lack of space.

Table 1. Design patterns quality characteristics in the base programs (E = Excellent, G = Good, F = Fair, P = Poor, and B = Bad)

Design patterns	Quality Sub-characteristics and Characteristics								
	Expandability	Simplicity	Generality	Modularity	Learnability	Understandability	Operability	Scalability	Robustness
Abstract Factory	E	E	G	G	G	G	G	G	G
Builder	G	G	F	F	F	G	F	G	G
Factory Method	P	P	F	G	G	G	G	G	G
Prototype	E	G	F	G	F	G	F	E	G
Singleton	P	B	F	E	F	F	F	G	G
Adapter	F	F	P	G	G	F	F	G	F
Bridge	G	F	G	G	F	F	G	G	G
Composite	F	F	F	F	F	G	F	F	G
Decorator	E	E	G	F	G	G	G	G	G
Façade	G	G	G	G	F	G	F	F	F
Flyweight	P	P	F	G	G	P	F	G	G
Proxy	G	P	F	G	F	P	G	G	F
Chain of Responsibility	G	G	G	P	F	F	G	G	F
Command	G	P	F	F	P	B	G	G	G
Interpreter	G	F	G	F	F	F	G	G	F
Iterator	E	E	G	F	G	F	F	G	G
Mediator	G	F	G	G	F	F	G	G	F
Memento	G	F	F	B	P	F	G	F	P
Observer	E	G	E	F	F	G	G	G	G
State	G	G	F	·P	F	B	G	G	F
Strategy	G	F	P	F	P	P	F	P	F
Template Method	E	G	F	F	G	G	G	G	G
Visitor	E	G	G	F	G	P	F	G	F

The rules are specific to the current case study but help in illustrating the advantages and limitations of our approach.

8. **Validating the quality model:** We use the leave-one-out method (Stone, 1974) for cross-validating the rules built for our quality model by JRip.

Table 2: Rule for learnability

> if (LCOM5 ? 1:1) ^ (NOA ? 33:25)
> then (Learnability = Good)
> else (Learnability = Fair)

Applying the Quality Model

We apply the quality model built in the previous section to the JHotDraw (for clarity, we apply our quality model on a subset of the micro-architectures in JHotDraw only), JUnit, and Lexi programs. We apply the learnability rule of the quality model in particular, because this rule represents a good trade-off between simplicity and expressiveness. The learnability rule has been built in task 7 with *minLCOM5*=0.75, *maxLCOM5*=1.82, *minNOA*=1.00, and *maxNOA*=86.00.

JHotDraw is a Java GUI framework for technical and structured graphics. It has been developed originally by Erich Gamma and Thomas Eggenschwiler as a "design exercise" but is now a full-fledge framework. Its design relies heavily on some well-known design patterns. JUnit is a regression testing framework written by Erich Gamma and Kent Beck. It is used to implements unit tests in Java. Lexi is a Java-based word processor. It has been developed by Matthew Schmidt and Brill Pappin originally. These programs are open-source and most are available on SourceForge.

Applying our quality model requires to identify in a program the micro-architectures similar to some design motifs. We consider micro-architectures as our "unit" of measurement rather than classes, as presented earlier. We decompose the task 1 of *identifying micro-architectures similar to design motifs in the architecture of a program P under evaluation* in two subtasks to improve the performance of the identification:

1. A task of role identification, in which we identify classes that could play a role in a design motif potentially.

2. A task of design motif identification, in which we identify classes which structural organization is similar to that of a design motif. In this subtask, we only consider classes identified in the previous subtask to reduce the search space and, thus, to improve performance, recall, and precision.

Identifying Roles

We associate numerical signatures with roles in design motifs to characterize classes that *could* play one of these roles and exclude classes that *obviously* could not. We seek to characterize classes playing roles in design motifs using their internal attributes. The most consensual attributes for classes in object-oriented programming languages are:

- **Size/complexity:** For example, number of methods, of fields.
- **Filiation:** For example number of parents, number of children, depth of the inheritance tree.
- **Cohesion:** For example, degree to which methods and attributes of a class belong together.
- **Coupling:** Strength of the association created by a link from one class to another.

Two or more classes may have identical values for a given set of internal attributes. Indeed, two or more classes may play a same role in different uses of a design motif and a same class may play two or more roles in one or more design motifs. Thus, internal attributes cannot be used to distinguish uniquely a class among classes playing roles in design motifs.

Yet, internal attributes can be used to reduce the search space of micro-architectures. We can use internal attributes to eliminate true negatives from the search space efficiently, that is, classes that *obviously* do not play a role in a design motif. Moreover, no thorough empirical studies have so far validated the impossibility to identify classes uniquely with their internal attributes, or attempted to find quantifiable *commonalities* among classes playing a given role in a design motif experimentally.

Therefore, we study the use of internal attributes of classes to quantify design motif roles: we devise *numerical signatures* for design motifs roles using internal attributes of classes. We group these numerical signatures in rules to identify classes playing a given role. For example, a rule for the role of Singleton in the Singleton design motif could be:

Rule for "Singleton" role:
  Filiation: Number of parents low,
          number of children low.

because a class playing the role of Singleton is high in the inheritance tree normally and has no (or a few) subclass usually. A rule for the role of Observer in the Observer design motif could be

Rule for "Observer" role:
   Coupling: Coupling with other classes low.

because the purpose of the observer design motif is to reduce the coupling between the classes playing the roles of observer and the rest of the program.

Building Numerical Signatures

Overview. Figure 6 presents an overview of the process of assigning numerical signature to design motifs roles. First, we build a *repository* of classes forming micro-architectures similar to design motifs in different programs. We identified the roles played by these classes in design motifs manually. Then, we *extract metrics* from the programs in which we found micro-architectures to associate a set of values for the internal attributes with each class in the repository. We feed a propositional *rule learner* algorithm with the sets of metric values. The rule learner returns a set of rules characterizing design motif roles with the metric values of the classes playing these roles. We *cross-validate* the rules using the leave-one-out method. Finally, we *interpret* the rules obtained (or the lack thereof) for roles in design motifs. The following subsections detail each step of the process.

Repository creation. We need a repository of classes forming micro-archi-tec-tures similar to design motifs to analyze these classes quantitatively. We investigate several programs manually to identify micro-architectures similar to design motifs and to build a repository of these micro-architectures, the P-MARt (pattern-like micro-architecture repository). We create this repository using different sources:

*   Studies in the literature, such as the original study from Bieman, Straw, Wang, Willard, and Alexander (2003), which record classes playing roles in design motifs from several different C++, Java, and Smalltalk programs.
*   Our tool suite for the identification of design motifs, Ptidej (*pattern trace identification, detection, and enhancement in Java*) (Albin-Amiot, Cointe, Guéhéneuc & Jussien, 2001; Guéhéneuc & Albin-Amiot, 2001), which implements PtidejSolver, an explanation-based constraint solver to identify design motifs.

Figure 6. Process of assigning numerical signatures to design motifs roles

- Assignments in an undergraduate course and in a graduate course, during which students performed analyzes of Java programs.

The repository of micro-architectures similar to design motifs surveys:

- For each program, motifs for which we found similar micro-architectures.
- For each motif, similar micro-architectures that we found in the program.
- For each micro-architectures, roles played by their classes in the design motif.

We validate all the micro-architectures manually before their inclusion in the repository; however, we do not claim that we identified *all* micro-architectures similar to design motifs in a given program.

So far, the P-MARt contains data from nine programs, for a total of 4,376 classes and 138 micro-architectures representing 19 different design motifs. We exclude inner classes because no inner class appears in a micro-architecture so far. Table 3 summarizes the data in the P-MARt. The two first rows give the names and number of classes (and interfaces) of the surveyed programs. The following rows indicates, for a given design pattern (per row), the number of micro-architectures found similar to its design motif in each program (per column). The table summarizes also the number of roles defined by a design motif and the number of classes playing a role in a design motif for all the programs (two last columns). The number of classes playing roles in design motifs shows that only a fraction of all the classes of the programs plays a role in a design motif. Moreover, some classes are counted more than once because they play different roles in different design motifs. Design motifs for which we did not identify similar micro-architectures are: chain of responsibility, interpreter, and mediator. We record this data in an XML file, which allows us to traverse the data to compute metrics and various statistics automatically.

Metric extraction. We parse the programs surveyed in the P-MARt and calculate metrics on their classes automatically. Parsing and calculation are performed in a three-step process: first, we build a model of a program using the PADL (*pattern and abstract-level description language*) meta-model and its

Table 3. Overview of the data set: Programs, design motifs, micro-architectures, and roles

	JHotDraw v5.1	JRefactory v2.6.24	JUnit v3.7	Lexi v0.0.1α	MapperXML v1.9	NetBeans v1.0.x	Nutch v0.4	PMD v1.8	QuickUML 2001	Total	Number of roles	Number of classes playing a role
Number of classes	173	575	157	127	172	5812	2558	447	224	7 068		
Design Motifs	Number of micro-architecture similar to the design motifs per program											
Abstract Factory					1	12			1	14	5	242
Adapter	1	17			2	8	2	1		31	4	252
Bridge							2			2	4	25
Builder		2		1				2	1	6	4	44
Command	1					1	2		1	5	5	85
Composite	1		1		1		2		2	7	4	147
Decorator	1		1							2	4	64
Façade					1					1	2	11
Factory Method	3	1			1			3		8	4	111
Iterator			1			5	1	1		8	5	41
Memento								2		2	3	15
Observer	2		3	2	1			2	1	11	4	135
Prototype	2									2	3	32
Proxy								1		1	3	3
Singleton	2	2	2	2	3		1		1	13	1	13
State	2	2								4	3	32
Strategy	4				1		2			7	3	47
Template Method	2				4		3	1		10	2	102
Visitor		2						1		3	5	143
									Total	138	40	1552

parsers; second, we compute metrics using POM (*primitives, operators, metrics*), an extensible framework for metric calculation based on PADL; third, we store the results of the metric calculation, names and values, in the P-MARt, by adding specific attributes and nodes to the XML tree representation.

We use metrics from the literature to associate values with internal attributes of classes playing a role in a design motif. Table 4 presents the metrics computed on classes related to the internal attributes that we consider: size/complexity, filiation, cohesion, and coupling. For size/complexity, we use the metrics by Lorenz and Kidd (1994) on new, inherited, and overridden methods and on the

Table 4. External attributes for classes and corresponding metrics

	Acronyms	Descriptions	References
Size/complexity	NM	Number of Methods	(Lorenz & Kidd, 1994)
	NMA	Number of new methods	(Lorenz & Kidd, 1994)
	NMI	Number of inherited methods	(Lorenz & Kidd, 1994)
	NMO	Number of overridden methods	(Lorenz & Kidd, 1994)
	WMC	Weighted methods count	(Chidamber & Kemerer, 1993)
Filiation	CLD	Class-to-leaf depth	(Tegarden et al., 1995)
	DIT	Depth of inheritance tree	(Chidamber & Kemerer, 1993)
	NOC	Number of children	(Chidamber & Kemerer, 1993)
Cohesion	C	Connectivity	(Hitz & Montazeri, 1995)
	LCOM5	Lack of cohesion in method 5	(Briand et al., 1997b)
Coupling	ACMIC	Accessor class-method import	(Briand et al., 1997a)
	CBO	Coupling between objects	(Chidamber & Kemerer, 1993)
	DCMEC	Descendants class-method export	(Briand et al., 1997a)

total number of methods and the count of methods weighted with their numbers of method invocations by Chidamber and Kemerer (1993). We do not use metrics related to fields because no design motif role is characterized by fields specifically: only the Flyweight, Memento, Observer, and Singleton design motifs (5 out of 23) expose the internal structures of some roles to exemplify typical implementation choices. Moreover, fields should always be private to their classes with respect to the principle of encapsulation. For filiation, we use the depth of the inheritance tree and the number of children by Chidamber and Kemerer (1993) and the number of hierarchical levels below a class, class-to-leaf depth, by Tegarden et al. (1995). For cohesion, we use the metric "C" measuring the connectivity of a class with the rest of a program by Hitz and Montazeri (1995) and the fifth metric of lack of cohesion in methods by Briand, Daly, and Wüst (1997b). Finally, for coupling, we use two metrics on class-method import and export coupling by Briand et al. (1997a) and the metric on coupling between objects by Chidamber and Kemerer (1993).

Rule learning and validation. The P-MARt contains a wealth of data to analyze. We use a machine learning algorithm to find commonalities among classes playing a same role in a design motif. We supply the data to a propositional rule learner algorithm, JRip, implemented in Weka, an open-source program collecting machine learning algorithms for data mining tasks (Witten & Frank, 1999).

We do not provide JRip with all the data in the P-MARt; this would lead to uninteresting results because of the disparities among roles, classes, and metric values. We provide JRip with subsets of the data related to each role. A subset ó of the data related to a role contains the metric values for the *n* classes playing the role in all the micro-architectures similar to a design motif. We add to this subset σ the metric values of $3 \times n$ classes *not* playing the role, chosen randomly in the rest of the data. We make sure the classes chosen randomly have the expected structure for the role that is, whether the role is defined to be played by a class or by an abstract class (Gamma et al., 1994), to increase their likeliness with the classes playing the role. The rule learner infers rules related to each role from the subsets σ. We validate the rules using the leave-one-out method with each set of metric values in the subsets σ (Stone, 1974).

Interpretation. The rule learner infers rules that express the experimental relationships among metric values, on the one hand, and roles in design motifs, on the other hand. Typically, a rule inferred by the rule learner for a role ROLE has the form:

Rule for "ROLE" role:

   - Numerical signature 1, confidence 1,

   - Numerical signature 2, confidence 2,

   - ...

   - Numerical signature N, confidence N.

where:

Numerical signature 1 $= \left\{ metric_1 \in V_{11}, ..., metric_m \in V_{m1} \right\}$

...

Numerical signature N $= \left\{ metric_1 \in V_{1n}, ..., metric_m \in V_{mn} \right\}$

and the values of a metric *metrici* computed on classes playing the role ROLE belong to a set $V_{ij} \subset N$. The degree of confidence K is the proportion of classes concerned by a numerical signature in a subset σ, which we use to compute error and recall ratios.

We collect all the rules inferred from the rule learner and process the rules with the following criteria to remove uncharacteristic rules:

- We remove rules with a recall ratio less than 75%.
- We remove rules inferred from small subsets σ that is, when not enough classes play a given role.

Then, we interpret the remaining rules in two ways: qualitatively, we explain rules with respect to their corresponding roles; quantitatively, we assess the quality of classes playing roles in design motifs. Practically, we show that numerical signatures reduce the search space for micro-architectures similar to design motifs efficiently.

Discussion

We decompose the data in the P-MARt in 56 subsets σ and infer as many rules with the rule learner, which decompose in 78 numerical signatures. The two first steps in the analysis process are quantitative and aim at eliminating roles that do not have a sufficient number of examples for mining numerical signatures and that do not have a high enough recall ratio. In the first step, we remove 20 over the 56 rules from all the rules inferred by the rule learner. The removed rules correspond to:

- Design motif roles with few corresponding micro-architectures and with a unique (or a few) classes in the micro-architectures. Some examples are the roles of Decorator in the Decorator design motif and of Prototype in Prototype.
- Design motifs roles played by "ghost" classes in many cases that is, classes known only from import references, such as classes in standard libraries. Some examples are the classes playing the roles of Command in the Command design motif and of Builder in Builder.

In the second step, we select 20 rules with a recall ratio greater than 75%, shown in Table 5, from the 36 remaining rules. All these rules have an error rate less than 10% (less than 5% for 16). Most of the rules removed because of their low recall ratio are associated with roles known to be non-key roles in design motifs and which, thus, do not have a particular numerical signature theoretically. For example, any class may play the role of client in the composite design motif. Similarly, any class may play the role of Invoker in the Command design motif. (Some researchers argue that client, invoker are not "real" roles and should not appear in most design motifs.)

We notice that, in many cases, we obtain a unique numerical signature for a given role in a design motif. Classes playing a same role have similar structures and organizations generally. For example, all the classes playing the role of target in the adapter design motif have a low complexity, represented by low values of WMC, as shown in the Rule for "Target" role (the degree of confidence is less than 1 because this numerical signature misclassifies one class, its error rate is

Figure 7. Rules inferred for the role of Target in the Adapter design motif

Rule for "Target" role:
- WMC <= 2, 24/25.

4%, as shown in Table 5). Such a low complexity is actually expected because of the architecture and of the behavior suggested by the adapter design motif. Likewise, many other numerical signatures confirm claims from and beliefs on design motifs. For examples, classes playing the role of Observer in the Observer design motif have a low coupling that is, a low CBO. Classes playing the roles of Singleton in the Singleton design motif have low coupling and belong to the upper part of the inheritance tree generally.

In a few cases, we obtain more that one numerical signature for a role. An example is the role of Concrete Visitor in the Visitor design motif. On the one hand, the most frequent numerical signature is characteristic of classes with a low coupling (low CBO) and a large number of methods (high NM), as expected from the problem dealt with by the Visitor design pattern. On the other hand, the

Table 5: Roles with inferred rules with recall ratio greater than 75%

Design Motifs	Roles	Error (in %)	Recall (in %)
Iterator	Client	0.00	100.00
Observer	Subject	0.00	100.00
Observer	Observer	2.38	100.00
Template Method	Concrete Class	0.00	97.60
Prototype	Concrete Prototype	0.00	96.30
Decorator	Concrete Component	4.17	89.58
Visitor	Concrete Visitor	0.00	88.89
Strategy	Context	3.70	88.89
Visitor	Concrete Element	2.04	88.78
Singleton	Singleton	8.33	87.50
Factory Method	Concrete Creator	4.30	87.10
Factory Method	Concrete Product	3.45	86.21
Adapter	Target	4.00	84.00
Composite	Leaf	6.47	82.09
Decorator	Concrete Decorator	0.00	80.00
Iterator	Iterator	0.00	80.00
Command	Receiver	6.67	80.00
State	Concrete State	6.67	80.00
Strategy	Concrete Strategy	2.38	78.57
Command	Concrete Command	3.23	77.42

second numerical signature states that the number of inherited methods is low (low NMI) for some classes playing the role of Concrete Visitor. When exploring the micro-architectures similar to the Visitor design motif in our repository, we notice that in JRefactory some classes play the roles of both Concrete Visitor and Visitor, which thus limits the number of inherited methods. This second numerical signature is particular to JRefactory and unveils design choices specific to the program or to a coding style.

Identifying Design Motifs

After identifying classes which could play roles in design motifs, we perform a structural search among these classes to identify those which structures and organizations are similar to the structures and organisations advocated by some design motifs.

We use explanation-based constraint programming to identify both complete and approximate forms of design motifs, that is, groups of classes which structures and organizations are similar to the motifs, while providing explanations and allowing user-interactions.

Explanation-based constraint programming. Explanation-based constraint programming proved its interest (Jussien & Barichard, 2000) in many applications already. We recall fundamentals on explanation-based constraint programming and some of its uses.

- **Contradiction explanations:** We consider a constraint satisfaction problem (CSP) (V, D, C): V is the set of variables, D is the set of domains for the variables, and C is the set of constraints among variables. Decisions made during enumeration — variable assignments — are represented by unary constraints added to or removed from the current constraint system. These unary constraints are called *decision constraints* because they are not defined in the constraint satisfaction problem but are generated by the solver to represent decisions taken during the resolution. A contradiction explanation [also known as *no-good* (Schiex & Verfaillie, 1994)] is a subset of the current constraint system that, left alone, leads to a contradiction — no solution. A contradiction explanation divides in two parts: a subset of the original set of constraints ($C' \subset C$ in Equation 1) and a subset of the decision constraints introduced during the search.

$$C \vdash \neg(C' \wedge v_1 = a_1 \wedge ... \wedge v_k = a_k) \tag{1}$$

A contradiction explanation without decision constraint denotes an overconstrained problem. In a contradiction explanation containing at least one decision constraint, we choose a variable vj and rewrite Equation 1 in 2.

$$C \vdash C' \wedge \bigwedge_{i \in [1..k] \setminus j} (v_i = a_i) \rightarrow v_j \neq a_j \qquad (2)$$

The left hand side of the implication is an *eliminating explanation* for the removal of value aj from the domain of variable vj. The eliminating explanation is noted:

$$\mathrm{expl}(v_j \neq a_j)$$

Classical solvers use domain-reduction techniques to solve constraint satisfaction problems by removing values from the domains of variables. Thus, recording eliminating explanations is sufficient to compute contradiction explanations. Indeed, a contradiction is identified when the solver empties the domain of a variable vj. A contradiction explanation can be computed with the eliminating explanations associated with each removed value, as shown in Equation 3.

$$C \dashv \neg (\bigwedge_{a \notin d(v_j)} \mathrm{expl}(v_j \neq a)) \qquad (3)$$

Several eliminating explanations exist for the removal of a given value generally. Recording all eliminating explanations would lead to an exponential space complexity. Thus, we must *forget* (erase) eliminating explanations that are no longer relevant to the current variable assignments. An eliminating explanation is said to be relevant if all its decision constraints are valid in the current search state (Bayardo & Miranker, 1996). We keep only *one* explanation at a time for any value removal and the space complexity remains polynomial.

• **Computing contradiction explanations:** Minimal contradiction explanations (with respect to inclusion) are the most interesting. They provide precise information on dependencies among variables and constraints identified during the search. Unfortunately, computing such explanations is time-consuming (Junker, 2001). A compromise between size and computability consists in using the knowledge *inside* the solver. Indeed, CSP solvers always know why they remove values from the domains of variables, although not often explicitly. They can compute minimal contradiction explanations with this knowledge explicitly. We must alter the source code of a CSP solver to make such knowledge explicit. The PaLM solver (Jussien & Barichard, 2000) is a reference implementation of an explanation-based constraint solver.

- **Using contradiction explanations:** We can use contradiction explanations for many different purposes (Jussien & Barichard, 2000; Jussien, Debruyne & Boizumault, 2000; Jussien & Lhomme, 2000). For example, we can use explanations to debug constraint resolution by explaining contradictions *clearly* and by explaining differences between intended and observed behavior (answering question such as "why is x not assigned to value 4?" explicitly).

Also, we can use contradiction explanations to assess the impact of a constraint on domains of variables and to handle, for example, dynamic constraint removals. Thus, Bessière's justification system (Bessière, 1991) for solving dynamic CSP is actually a partial explanation-based constraint solver.

Finally, we can use contradiction explanations to improve standard backtracking algorithms and to improve the search: to provide intelligent backtracking (Guéret, Jussien & Prins, 2000), to replace standard backtracking with jump-based approaches *à la* dynamic backtracking (Ginsberg, 1993; Jussien et al., 2000), to develop new local searches on partial instantiations (Jussien & Lhomme, 2000), and to guide the search dynamically.

Application to design motif identification. Design motif identification consists:

1. In modeling a set of design motifs as CSP. A variable is associated with each class defined by a design motif. The variables of our model are integer-valued. The domain of a variable is a set of existing classes in the source code. Each class is identified by a unique integer. Relationships among classes (inheritance, association) are represented by constraints among variables.

2. In modeling the maintainers' source code to keep only the information needed to apply the constraints: class names — forming the domain of the variables and the relationships among classes — verifying or not the constraints.

3. In resolving the CSP to search both approximate and complete microarchitectures: when all solutions to the CSP are found, that is, when all

micro-architectures identical to a design motif are identified, the search is guided by the maintainers to find approximate micro-architectures dynamically. Contradiction explanations provided by the constraint solver help the maintainers in guiding the search.

We build a library of specialized constraints from the relationships among classes used to describe design motifs. Specialized constraints express the inheritance, creation, association relationships among classes. Our library offers constraints covering a broad range of design motifs. However, some design motifs are difficult to express as CSP and require additional relationships or the decomposition of existing relationships into subrelationships. We provide the following constraints:

- **Strict inheritance** establishes a strict inheritance relationship between classes. A strict inheritance relationship links two classes in a parent-child-like relationship that is, superclass-subclass. When considering single inheritance, the strict inheritance relationship is a partial order, denoted $<$, on the set of classes E. For any pair of distinct classes A and B in E, if B inherits from A then: $A < B$. The constraint associated with the strict inheritance relationship is a binary constraint between variables A and B. The operational semantics of the constraint is:

$$\forall C_A \in d_A, \exists d_B, c_A < c_B$$

$$\forall C_B \in d_B, \exists d_A, c_A < c_B$$

  where dX represents the domains of variable X. From this definition of strict inheritance, we derive an inheritance relationship, and its associated constraint, such that the variables may represent a same class: $A < B$ or $A = B$.

- **Use** establishes a use relationship (Guéhéneuc, 2004) between classes. A class A knows about a class B if methods defined in A invoke methods of B. This relationship is binary, oriented and intransitive. We denote this relationship by $A > B$.

- **Association**, **aggregation**, and **composition** enforce that two classes are associated, aggregated, or composed with one another (Guéhéneuc &

Albin-Amiot, 2004), respectively. For example, a class A is composed with instances of a class B if the A class defines one or more fields of type B. We write $A \supset B$. This relationship is binary, oriented, and intransitive.

Behavior of the CSP solver. The library of specialized constraints is not sufficient in itself to allow design motif identification. Indeed, micro-architectures that fit exactly in the modeling of a design motif as a CSP are of no use to identify area with poor quality characteristics. We need to find *approximate* micro-architectures that is, micro-architectures that do not verify all constraints from a design motif. Explanation-based constraint programming allows to identify approximate and complete forms.

First, a specialized CSP solver computes complete forms. The resolution ends by a contradiction, there are no more micro-architectures. Explanation-based constraint programming provides a contradiction explanation for this contradiction: the set of constraints justifying that other combinations of classes do not verify the constraints describing the searched design motif. We do not need to relax other constraints than the constraints provided by the contradiction explanation: we would find no other micro-architecture. The explanation contradiction provides knowledge on which approximate forms are available. This knowledge allows maintainers to lead the search towards interesting approximate forms, from their viewpoints, by exhibiting constraints to relax. Removing a constraint suggested by a contradiction explanation does not necessarily lead to new micro-architectures but the removal is applied recursively.

Preferences are assigned to the constraints of a CSP to ease maintainers' interactions with the specialized CSP solver. They reflect a hierarchy among constraints *a priori*, but they are not mandatory in our CSP solver. We derive a metric from the preferences, with which we measure the quality of a micro-architecture in terms of its distance with the search design motif; that is, the number of constraints relaxed to obtain this micro-architecture. The metric allows the automation of the CSP solver to identify all approximate micro-architectures.

The maintainer-driven version of our CSP solver is of great interest when *a priori* preferences are hard to determine, which is often the case. Moreover, maintainers can restrict the search to a subset of interesting approximate forms interactively. Explanation-based constraint programming gives a complete control to the maintainers: this is important in an *intellectual* activity such as design motif identification.

Discussion. The use of explanation-based constraint programming to identify micro-architec-tures similar to design motifs provides three interesting properties:

- Identification of both complete and approximate forms of design motifs
- Explanations about the identified micro-architectures
- Interactions with the maintainers

We describe design motifs as constraint systems: each role is represented as a variable and relationships among roles are represented as constraints among variables. Variables had identical domains: all the classes in a program in which to identify design motifs. For example, the identification of micro-architectures similar to the composite design motif, shown in Figure 8, in JHotDraw translates to the constraint system:

Variables:
  client
  component
  composite
  leaf
Constraints:
  association(client, component)
  inheritance(component, composite)
  inheritance(component, leaf)
  composition(composite, component)

where the four variables *client*, *component*, *composite*, and *leaf* have identical domains, which contains all the 155 classes (and interfaces) composing JHotDraw, and the four constraints represent the association, inheritance, and composition relationships suggested by the Composite design motif.

However, as other structural approaches, our approach with explanation-based constraint programming has limited performance and a low recall. Indeed, the Composite design motif describes four roles, which are expressed as four variables. Thus, the search of micro-architectures similar to the Composite design motif in the JHotDraw framework, which contains 155 classes, has potentially $155^4 = 577,200,625$ solutions.

We use the numerical signatures associated with roles in design motifs to reduce the search space and to improve both performance and recall. We apply numerical signatures on the domain of each variable to remove from its domain the classes that *obviously* cannot play the design motif role associated with this variable.

Figure 8. Composite design motif

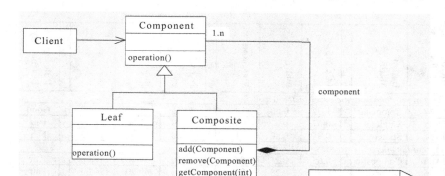

Applying the Quality Model

We have now identified micro-architectures similar design motifs. We follow the four tasks from Subsection 1.4 to apply the quality model on these micro-architectures.

1. **Identifying micro-architectures:** JHotDraw uses 11 different design motifs in 21 micro-architectures: Adapter, Command, Composite, Decorator, Factory Method, Observer, Prototype, Singleton, State, Strategy, and Template Method. JUnit contains 8 micro-architectures similar to 5 different design motifs: Composite, Decorator, Iterator, Observers, and Singletons. Lexi contains 5 micro-architectures similar to the Builder, Observer, and Singleton design motifs. Table 6 summarizes these micro-architectures.

2. **Measuring internal attributes:** For each micro-architecture identified in JHotDraw, in JUnit, or in Lexi, we use PADL and POM to compute the class-based metric values and Etiquette to compute the micro-architecture-based metric values (using average). Table 6 presents the data for each micro-architecture for the LCOM5 and NOA metrics.

3. **Adapting the rules:** We adapt the metric values in the rule in Table 2 by computing the ratio between the minimum and maximum values of the LCOM5 and NOA metrics for the base programs, on the one hand, and each micro-architecture, on the other hand. Table 6 also displays the adapted rules for all the micro-architectures.

Table 6. Data and rules when applying the quality model to a subset of JHotDraw, JUnit, and Lexi

Micro-architectures	Design Motifs	LCOM5	min_{LCOM5}	max_{LCOM5}	NOA	min_{NOA}	max_{NOA}	Rule for Learnability
Subset of the micro-architectures in JHotDraw								
MA74	Command	1.07	0.50	1.63	29.35	1.00	164.00	Good
MA85	Singleton	0.67	0.67	0.67	1.00	1.00	1.00	Fair
MA91	Strategy	0.95	0.80	1.0	553.88	221.00	792.00	Fair
Subset of the micro-architectures in JUnit								
MA65	Composite	0.65	0.25	0.95	70.10	4.00	148.00	Fair
MA66	Decorator	0.65	0.25	0.90	135.41	49.00	176.00	Fair
MA67	Iterator	0.92	0.83	0.99	30.67	1.00	48.00	Fair
MA68	Observer	0.60	0.66	1.03	112.43	1.00	191.00	Fair
MA69	Observer	0.83	0.83	0.83	1.00	1.00	1.00	Fair
MA70	Observer	0.83	0.83	0.83	11.00	11.00	11.00	Fair
MA71	Singleton	0.00	0.00	0.00	1.00	1.00	1.00	Fair
MA72	Singleton	0.00	0.00	0.00	1.00	1.00	1.00	Fair
Subset of the micro-architectures in Lexi								
MA8	Builder	0.95	0.93	0.97	7.75	1.00	12.00	Fair
MA9	Observer	0.95	0.94	0.97	9.50	1.00	18.00	Fair
MA10	Observer	0.95	0.94	0.97	61.67	35.00	94.00	Fair
MA11	Singleton	1.01	1.01	1.01	1.00	1.00	1.00	Fair
MA12	Singleton	0.99	0.99	0.99	2.00	2.00	2.00	Fair

4.   **Applying the rules:** We compare the expected metric values in the adapted rules with the metric values computed for each micro-architecture.

Discussion. Table 6 presents the results for adapting the learnability rule in Table 2. We computed the average, the minimum, and the maximum values of the LCOM5 and NOA metrics for each program, JHotDraw, JUnit, and Lexi. We adapted the rule from the minimum and maximum values of the base programs and of JHotDraw, JUnit, and Lexi. The last column shows the adapted rules and the results of applying the rules.

The first line of the table shows an example of applying the learnability rule to a micro-architecture similar to the Command design pattern. The outcome of the rule states that this particular implementation of the Command design pattern has a Good learnability.

However, the quality model obtained is unsatisfactory for many reasons. First, the size of the base programs used to create the quality model renders the rule uninteresting in many cases. In particular, we do not have sufficient data yet but to assess the learnability of JUnit and of Lexi as Fair.

Second, adapting the rule when there is one metric value only, see for example the micro-architecture MA5 in JUnit, does not provide interesting information because the adapted threshold of the learnability rule is always inferior to the maximum (and unique) value. Adaptation requires a range or more accurate rules (based on a minimum and a maximum thresholds) to be efficient.

Third, we do not distinguish in the micro-architectures between code which plays a role in the design motif and code which does not. Considering all the metric values, potentially including "dead" code, has an impact on the results certainly.

Moreover, learnability is a human-related quality characteristic. It is difficult to assess this characteristic intrinsically because it depends on the individuals performing the assessment. Thus, we need to perform more evaluations to obtain an accurate rule.

Conclusion

In this chapter, we presented a global coverage of our work on software quality models and on design motif identification. We used design patterns as laws of software quality and we used these laws to observe micro-architectures similar to design motifs and to assess their quality.

We described the process of building a quality model using motifs to link metrics and quality characteristics with a learning algorithm. We also described the process of applying the quality model on software, using explanation-based constraint programming to identify micro-architectures similar to design motifs and metrics to improve the performance, recall, and precision of the identification.

This chapter highlights the need for *principles* in software engineering. These principles can be laws or theories formalizing and explaining observations realized on software. Our contribution is the use of design patterns and of their solutions, design motifs, as laws of software quality to build quality models.

In the future, we believe that the software engineering community must develop its understanding of design patterns and their applications to solve problems, such as traceability and maintainability. Indeed, patterns are more and more recognized as important concepts in software engineering, in particular in conjunction with cognition during software development (Floyd, 1992; Miller, 1956), and they both require and deserve a more thorough and systematic study.

Also, the software engineering community must strive to identify concepts on which to build laws and theories. We strongly believe that design motifs can be considered as laws of quality. However, our belief requires further studies and analyzes.

Acknowledgments

We thank James Bieman, Greg Straw, Huxia Wang, P. Willard, and Roger T. Alexander (Bieman et al., 2003) for kindly sharing their data. We are grateful to our students, Saliha Bouden, Janice Ka-Yee Ng, Nawfal Chraibi, Duc-Loc Huynh, and Taleb Ikbal, who helped in the creation of the repository. "Femme Profile" by Pablo Picasso is from rogallery.com, we are currently in contact with its director regarding copyrights.

All the data and programs used to perform the case study are available on the Internet at http://ptidej.iro.umontreal.ca/downloads/pmart/.

References

Albin-Amiot, H., Cointe, P., Guéhéneuc, Y.-G., & Jussien, N. (2001). Instantiating and detecting design patterns: Putting bits and pieces together. In D. Richardson, M. Feather, & M. Goedicke, (Eds.), *Proceedings of the 16th Conference on Automated Software Engineering* (pp. 166-173). IEEE Computer Society Press.

Antoniol, G., Fiutem, R., & Cristoforetti, L. (1998). Design pattern recovery in object-oriented software. In S. Tilley & G. Visaggio (Eds.), *Proceedings of the 6th International Workshop on Program Comprehension* (pp. 153-160). IEEE Computer Society Press.

Bayardo, R. J., Jr., & Miranker, D. P. (1996). A complexity analysis of space-bounded learning algorithms for the constraint satisfaction problem. In D. Weld & B. Clancey (Eds.), *Proceedings of the 13th National Conference on Artificial Intelligence* (pp. 298-304). AAAI Press/The MIT Press.

Bessière, C. (1991). Arc-consistency in dynamic constraint satisfaction problems. In T. L. Dean & K. McKeown (Eds.), *Proceedings of the 9th National Conference on Artificial Intelligence* (pp. 221-226). AAAI Press/The MIT Press.

Bieman, J., Straw, G., Wang, H., Willard, P., & Alexander, R. T. (2003). Design patterns and change proneness: An examination of five evolving systems. In M. Berry & W. Harrison (Eds.), *Proceedings of the 9th International Software Metrics Symposium* (pp. 40-49). IEEE Computer Society Press.

Briand, L., Devanbu, P., & Melo, W. (1997a). An investigation into coupling measures for C++. In W. R. Adrion (Ed.), *Proceedings of the 19th International Conference on Software Engineering* (pp. 412-421). ACM Press.

Briand, L. C., Daly, J. W., & Wüst, J. K. (1997). A unified framework for cohesion measurement. In S. L. Peeger & L. Ott (Eds.), *Proceedings of the 4th International Software Metrics Symposium* (pp. 43-53). IEEE Computer Society Press.

Briand, L. C., & Wüst, J. (2002). Empirical studies of quality models in object-oriented systems. *Advances in Computers, 59*, 97-166.

Chidamber, S. R., & Kemerer, C. F. (1993). *A metrics suite for object-oriented design* (Tech. Rep. No. E53-315). MIT Sloan School of Management.

Ciupke, O. (1999). Automatic detection of design problems in object-oriented reengineering. In D. Firesmith (Ed.), *Proceeding of 30th Conference on Technology of Object-Oriented Languages and Systems* (pp. 18-32). IEEE Computer Society Press.

Endres, A., & Rombach, D. (2003). *A handbook of software and systems engineering.* Addison-Wesley.

Eppstein, D. (1995). Subgraph isomorphism in planar graphs and related problems. In K. Clarkson (Ed.), *Proceedings of the 6th Annual Symposium On Discrete Algorithms* (pp. 632-640). ACM Press.

Fenton, N. E., & Pfleeger, S. L. (1997). *Software metrics: A rigorous and practical approach.* PWS Publishing Company.

Firesmith, D. G. (2003). *Common concepts underlying safety, security, and survivability engineering* (Technical Note CMU/SEI-2003-TN-033). Carnegie Mellon Software Engineering Institute.

Floyd, C. (1992). *Human questions in computer science.* Springer-Verlag.

Gamma, E., Helm, R., Johnson, R., & Vlissides, J. (1994). *Design patterns elements of reusable object-oriented software.* Addison-Wesley.

Ginsberg, M. (1993). Dynamic backtracking. *Journal of Artificial Intelligence Research, 1*, 25-46.

Guéhéneuc, Y. G. (2004). A reverse engineering tool for precise class diagrams. In J. Singer & H. Lutya (Eds.), *Proceedings of the 14th IBM Centers for Advanced Studies Conference.* ACM Press.

Guéhéneuc, Y. G., & Albin-Amiot, H. (2001). Using design patterns and constraints to automate the detection and correction of inter-class design defects. In Q. Li, R. Riehle, G. Pour, & B. Meyer (Eds.), *Proceedings of the 39th Conference on the Technology of Object-Oriented Languages and Systems* (pp. 296-305). IEEE Computer Society Press.

Guéhéneuc, Y. G., & Albin-Amiot, H. (2004). Recovering binary class relationships: Putting icing on the UML cake. In D. C. Schmidt (Ed.), *Proceedings of the 19ᵗʰ Conference on Object-Oriented Programming, Systems, Languages, and Applications.* ACM Press.

Guéhéneuc, Y.-G., & Jussien, N. (2001). Using explanations for design-patterns identification. In C. Bessière (Ed.), *Proceedings of the 1ˢᵗ IJCAI workshop on Modeling and Solving Problems with Constraints* (pp. 57-64). AAAI Press.

Guéhéneuc, Y. G., Sahraoui, H., & Zaidi, F. (2004). Fingerprinting design patterns. In E. Stroulia & A. de Lucia (Eds.), *Proceedings of the 11ᵗʰ Working Conference on Reverse Engineering* (pp. 172-181). IEEE Computer Society Press.

Guéret, C., Jussien, N., & Prins, C. (2000). Using intelligent backtracking to improve branch and bound methods: An application to open-shop problems. *European Journal of Operational Research, 127*(2), 344-354.

Harrison, R., Counsell, S. J., & Nithi, R. V. (2000). Experimental assessment of the effect of inheritance on the maintainability of object-oriented systems. *Journal of Systems and Software, 52*(2-3), 173-179.

Hitz, M., & Montazeri, B. (1995). Measuring coupling and cohesion in object-oriented systems. In *Proceedings of the 3ʳᵈ International Symposium on Applied Corporate Computing* (pp. 25-27). Texas A&M University.

ISO/IEC 9126:1991(E). (1991). *Information technology software product evaluation quality characteristics and guidelines for their use.*

Jahnke, J. H., & Zundorf, A. (1997). Rewriting poor design patterns by good design patterns. In S. Demeyer & H. Gall (Eds.), *Proceedings of the 1ˢᵗ ESEC/FSE Workshop on Object-Oriented Reengineering.* Distributed Systems Group, Technical University of Vienna, TUV-1841-97-10.

Junker, U. (2001). *QUICKXPLAIN: Conflict detection for arbitrary constraint propagation algorithms* (Technical Report). Ilog SA.

Jussien, N., & Barichard, V. (2000). The PaLM system: Explanation-based constraint programming. In N. Beldiceanu, W. Harvey, M. Henz, F. Laburthe, E. Monfroy, T. Muller, L. Perron, & C. Schulte (Eds.), *Proceedings of TRICS: Techniques for Implementing Constraint Programming Systems* (pp. 118-133). School of Computing, National University of Singapore, Singapore.

Jussien, N., Debruyne, R., & Boizumault, P. (2000). Maintaining arc-consistency within dynamic backtracking. In R. Dechter (Ed.), *Proceedings of the 6ᵗʰ Conference on Principles and Practice of Constraint Programming* (pp. 249-261). Springer-Verlag.

Jussien, N., & Lhomme, O. (2000). Local search with constraint propagation and conflict-based heuristics. In H. A. Kautz & B. Porter (Eds.), *Proceedings* of the 17*th* *National Conference on Artificial Intelligence* (pp. 169-174). AAAI Press/The MIT Press.

Keller, R. K., Schauer, R., Robitaille, S., & Page, P. (1999). Pattern-based reverse-engineering of design components. In D. Garlan & J. Krämer (Eds.), *Proceedings of the 21st International Conference on Software Engineering* (pp. 226-235). ACM Press.

Kerievsky, J. (2004). *Refactoring to patterns.* Addison-Wesley Professional.

Khosravi, K., & Guéhéneuc, Y.-G. (2004). *A quality model for design patterns* (Tech. Rep. No. 1249). University of Montreal.

Krämer, C., & Prechelt, L. (1996). Design recovery by automated search for structural design patterns in object-oriented software. In L. M. Wills & I. Baxter (Eds.), *Proceedings of the 3rd Working Conference on Reverse Engineering* (pp. 208-215). IEEE Computer Society Press.

Kuchana, P. (2004). *Software architecture design patterns in Java.* Auerbach Publications.

Lorenz, M., & Kidd, J. (1994). *Object-oriented software metrics: A practical approach.* Prentice Hall.

McCall, J. A. (2001). Quality factors. *Encyclopedia of Software Engineering, 1-2,* 958.

Miller, G. A. (1956). The magical number seven, plus or minus two: Some limits on our capacity for processing information. *The Psychological Review, 63*(2), 81-97.

Quilici, A., Yang, Q., & Woods, S. (1997). Applying plan recognition algorithms to program understanding. *Journal of Automated Software Engineering, 5*(3), 347-372.

Schiex, T., & Verfaillie, G. (1994). No good recording for static and dynamic constraint satisfaction problems. *International Journal of Artificial Intelligence Tools, 3*(2), 187-207.

Smith, C. U., & Williams, L. G. (2001). *Introduction to software performance engineering.* Addison-Wesley. Retrieved from http://www.awprofessional.com/articles/article.asp?p=24009

Stone, M. (1974). Cross-validatory choice and assessment of statistical predictions. *Journal of the Royal Statistical Society (Series B: Statistical Methodology), 36,* 111-147.

Tegarden, D. P., Sheetz, S. D., & Monarchi, D. E. (1995). A software complexity model of object-oriented systems. *Decision Support Systems, 13*(3-4), 241-262.

Tran, J. B., Godfrey, M. W., Lee, E. H., & Holt, R. C. (2000). Architectural repair of open source software. In *Proceedings of the 8th International*

Workshop on Program Comprehension (pp. 48-57). IEEE Computer Society Press.

Wendorff, P. (2001). Assessment of design patterns during software reengineering: Lessons learned from a large commercial project. In P. Sousa & J. Ebert (Eds.), *Proceedings of 5th Conference on Software Maintenance and Reengineering* (pp. 77-84). IEEE Computer Society Press.

Witten, I. H., & Frank, E. (1999). *Data mining: Practical machine learning tools and techniques with Java implementations,* (1st ed.). Morgan Kaufmann.

Wood, M., Daly, J., Miller, J., & Roper, M. (1999). Multimethod research: An empirical investigation of object-oriented technology. *Journal of Systems and Software, 48*(1), 13-26.

Wuyts, R. (1998). Declarative reasoning about the structure of object-oriented systems. In J. Gil (Ed.), *Proceedings of the 26th Conference on the Technology of Object-Oriented Languages and Systems* (pp. 112-124). IEEE Computer Society Press.

Wydaeghe, B., Verschaeve, K., Michiels, B., Damme, B. V., Arckens, E., & Jonckers, V. (1998). Building an OMT-editor using design patterns: An experience report. In *Proceedings of the 26th Technology of Object-Oriented Languages and Systems Conference* (pp. 20-32). IEEE Computer Society Press.

Chapter VI

Automatic Verification of OOD Pattern Applications

Andrés Flores, University of Comahue, Argentina

Alejandra Cechich, University of Comahue, Argentina

Rodrigo Ruiz, University of Comahue, Argentina

Abstract

Object-oriented patterns condense experimental knowledge from developers. Their pragmatic benefits may involve a reduction on the effort impact of the maintenance stage. However, some common problems can be distinguished as well. For instance, some design patterns are simply too difficult for the average OO designer to learn. A pattern-based design process could be enhanced by the provision of an automatic support for modeling and verification with a proper formal foundation. In this chapter we show how formal specifications of GoF patterns have been helpful to develop that tool support, where we have adopted the well-known Java language upon its portability facet. Thus, we are changing the object-oriented design process by the inclusion of pattern-based modeling and verification steps. The latter involving checking design correctness and appropriate pattern application through the use of the supporting tool, called DePMoVe (Design and Pattern Modeling and Verification).

Introduction

Object-oriented patterns represent an important source of knowledge by condensing years of experience from developers. They certainly became a useful technical vocabulary which helps for developers to discuss and communicate ideas. Particular design problems, for example, can be easily described by *"using an observer"* or *"separated by a bridge."* The abstractness of patterns description allows cutting across traditional boundaries of system development and business engineering. At any stage of a development project, knowledge upon business processes can be practically shared when patterns are properly applied on the supporting systems.

The pragmatic benefits of using design patterns may involve the possibility to reduce the impact on cost — time + effort — of the maintenance stage, which usually may rise to 80% of the overall cost of the project (Polo, Piattini, & Ruiz, 2002). Design patterns address the concern of the evolutionary nature of the software, since they may allow software to be flexibly accommodated to constant changes. Hence, they are considered as a technique for *design to change*, thus satisfying the design principle of *anticipation to change* (Gamma, Helm, Johnson, & Vlissides, 1995; Ghezzi, Jazayeri, & Mandrioli, 2002).

However, a number of common problems can be distinguished as well. For example, some design patterns are simply too difficult for the average OO designer to learn. In some cases, the pattern is inherently complex; in other cases the pattern involves an explanation and a name that are not obvious. Hence, pattern understanding could be a serious problem for being skeptic when they will be adopted by an organization. In practice, an OO designer needs personal time and personal initiative to become skilful in design patterns. This could be approached by firstly experimenting with the use of a pattern in a toy example before it can be used in the real case. Thus, the main issue implies OO designers with an imperative need of learning how to apply design patterns.

Such a misunderstanding problem on patterns applications has been distinguished as a consequence of the provided description on current patterns catalogues (Alagar, & Lämmel, 2002; Eden, 2000; Lauder, & Kent, 1998). Patterns are invariably described informally in the literature (Buschmann, Meunier, Rohnert, Sommerland, & Stal, 1996; Cooper, 2000; Coplien, 1996; Fowler, 1997; Gamma, et al., 1995; Grand, 1998a, 1998b; Pree, 1995), generally using natural language narrative together with a sort of graphical notation, which makes it difficult to give any meaningful certification of a pattern-based software. Particularly, patterns in the GoF catalogue (Gamma, et al, 1995) are described using a consistent format which is based on an extension of the object modeling technique (OMT) (Rumbaugh, Blaha, Premerlani, Eddy, & Lorensen, 1991). This form of presentation gives a very good intuitive picture of the patterns, but it is not sufficiently precise to allow a designer to conclusively demonstrate that a particular problem matches a specific pattern or that a proposed solution is consistent with a particular pattern. Moreover, it is difficult to be certain that patterns themselves are meaningful and contain no inconsistencies. In some cases, descriptions of patterns are intentionally left loose and incomplete to ensure that they are applicable in a range as wide as possible. This reduces understanding and interpretation upon appropriate patterns usage. Nevertheless, the availability of a more formal description could help alleviate these problems.

In a previous work (Moore, Cechich, Reynoso, Flores, & Aranda, 2002), we have presented a formal model of a generic object-oriented design that was developed in RSL — the RAISE Specification Language (RAISE Group, 1992, 1995) — and based upon the extended OMT notation given on the GoF catalog. We have shown how designs can be formally linked with patterns in this model, and how properties of individual patterns can be specified in the model, thus giving a basis for formally checking whether a given design and a given pattern are consistent with each other. Although we have limited our attention to GoF patterns in this work, the whole model is general enough to be applied in a similar way to formalize other design patterns based on object-oriented notations, such as those in (Buschmann, et al, 1996; Cooper, 2000; Coplien, 1996; Fowler, 1997; Grand, 1998a, 1998b; Pree, 1995) based on the Unified Modeling Language (UML).

In order to understand the characteristics that need to be present on a formal basis for improving patterns application, we have developed an evaluation framework consisting of two parts. One part focuses on patterns themselves and the other on the formal languages that were used to specify the patterns. This gives a good picture of the involved aspects that are necessary to improve the so-called Pattern-based Design Process.

Such a process could be enhanced even more whether an automatic support for modeling and verification is provided. This has been our project's target and in this chapter we show how the specifications of individual GoF patterns have been a useful basis to carry out the development of the tool support. On such a development we have adopted the well-known Java language which allows an easy portability to different working environments. We are then, updating the design process by the inclusion of a pattern-based modeling and verification steps. The latter involving checking design correctness and appropriate pattern application.

The usage of this tool is also focused on the learning process about pattern applications. This may let designers gain a useful insight into design principles and also learn about diverse pattern properties. Through a better understanding of patterns, a designer may certify when and how a pattern is being appropriately applied to solve a specific design problem. Furthermore, the design process may be improved with a precise technique supported by this tool: any error detected during verification can help designers to improve their designs and reason about information that can be vital to correctly apply a particular pattern.

We have organized this chapter in the following way. In the next section we present definitions of the pattern-based design process and show some examples of design patterns descriptions which could make a designer feel insecure on how to carry out a pattern application. We also present considerations about the likely benefits of a more rigorous description and a collection of features that could enhance a formal model for pattern-based design. The third section introduces the formal basis that we have developed in RSL, where we also highlight features and considerations from the second section, for a better understanding. The fourth section describes how the formalization was applied to build a tool support for modeling and verification, and the process of translation from the RSL formal basis to the Java language. The fifth section presents the corresponding change on the design process, and illustrates the process by a case study. Conclusions are presented afterwards.

Pattern-Based Design

A design process which is based on the application of patterns involves a binding of elements from a pattern description (roles) to elements of the design (classes, methods, relations, and so on). A subset of the classes and other elements in a design then conforms to a specific pattern if they satisfy the properties of their counterparts in the pattern (Flores, Moore, & Reynoso, 2001; Flores, & More, 2001). Figure 1 shows a schema for a design-pattern linkage (Meijers, 1996) to explain the concept of patterns application. Such a binding is also called *pattern instantiation* for which one of the following three approaches could be used on a design process:

- **Top-down:** given a pattern, generate its appropriate components at the design level;

- **Bottom-up:** given a (subset of a) design and a pattern, perform the binding or verify the matching;

- **Mixed:** given a pattern and a (subset of a) design that only partly matches it, generate the missing pattern components at the design level.

Figure 1. Design-pattern levels linkage

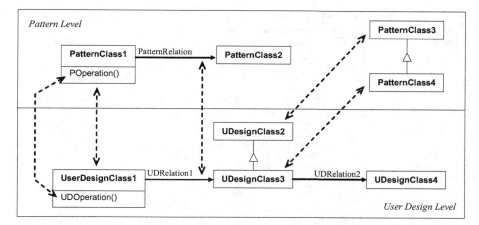

For a design to be really enhanced by the application of a pattern, there should not be any doubt at reading its documentation -like for any software engineering artifact. However, different circumstances have been distinguished, where a designer may find it difficult to be sure if the working instantiation does not introduce side effects as, for example, violating an important pattern feature that in the worst case could change the *pattern intent* or even deteriorate the design quality. Some of these situations are reported in the following section.

Analysis of Patterns Descriptions

When a designer intends to actually use patterns could discover that it is necessary a pretty brilliant mind to recognize how to adjust the provided template and description on the design under development. The *intent* section on a pattern description format, for example, does not give an *a priori* needed "help," but it may be gradually understood after reading the rest of the description format. Then, the *structure* section is quite generic so to reason about all the possible concrete situations where such pattern could be used. Hence, it is "reinforced" with textual descriptions on other different sections, which far from supplying the required "help," actually produces quite a big confusion on several aspects.

In Eden (1998) there is a simple analysis of the description format for patterns in the GoF catalog (Gamma, et al, 1995), where six categories of textual sentences have been identified with respect to their exactitude at describing the

Table 1: Fairly accurate and elusive 'extracts' from the GoF catalogue

Interpretation Category	Textual Statements
1. Precise, singular	(DECORATOR) "maintains a reference to a Component object"
	(VISITOR's ConcreteElement) "implements an Accept operation that takes a visitor as an argument"
2. Enumerated alternatives	(FACTORY METHOD's Creator) "may call the factory method to create a Product object"
	(STRATEGY, Collaborations) "Alternatively, the context can pass itself as an argument to Strategy operations"
	(DECORATOR, Collaborations) "It may optionally perform additional operations before and/or after forwarding the operations"
3. Precise generalization	(VISITOR) "declares a Visit operation for each class of ConcreteElement in the object structure"
	(Decorator) "defines an interface that conforms to Component's interface"
4. Technical terms, yet open to various interpretations	(PROXY) "Virtual proxies ... cache additional information about the real subject so they can postpone accessing to it"
	(PROTOTYPE) "implements an operation for cloning itself"
	(MEMENTO) "stores internal state of the Originator object."
5. Fuzzy, informal, or theological description	(ADAPTER's Adaptee) "defines an existing interface that needs adapting"
	(COMPOSITE's Component) "implements default behavior for the interface common to all classes, as appropriate"
	(OBSERVER's Collaborations) "ConcreteObserver uses this information to reconcile its state with that of the subject."
6. Deliberate omission of detail	(STATE) "The State pattern does not specify which participant defines the criteria for state transitions"

promised solution. Table 1 shows that three categories concern quite *precise* statements while the three others present less accurate or elusive statements.

Table 1 shows the situations that a designer can discover when intends to use a pattern. Therefore, the requirement is on the provision of a more accurate description of patterns, which could be achieved by the use of formalisms. However, there is certain general denial on the use of formal languages, as we report in the following section.

Can Patterns Be Formalized?

Developers and even scientists may have a certain skepticism concerning the use of formalisms to describe patterns. Some objections that were identified in Eden (2000) are expressed along the following lines:

- **Formal specifications:** Formal specifications contribute little or nothing to the understanding when and how to use a pattern. "Formalizing the solution makes it harder to grasp the key ideas of the pattern. ... Programmers need concrete information that they can understand, not an impressive formula" (Buschmann, 1996, p. 427).

- **Patterns:** Patterns are abstractions, or generalizations, and therefore are meant to be vague, ambiguous, and imprecise. If they were specified in a precise form, or expressed in mathematical terms, they would no longer be patterns. "Formalizing the solution makes it harder … to create valid variants. A formalized solution may thus narrow the applicability of the pattern unnecessarily. … Formalisms tend to describe particular issues very precisely, but do not allow for the variation that is inherently embedded into every pattern" (Buschmann, 1996, p. 427).

- **There is no fixed element in patterns:**, Everything can be changed about them. In other words, if "the basic structure is fixed … this isn't patterns any more" (Coplien, 1996).

Such concerns seem to be valid on many approaches which apply formality without a previous planning of needed and achievable objectives. This has been our concern as well, and we had the intention not only to properly cover all of them, but also to solve other issues that contribute to a poor understanding on patterns application. In the next section we give other specific reasons for seriously consider the application of formality on the description of a pattern instantiation model.

Some Concrete Reasons to Formalize Patterns

In order to implement a pattern instantiation approach, the need for an adequate notation is essential. Current object notations are inappropriate as languages for pattern description. Each of the common object notations considers symbols which are mapped to concrete constructors on Object-Oriented Programming Languages (OOPL). The typical example is OMT used in the *Structure* section of each pattern in the GoF catalog. The purpose of a notation should be to allow a designer to transcend a pattern description in order to understand benefits and risks of its application. In particular we are trying to avoid the following aspects that are inherent of an informal notation (Flores, & Fillottrani, 2003), and also attending on one side the analyzed aspects discovered from a textual description of patterns, and on the other the objections on the use of formalisms — see previous sections.

Precision

- **Ambiguity:** different interpretations from a poor structural description that is even worsened by adding natural language narrative with the purpose to clear some information.

- **Incompleteness and vagueness:** poor documentation to guide certain pattern uses, by a confusing or undefined aspect, its complete absence or the addition of undesirable aspects.
- **Inconsistency:** contradictory description which if not immediately clear, become perfectly evident upon certain contexts.

Pattern Structure

- **Meaningless entity relations:** interrelations between design entities not only should involve the syntactic part but most importantly a semantic aspect. They describe a behavior of communication and cooperation between entities.
- **Deficient abstraction:** OO generalizations give one of the reuse mechanisms that help for a flexible development process, which together with composition allow the variation of aspects described by patterns.

Pattern Model

- **Benefit of patterns:** a model of patterns may give a similar result with its description, but should not worsen the application of patterns upon the intent to provide precision.
- **Object orientation:** notations without object orientation must be carefully analyzed since certain aspects described on patterns belong exclusively to such a paradigm. Analogies of OO characteristics on a language may inject an undesirable imprecision aspect.

These issues may deliver a more clear understanding on the need of applying formality on a *model of pattern instantiation*, as an approach to approximate the solution of appropriate pattern usage. However, this knowledge must be properly used when such a model is actually developed. In the next section, a collection of features is distilled from all the concerns detailed from the beginning of this section, which could be used to evaluate different existing models.

Characterizing Patterns Models

A formal basis for a *model of pattern instantiation* should present certain aspects to actually improve the process of pattern-based design. Some of these aspects, however, could be either successfully achieved or deteriorated, depend-

Table 2. Characteristics of formal languages

Characteristic	Description
01 – Mathematical Foundation	Mathematical theory. Expressiveness. Concise set of symbols.
02 – Style	Modeling mechanisms according to specification style.
03 – Visual Notation	To easy modeling a solution to a problem.
04 – Structural	Static description to abstract out environmental aspects.
05 – Behavioral	Scenario-based description to represent dynamic aspects.
06 – OO Support	Not loosing object orientation from OO patterns.
07 – Refinement	Generalization, classification, specialization, abstraction. Static Reuse.
08 – Constraints	To set conditions or requisites for different scenarios.
09 – Design-level Implementation	Pseudo-code analogies at design level. Not losing abstraction.
10 – Understandability	Easy to write and read specifications. Easy to communicate ideas.
11 – Extensibility	Adding new aspects of the environment. Anticipation to change.
12 – Usability	Concise formal apparatus to remember. Affects modeling, productivity.
13 – Multi-level	Description at different levels of abstraction.
14 – Repository Management	Easy to reuse and integrate specifications.

Table 3. Characteristics of formal models of patterns

Characteristic	Description
01 – Model Type	Kind of instantiation approach. Affects over a pattern-based design.
02 – Precision	Not deteriorating pattern semantics. Try to give improvements.
03 – Completeness	Solving ambiguities and incompleteness to understand patterns use.
04 – Design Heuristics	Addition of design heuristics, principles and criteria. An improvement.
05 – Flexibility	Capacity to precisely apply variations to patterns.
06 – Design-level Implementation	Pseudo-code annotations to help describing entities collaborations.
07 – Extensibility	Adding new pattern specifications or properties to existing specifications.
08 – Usability	Learning curve to use the model.
09 – Repository Management	Needed for pattern instantiation.

ing on the selected formal language. Hence, on Tables 2 and 3, we present a framework describing useful characteristics from both a pattern model and the used language.

For these characteristics to be evaluated, we assume in general a *not* supported, *poorly* supported, to *very well* supported value. Such linguistic values are mapped to numerical values for easy of understanding, when generating graphics for comparison, as can be seen on Table 4. From Table 2, however, characteristics 01 and 02 describe general information and a numerical value. Characteristic 03 assumes the values *yes* or *no* whether there is a visual notation or not,

Table 4. Linguistic and numerical values for characteristics

Linguistic Values	No	Very Poor	Poor	Regular	Good	Very Good
Numerical Values	0	1	2	3	4	5

and they are mapped to values 5 and 3 respectively. Similarly, characteristic 01 on Table 3 describes the type of approach for pattern instantiation, and the value is 3 for a top-down (T-D) approach and 5 for the two others.

We have carried out an evaluation from seven formal models of patterns, where seven different languages were applied on their construction. Tables 5 and 6 show the results of the analysis, and Figures 3 and 4 presents a graphical comparison based on the numerical-valued characteristics. As can be seen, RAISE is one of such languages under evaluation since it was the language we have used to build our model of pattern instantiation. Thus, we have compared our model and the used language in order to understand benefits and drawbacks by observing different other viewpoints. For a complete explanation behind the analysis, we refer the reader to Flores and Fillottrani (2003).

From Table 5 and Figure 2 we can see that the languages satisfying the characteristics with an acceptable degree are LePUS, RAISE, VDM++ and UML. If a visual notation is a prerequisite, then the choice is centered around LePUS and UML. However, whether the formal foundation must be rigorous, we must take into account that UML presents serious lack on semantics. Indeed RAISE is not a language with object-orientation characteristics, though its formal apparatus allows both to easily develop an OO design meta-model and to accurately represent such object-orientation aspects, as we have experienced.

Figure 2. Graphical comparison of formal languages

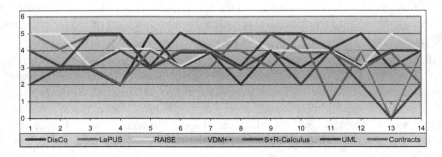

Table 5. Results from the analysis of formal languages

N°	DisCo	LePUS	RAISE	VDM++	ς+ρ-Calculus	UML	Contracts
01	[3] T-D	[3] T-D	[5] B-U	[3] T-D	[3] T-D	[5] B-U	[3] T-D
02	3	5	5	4	4	4	3
03	3	4	5	4	4	4	3
04	2	3	5	2	2	2	2
05	2	4	5	2	2	5	2
06	2	2	4	4	2	4	2
07	4	3	4	4	4	4	4
08	4	5	4	4	3	5	4
09	3	4	4	4	2	4	4

Table 6. Results from the analysis of formal models of patterns

N°	DisCo	LePUS	RAISE	VDM++	ς+ρ-Calculus	UML	Contracts
01	[3] Strong Math. basis. For reactive systems. (TLA)	[5] Sound Math. basis. Formulae on subset of HOML	[5] Rigorous, based on VDM-SL and others (ASL, ML, OBJ, Larch, etc)	[5] Rigorous, OO version based on VDM-SL. Discrete Math., Set theory.	[4] OO analogy of λ-Calculus. Sound and complete	[2] Not very rigorous. Useful Set theory	[3] Specific. based on invariants
02	[3] Imperative	[4] Based on predicates	[5] Property and model based	[4] Model-based	[3] Imperative	[3] Imperative	[3] Imperative
03	No	Yes	No	No	No	Yes	No
04	2	5	4	5	4	5	2
05	5	3	4	5	3	3	5
06	3	4	3	5	4	5	3
07	4	4	4	4	4	4	3
08	2	4	5	3	3	3	5
09	4	3	4	5	4	5	5
10	3	5	4	5	2	5	4
11	4	1	4	4	4	4	4
12	3	4	3	4	2	5	3
13	4	0	5	0	0	5	4
14	4	4	4	4	2	4	2

Figure 3. Graphical comparison of formal models of patterns

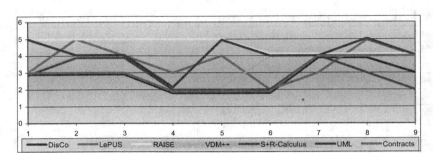

From Table 6 and Figure 3, it can be seen that our formal basis for pattern application satisfies the characteristics with a high degree. Its level of completeness on solving problems of imprecision is much higher than the other models. This has been achieved at the design level by remarking principles and heuristics, and also at the pattern level by precisely describing their deeply analyzed properties.

In the next section, we present our formalization of a pattern instantiation model where the characteristics of the framework will be remarked. In this way, the reader may understand the requirements for an approach of pattern instantiation and its likely benefits when applied to a design process.

A Formal Basis of OOD and Patterns

We have developed our approach based on a previously developed model (Cechich, & Moore, 1999a, 1999b), which uses RSL — the *RAISE Specification Language* (RAISE Group, 1992) — to formally specify properties of patterns, in particular the responsibilities and collaborations of the pattern participants. However, we significantly extended the scope of the model used therein. Firstly, we have generalized the model so that it can describe an arbitrary object-oriented design and not just the patterns as the previous model does. Hence, our model can be characterized as a bottom-up approach, while the previous model is considered a top-down approach for pattern instantiation. Secondly, we include in our model specifications of the behavioral properties of the design, specifically the actions that are to be performed by methods, which were not specified in the previous model. And thirdly, we formally specify how

Table 7. RSL schemas forming the whole formal basis

Scheme	Description
Types	general definitions to the model.
Methods	operations or methods that form a class' interface.
Design_Class	the structure and behavior of classes in a OO design.
Design_Relations	set of valid relations that link classes on a design.
Design_Structure	consistent link between classes and their inter-relations.
Renaming	correspondence between names from design elements to those at a pattern level — this helps to set the pattern roles that are played by design entities.
Design_Pattern	set of generic functions that help to formally describe any design pattern.

to match the design against a pattern. This allows us to formally specify the patterns in such a way that their consistency and completeness can be checked. We are also able to formally verify that a given subset of a design corresponds to a given pattern.

There is also an important difference between the two models in the way the dynamic aspects of the patterns are specified. In the previous model the structural aspects are specified statically while the collaborations are specified in terms of sequences of interactions. Now, both the structural properties and the collaborations are represented statically, the collaborations being modeled partly by the relations between the classes and partly by the requests the operations make to other classes. The latter is incorporated by specifically modeling the bodies of the methods.

OOD Metamodel

Our work of formalization has been organized in the form of seven main RSL schemas, which describe a metamodel of a generic object-oriented design with the addition of a mechanism to link pattern descriptions to elements of a design. Those schemas are briefly described in Table 7, and details of the main aspects of the whole specification are given afterwards.

Design Structure

A design is composed of a collection of classes and a collection of relations between those classes. This is formalized as follows:

$$Design\_Structure = C.Classes \times R.Wf\_Relations$$

We assure a consistence on the link between classes and also include heuristics on a design. To do this, the *Design_Structure* type is constrained to establish a well-formed type by the function *is_wf_design_structure*, which is composed of different sub-functions, each addressing a particular design aspect.

Wf_Design_Structure = {| *ds* : *Design_Structure* • *is_wf_design_structure(ds)* |}

is_wf_design_structure : *Design_Structure* → *Bool*
is_wf_design_structure(ds) ≡
is_correct_design_class(ds) ∧ *is_defined_class(ds)* ∧ *is_correct_name_relation(ds)* ∧
is_correct_name_rel_in_subclass(ds) ∧ *correct_state_hierarchy(ds)* ∧ *not_allowed(ds)* ∧
correct_multiple_inheritance(ds) ∧ *is_correct_invocation(ds)* ∧ *is_rqst_instantiation(ds)* ∧
is_implemented_signature(ds) ∧ *is_impl_error_interf_inherited(ds)* ∧ *is_correct_res_f_param(ds)*

A design class is composed of a set of *methods* that form its interface, a set of properties that represent its *state*, and a *type* which can be "*concrete*" or "*abstract*." Every design class has a *name* that is unique on the entire design. Thus we use the RSL map type to describe the correspondence between a class name and its definition.

Wf_Design_Class =
   G.Class_Name $\overrightarrow{m}$ *Design_Class*,

Design_Class ::
   class_state : *G.State*
   class_methods : *M.Class_Method*
   class_type : *G.Class_Type*

Methods

Every method has a unique *name* into the interface of a class which together with a *list of parameters* and a *result* forms the method's signature. A method may be only *defined* by its signature or may express a concrete functionality, that is, being *implemented*. A special case is a method which describes a situation of *error*.

Class_Method = {| *m* : *Map_Methods* •
       is_wf_class_method(m) |}

Map_Methods = *G.Method_Name* $\overrightarrow{m}$ *Wf_Method*

Method ::
   f_params : *G.Wf_Formal_Parameters*
   meth_res : *Result*
   body : *Method_Body*

An *implemented* method helps describing collaborations between classes. Changes on the state of a class (by its variables) and some assignments for returning *results* are described by the mapping *variable_change*. They are mainly produced by specific *request*'s, such as *invocation* of methods (belonging to a given class) or *instantiation* to create objects. A *request-list* describes the order of their occurrence into the body of an implemented method.

Method_Body ==   *defined* | *error* |
                 implemented(variable_change : Variable Change,
                      request_list : Request*)

Variable_Change = {| *m : G.Wf Vble Name-set* $\overset{m}{\rightarrow}$ *Request_or_Var* •
               is_wf_vchange(m) |}

Request = *Invocation* | *Instantiation* | _

Design_Relation

A relation is described by the classes it connects, which are identified by means of their *class names*. The relation has a specific *type* that may be *inheritance*, *association*, *aggregation*, or *instantiation*. All relations are represented in the model as binary relations, by identifying source and sink classes. We have applied constraints to the definition of a relation as well as to the set of possible relations that can be modeled in a design.

$$Wf\_Relations = \{|\ rs : Wf\_Relation\text{-}set \bullet wf\_relations(rs)\ |\}$$

Design_Relation ::
   relation_type : Relation_Type
   source_class : G.Class_Name
   sink_class : G.Class_Name,

Relation_Type ==
   inheritance | *association(as_ref: Ref)* |
   instantiation | *aggregation(ag_ref : Ref),*
   Ref :: relation_name : G.Wf_Vble_Name ..,.

Renaming

The link from design elements (classes, variables, methods and parameters) with corresponding elements of a pattern is defined by means of a mapping of names. A design class may play more than one pattern role, and so can do the rest of the design elements. A method or a variable (a relation name or a state variable) may play pattern roles depending on a given class role —similarly for parameters with respect to methods. Then a design matches a particular pattern if all the elements in a design playing a pattern role satisfy its properties.

$$Renaming = G.Class\_Name \rightleftarrows ClassRenaming\text{-}set,$$

$$ClassRenaming :: classname : G.Class\_Name$$
$$methodRenaming : Method\_and\_Parameter\_Renaming$$
$$varRenaming : VariableRenaming,$$

Then a design together with a renaming map which defines its correspondences to a given pattern is described by the simple cartesian product type *Design_Renaming*. This type is properly constrained in order to complement the model with some consistency conditions.

$$Design\_Renaming = DS.Wf\_Design\_Structure \times Wf\_Renaming$$

This has been so far a brief summary of the formalization concerning a generic design and a mechanism for pattern applications. However, we still require a precise description of patterns in order to actually achieve a solution on patterns understanding. Thus, next section is focused on such a formal description for design patterns.

Formalization of Patterns

Our model of patterns was separated into three working units according to the *purpose* classification given by the GoF catalog. Thus the Formal Metamodel for OO design was used to formalize *creational*, *structural*, and *behavioral* design patterns from the GoF catalog. The reader may see the complete formalization of patterns in (Aranda, & Moore, 2000; Flores, & Moore, 2000; Reynoso, & Moore, 2000). In this section, we illustrate such a formalization through the definition of the Decorator Pattern.

The Decorator Design Pattern

Sometimes requirements of a system include the addition of responsibilities to individual objects instead of to an entire class. Perhaps the primary way of achieving this is by inheritance: inheriting a responsibility from another class can decorate every subclass instance. However, this is inflexible since the responsibility is allocated statically, which means that a client is not able to control how and when to decorate the component.

The Decorator pattern embodies another approach, where the component is enclosed inside another object taking care to add the responsibility. The enclosing object, called *decorator*, conforms to the interface of the component it decorates so that its presence is transparent to the component's clients. In addition, it forwards requests to the component and may perform additional actions (related with the new responsibility) before or after forwarding. Decorators may be recursively nested, which effectively allows an unlimited number of added responsibilities. Figure 4 shows the structure of Decorator pattern.

Component, ConcreteComponent, Decorator, ConcreteDecorator, Client : G.Class_Name,
Operation, AddedBehaviour: G.Method_Name,
component, addedState : G.Variable_Name

From Figure 4, the names of the classes in the pattern together with the names of their methods and state variables, are defined as RSL constants as follows.

The formalization of the Decorator pattern is represented by the function *is_decorator_pattern*, which collects all of the properties that were recognized and properly analyzed. This helps to distinguish whether or not a design matches this pattern.

is_decorator_pattern: Wf_Design_Renaming → Bool
is_decorator_pattern(dr) ≡
    one_component_in_hierarchy(dr) ∧ one_decorator_in_hierarchy(dr) ∧
    is_abstract_decorator(dr) ∧ has_parent_component(dr) ∧ decorator_client(dr) ∧
    decorator_relation(dr) ∧ store_unique_component(dr) ∧
    exist_concrete_component(dr) ∧ is_concrete_component(dr) ∧
    exist_concrete_decorator(dr) ∧ is_concrete_decorator(dr) ∧
    Ct_has_operation_defined(dr) ∧ CCt_has_impl_operation(dr) ∧ Dec_has_impl_operation(dr) ∧
    CDec_has_impl_operation(dr) ∧ CDec_has_extended_interface(dr)

Figure 4. Structure of decorator design pattern

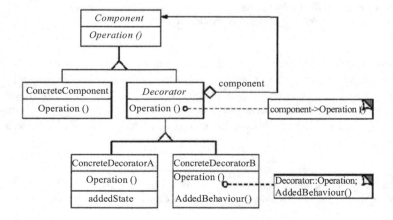

For example the function *one_component_in_hierarchy* constraints that the Component role is played once in the pattern and stands for the root of a hierarchy in which the leaves play either the ConcreteComponent or the ConcreteDecorator role. Every class in this hierarchy can play only one role in the pattern (because they have different properties) and no class in the hierarchy can play the Client role. In a particular design, we may have a class playing the ConcreteComponent role that has subclasses (specializations) which also may play the same role. That is, the design heuristic which encourages to "factor out" common behavior and properties from related classes into a superclass — the process of generalization or classification (Martin, & Odell, 1995; Rumbaugh et al, 1991). Hence, we allow intermediate additional classes between the root and the leaves, which may play the same roles as the leaves, that is ConcreteComponent or ConcreteDecorator. These properties are specified using the generic function *hierarchy* from the *Design_Pattern* scheme:

one_component_in_hierarchy(dr) ≡
    hierarchy(Component, {ConcreteComponent, ConcreteDecorator}, {Client}, dr),

The Decorator class also forms the root of a hierarchy, where the leaves and possible intermediate classes may only play the ConcreteDecorator role. However, since Decorator is an abstract superclass which factors out the common interface of its subclasses, it should be a direct subclass of Component (i.e., without intermediate classes). We explicitly specify that Decorator class is abstract whereas this is not needed for Component. Since Component contains an abstract method (Operation) in its interface, then the class is abstract as well — this property is built into our general model of object-oriented design; see (Flores, & Moore, 2000, 2001).

has_parent_component(dr) ≡ *has_parent_direct(Decorator, Component, dr)*
is_abstract_decorator(dr) ≡ *is_abstract_class(Decorator, dr)*

When a class role must be represented at the design level, we state this explicitly. This is the case for the ConcreteComponent and ConcreteDecorator roles where we use the function *exists_role*. As these classes represent actual components and decorators in the system, they must be concrete. The function *is_concrete* checks if a class is a concrete subclass of a given class — in this case Component and Decorator respectively.

exist_concrete_component(dr) ≡ *exists_role(ConcreteComponent, dr),*
is_concrete_component(dr) ≡ *is_concrete(Component, ConcreteComponent, dr),*

The Decorator pattern provides a structure which allows a Client to refer to objects without knowing whether they are decorated or not — all objects are accessed uniformly through Operation methods in the Component interface. Clients should therefore be linked to the Component class by either an aggregation or an association relation.

decorator_client(dr) ≡
    has_assoc_aggr_reltype(Client, Component, AssAggr, G.one, dr) ∧
    use interface(Client. Component. Operation. dr)

For the previous interaction, one abstract method (*defined*) is needed playing the Operation role in the Component class. Operation methods must be implemented in ConcreteComponent, Decorator and ConcreteDecorator classes. Decorator class has a specific implementation that simply forwards the method call to its component state variable — specified by the function *deleg_with_var*.

Ct_has_operation_defined(dr) ≡
  has_def_method(Component, Operation, dr) ∧ *has_all_def_method(Component, Operation, dr)*,
Dec_has_impl_operation(dr) ≡
  deleg_with_var(Decorator, Operation, component, Component, Operation, dr),
  CCt_has_impl_operation(dr) ≡ *has_all_impl_method(ConcreteComponent, Operation, dr)*,

The unique relation between the Decorator and Component classes is an aggregation (Martin, & Odell, 1995). It has cardinality *one-one* since its purpose is to add one and not many responsibilities at a time (Gamma et al, 1995). The name of this relation, component, is a unique state variable which refers to the object that is being decorated.

decorator_relation(dr) ≡
  has_unique_assoc_aggr_relation(Decorator, Component ,dr) ∧
  has_assoc_aggr_var_ren(Decorator, Component, Aggregation, component, one, dr),
store_unique_component(dr) ≡ *store_unique_vble(Decorator, component, dr)*

Finally, we refer to the Operation methods in ConcreteDecorator classes. These classes provide the "decoration" to ConcreteComponent classes, which can be done either by adding new state variables or by adding new methods. In the first case, an Operation in ConcreteDecorator might override a corresponding method in a superclass, making an invocation to that method and additionally invoking other methods on the addedState variables. In the second case, an Operation in the ConcreteDecorator class might invoke a corresponding method in a superclass and additionally invoke local AddedBehavior methods — as is shown on Figure 5. This requires at least one *implemented* (concrete) AddedBehavior method, and to describe both the invocation to the superclass (super) and the local invocation (self) to AddedBehavior methods.

$CDec\_has\_extended\_interface(dr) \equiv$
  $(CDec\_has\_impl\_added\_behaviour(dr) \lor CDec\_stores\_added\_state(dr)) \land$
  $(CDec\_has\_impl\_added\_behaviour(dr) \Rightarrow CDec\_has\_super\_self\_operation(dr)) \land$
  $(CDec\_stores\_added\_state(dr) \Rightarrow CDec\_has\_super\_operation(dr)),$

In the same way that Decorator pattern has been described formally in this section, the rest of the patterns in the GoF catalogue has been properly specified as well. We do not explain other specifications along this chapter so to hold the reader mainly focused on the importance concerning formality instead all the details. Thus, its application to solve impreciseness will be clearly understood, and it will help to evaluate its usage as a back-end for an automatic tool support.

In the next section, we also provide some specific issues that a designer may find useful to become skilled at the use of patterns, and help to clean any doubt from the use of formalisms.

Rigorous Does Not Mean Inflexible

Along this section we have presented a more accurate description of a general object-oriented design and patterns, based on the use of the RSL formal language. However, one of the concerns presented in the second section expresses that a formal description of design patterns could make too inflexible the usage of patterns. As patterns were defined to be general enough for a wide application on different contexts, the doubt is whether to apply formality could narrow this scope. Nevertheless, we can positively claim that far from reducing the range of use, we have achieved a model which precisely allows and describes valid variations of pattern applications. Thus, we following present remarks of different variants on the use of patterns — generically depicted in Figure 5 — which are possible to be performed by means of our formal basis.

The list may help designers to learn possibilities which could be poorly described in the consistent format description. Each item on the following list is presented without a specific order, and references some specific sections from the consistent format description given in the GoF catalog (Gamma et al, 1995).

Figure 5. Different generic applications of patterns on a design

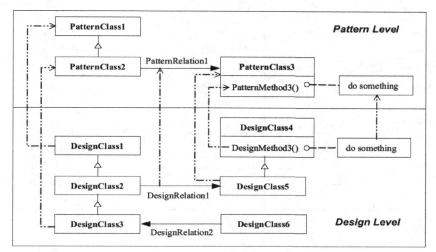

Hierarchy

A pattern structure usually shows an inheritance relationship between two classes, however it does not mean there are only two levels in the hierarchy. In fact, it usually means an inheritance hierarchy. Figure 5 depicts this issue in a generic way.

Figure 6. Composite — Pattern and design levels

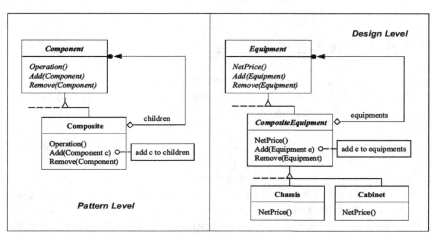

Figure 7. Prototype — Pattern and design levels

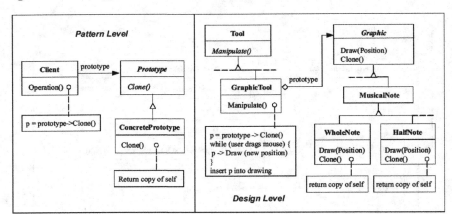

Example:

- **Composite:** In Figure 6 we can see the *Sample* section of this pattern. In such structure is depicted an instantiation where there is an intermediate class between the Component class and the Composite leaf-classes. Further explanations in Flores and Moore (2000).

- **Prototype:** The ConcretePrototype classes showed in the *Motivation* section of this pattern (Figure 7), are not connected directly to the Graphic class, but through the MusicalNote class.

Association vs. Aggregation

In some cases, an association relationship between two participant classes, can be replaced by an aggregation relationship in a particular design, without changing the intent of the pattern.

Example:

- **Prototype:** Following the example of Figure 7, the Client asks Prototype to clone itself. This request is modeled by one association relationship between Client and Prototype classes. Notice that GraphicTool is connected to

Graphic using an aggregation relationship, which is stronger than association. This is not contradictory with respect to the pattern intent since Client can manage with its responsibility, and collaborations can be carried out as well.

- **Note:** In the application of the formal general basis to the specification of each pattern we have analyzed when it is possible to change a relation type (full details can be seen in Aranda, & Moore, 2000; Flores, & Moore, 2000; Reynoso, & Moore, 2000).

Additional Design Methods

It is always possible to include methods in the design that have not counterparts in the pattern. They are important to the domain in which the pattern is being applied but they do not change the behavior of the pattern participants.

Example:

- **Prototype:** in the *Motivation* of this pattern (Figure 7), the Draw method does not play any method role in the pattern, but it represents an added method in design which is related to the specific-domain of the graphical editor.

Minimal Set of Methods

Although the set of methods represented in a pattern structure seems to be the minimal set that a design should include, it is possible to omit few of them.

Example:

- **Singleton:** SingletonOperation and GetSingletonData are specific methods which may or may not have a representative in design, without loosing the features of a Singleton class. Further details in Aranda and Moore (2000).

- **Observer and composite:** those methods related to the management of an object collection (Attach, Dettach in Observer; Add, Remove, GetChild in Composite), are not completely necessary when there is another class in charge of building their object structure.

Additional Design Parameters

If no parameters are included in a method definition of any class in a pattern structure, it does not mean they are not allowed in a correct design. The fact they are not shown only means they are not significant for the family of designs the pattern represents.

Example:

- **Builder:** The *Sample* section of this pattern presents an implementation of the *Maze* problem. Although the method BuildPart is showed without parameters in the pattern, its counterparts in design: BuildRoom and BuildWall methods, have some parameters. For a precise description, see Aranda and Moore (2000).

Additional Design Hierarchy

Although a particular concrete participant could be shown in a pattern structure as a "stand-alone" class (a class not included in a hierarchy), in a design it can be part of a hierarchy. In other words, hierarchies in the structure of a pattern are shown when the aspect that varies in the pattern can only be designed using inheritance; however it does not mean that other participant can be included in specific-domain hierarchies.

Example:

- **Prototype:** Can be seen in Figure 7 of this pattern, that GraphicalTool representing the Client is in fact a leaf in the hierarchy with root Tool.

Note: our formal model includes this possibility, as can be seen in Aranda and Moore (2000), Flores and Moore (2000), and Reynoso and Moore (2000).

Implicit Relations

In some patterns, the name of some methods and classes reveals relations between classes involving semantic aspects.

Example:

- **Visitor:** The way each method of the Visitor class is named (VisitConcreteElementA, VisitConcreteElementB) indicates that each one is related to a particular ConcreteElement (Reynoso, & Moore, 2000).
- **Abstract factory:** It is shown a more complex situation that establishes a relation between ConcreteFactory and Product using two different indexes

(numbers and letters). For instance, the CreateProductA method of ConcreteFactory1 class instantiates the ProductA1 (Aranda and Moore, 2000).

• **Note:** Our model does not implement this feature by restricting the names of the methods. Instead, we constrain the way classes playing these roles are related.

Inherited Methods

A method is shown as part of a given participant class in the pattern structure. Though that method in design can be either defined in the owned interface of the design class playing that participant role, or inherited from a superclass. This feature is shown in a general way in Figure 5.

Example:

• **Composite:** in Figure 6, the methods Add and Remove in the leaves classes (e.g., Chassis) playing the Composite role are inherited from the design CompositeEquipment class where they are implemented (Flores, & Moore, 2000).

Factorized Relations

An association, aggregation or instantiation relation between two classes in the pattern structure, may be modeled in design by means of a factorization. Let us define PA and PB pattern participants, and DA and DB their counterparts in design. If there is a relation from PA to PB in a pattern, in design the relation can be from DA to DB as well as from a superclass of DA to DB. See a generic draw in Figure 5.

Example:

• **Composite:** in Figure 6, the relation with variable name children in the pattern, is factored out in design to the CompositeEquipment class.

Brief Discussion

All of the third section has been intended to present a solution to the problem of imprecision about the consistent format used to describe patterns. It has uncovered not only an accurate description but also the variations of patterns uses. So far it has gone beyond this objective by also providing an instrument to identify good design practices by means of design principles inserted into the formal basis core. Nevertheless, our intent is not to replace the original format of patterns descriptions, but to provide a useful complementing mechanism.

We are still concerned with certain dislike of using formal languages to model and communicate ideas — mostly on nonacademic or controlled working environments. Modeling is not a trivial task and the use of a visual notation may certainly provide a practical way to capture aspects of a situation. Hence, we have been also focused on the achievement of an agile design process without losing the precision of our formal basis as we will see in the next section.

The Supporting Tool

We have developed a tool for graphical modeling, where the formal model serves as an instrument to verify whether patterns are properly applied and the design satisfies the required modeling principles. The importance of implementing a supporting tool comes from the fact that successfully applying formal notations strongly depends on its acceptance by a wide community of developers. This tool allows developers to introduce verification into the development process without requiring high investments in learning formalisms or dramatically changing the process itself.

Basically the tool is divided into two layers. The Modeling layer, whose result is a specification of an OO design model provided by a graphical component; and the Verification layer, which carries out the process of checking the correctness of the design model. It also matches part of a design to a specific pattern by satisfying the pattern properties (Aranda, Flores, Buccella, & Reynoso, 2002; Reynoso, Aranda, Buccella, & Flores, 2002). The following sections describe the main components of the two tool's levels as well as some design decisions and details of the documentation.

The Modeling Layer

Many tools providing a graphical component for modeling object-oriented designs have already been developed with a proved success. Thus, we have decided to choose one of them and thus concentrate our major effort on the field where less work has been done so far. We have selected a non-commercial tool called Fujaba (Fujaba, 1998; Klein, Nickel, Niere, & Zündorf, 2000; Nickel, Niere, Wadsack, & Zündorf, 2000), which was developed in the Java language. After modeling a particular object-oriented design solution, the tool may produce a Java specification of such a design.

The functionality of Fujaba is close to our expectations. However, according to our formal basis, a new behavior needs to be developed in order to be able to represent an entire object-oriented model in which a pattern has been applied. The extended functionality is related, for example, to the annotations attached to methods of classes, which help to describe collaborations between classes. Other important behavior concerns the possibility of selecting a particular pattern from a pattern repository and setting which pattern roles are played by different entities at the design level.

Figure 8 shows the graphical user interface (GUI) of Fujaba, with the added functionality: a specific menu item for selecting a pattern to be applied, and a tool bar consisting of three parts. The first part, which was also added to the *Class* menu item, concerns the setting of roles from the selected pattern to a class (yellow*), a relation (green*), an attribute (light blue*), and a method (pink*). The second part, which was also included into the *Pattern* menu item, involves the selection of a design pattern. The third part, which was also added to the *Tools* menu item, concerns the possibility of exporting an *extended Java specification* (which is explained in the next paragraph) from the visual diagram, and also checking correctness of a design and the applied pattern.

Some other necessary changes, mainly concern the notation of the object-oriented model given by a Java specification. Thus, our particular *extended Java specification* includes, for example, a simplification in the representation of an aggregation relation, as can be seen in Figure 9. This helps reducing the complexity of the grammar for the Parser involved in the verification step — explained in the next section. Pattern roles and other design or pattern elements are expressed adding "comments" in the Java specification.

We must say that we did not change but extended the existing functionality of Fujaba. Thus, its back-end continues unaffected and only the GUI was updated to incorporate the front-end of the new behavior. For example, the regular Java code can still be generated for other purposes but the verification of appropriateness on a pattern usage.

Figure 8. Fujaba's GUI with menu and tool bar extensions for pattern verification

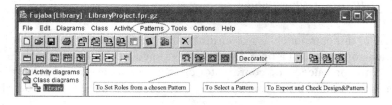

Figure 9. Aggregation relation on a regular exported Java code and an extended Java specification

```
/**
 * UMLClass: 'DesignClassA'.          [Regular Java Code]
 */
abstract public class DesignClassA
{
/**
    * <pre>
    *                    /\  0..1     aggrRel_ab    0..n
    * DesignClassA <  >--------------------------
DesignClassB
    *                    \/ designClassA    designClassB
    * </pre>
    */
   private DesignClassB  designClassB;
```

```
/**
 * UMLClass: 'DesignClassA'.          [Extended Java Specification]
 */
abstract public class DesignClassA
{
/*@
      @Aggregation  aggrRel_ab  DesignClassA @One
DesignClassB @Many
 @*/

   private DesignClassB  designClassB;
```

Next we explain the layer concerning the verification process, its internal components, and a diagrammatic view of the whole process of verification.

The Verification Layer

The Verification Layer is composed of four main components as can be seen in Figure 10, where a component diagram showing the components of and their interdependencies, is presented. Each component, the interfaces and dependency relationships are described below. Some of them are described in terms of their interfaces and subcomponents, and others are informally mentioned for brevity reasons.

The Coordinator Component

The intent of this component is to coordinate the verification process accordingly using each component at a time. Once the Java specification from the graphical component is produced, the coordinator calls the Java parser and instantiation component to obtain an object structure (representing an instantiation of the

Figure 10. Component diagram of the verification layer

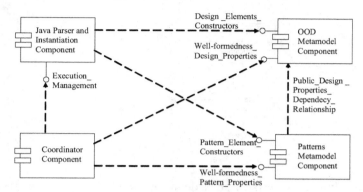

OOD and pattern metamodel component) as a result. Then the coordinator invokes different functions of the object structure in order to verify design constraints. If the result is successful, the coordinator will invoke the pattern metamodel component to check the pattern constraints with the aim to assure the correct use of a specific pattern.

The Java Parser and Instantiation Component

This component should parse the Java code generated by the graphical component in order to create an object structure which represents a valid instantiation of the OOD metamodel and pattern metamodel. The way the component uses services of the last two mentioned components are described later in this section. In addition, error codes are returned to the coordinator component, generated during the parse process or the creation of an instance of any metamodel.

The OOD Metamodel Component

This component corresponds to the Java translation of the OOD formal model presented in the third section. It will be referred in this chapter using its acronym OOD-M. The schemes division presented in that section allowed making a useful partitioning of working units during the translation process. Thus, we have decomposed the OOD-M component into four subcomponents where meta_methods involves functionality of the scheme method, a meta_class involves functionality of the design_class scheme, and so on. Figure 11 shows a detailed diagram of this component.

Figure 11: Component diagram of OOD-M Component

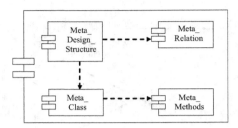

Two different kinds of interfaces and a dependency relationship were identified in the OOD-M Component, as is shown in Figure 10. Following we present a short description of them:

- *Design_Elements_Constructor Interface*

  Used by: Java Parser Component,

  Intent: Provides an interface for constructing elements of the OOD metamodel in order to generate a possible metamodel instantiation. The parser and instantiation component could access directly to the class constructor of the metamodel. If it does so, it might also access the behavior of the created object, which should not be allowed. That is why the instantiation component should only see a narrow interface, which provides a service of creating an object structure to represent an instantiation of the metamodel.

  Data returned: According to the method being invoked, an instance of an element or composed element of the metamodel is returned.

- *Well-formedness_Design_Properties Interface*

  Used by: Coordinator component

  Intent: Provides an interface for verifying correctness of design properties.

  Data returned: Whenever a constraint is violated, an appropriate error code is generated. Other facilities of error management are provided as well.

- *Public design properties dependency relationship*

  Used by: Pattern metamodel component.

  The pattern metamodel component is dependent on the OOD-M component, since it calls specific methods on the component. Although the communication is two-way (since the OOD-M component returns data), the OOD-M component is not aware of who is calling it and it does not depend on the pattern metamodel component.

Intent: Provides a set of design properties which must be of public access for defining pattern properties.

Data returned: A boolean condition of the invoked property and error codes.

The Pattern Metamodel Component

This component represents the Java translation of the renaming scheme and design_pattern scheme presented in the third section and the formal specification of GoF patterns have been described (Aranda, & Moore, 2000; Flores et al, 2000; Reynoso, & Moore, 2000). Thus, it is conformed by three subcomponents: renaming, general pattern properties and properties of a specific pattern. It calls specific methods of the OOD-M component in order to accomplish verification activities of pattern properties. This is shown through a dependency relationship in Figure 12. This component has two interfaces: patterns element constructor interface and well-formedness pattern properties; their intent and data results are analogous to those described in the OOD-M component.

The next section shows how the components of tool participate in a modeling and verification process when a designer applies a pattern on a particular design.

The Process of Verification

Figure 13 shows, in a diagrammatic way, the whole process for correctness verification when modeling a design by means of the tool support. Briefly, the process involves a designer drawing the design elements (classes, methods, and so on), and also selecting a specific pattern from which the setting of roles could be carried out. After that, the designer may choose to export an *extended Java specification* from where the verification tasks could be initiated.

Figure 12. Component diagram of pattern metamodel component

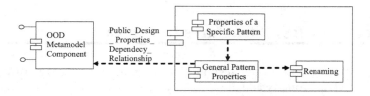

Figure 13. Internal process of design and pattern verification

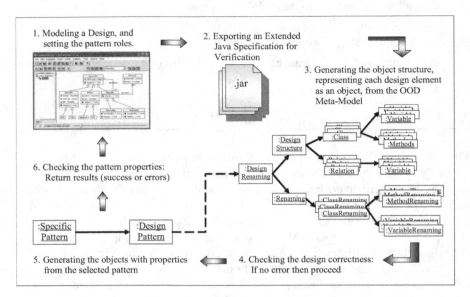

The designer may choose to check only the design for correctness on design principles and heuristics that should be exhibited by the design. The other option also includes checking whether the pattern has been correctly applied. For both options, the first step is to generate an object structure from the *extended Java specification* — task of the parser and instantiation component. Then the verification of design is carried out by invoking the ad-hoc services. If no error occurs this step is considered successful; otherwise, a set of errors is returned to be showed in the Fujaba's GUI. If the selected option includes the verification of a pattern application, the next step (in case the design checking has been successful) is to instantiate the objects representing the selected pattern. Then the checking is initiated by invoking the ad-hoc services on the previously generated objects. The results are shown in the Fujaba's GUI. Thus, the designer may correct what is needed (in case of error).

The following is a brief summary of the procedure of translation of different RSL aspects to the Java language (Flanagan, 1997; Grand, 1997).

Translation of RSL Structures into Java

As we have pointed out in the second section, RSL is a language of a wide spectrum which is property and model oriented. Thus, specifications generated from this language may be quite abstract with respect to what can be developed on a programming language. In fact, on the RAISE method (RAISE Group, 1995) there is a particular set of conditions and tools to assure an appropriate transition from abstract to imperative specifications. However, we have done this process manually, but at the same time with a very rigorous analysis of structures and data types on the involving languages to maintain the semantic exhibited by the RSL specification (Hoang, & George, 2000). Hence, following we list some aspects to be considered on a translation from RSL to any programming language.

- RSL structures that help to describe aspects from an abstract viewpoint, such as *axioms*, *pre-* and *post-conditions*, *quantifiers*, and so forth.

- RSL structures with a direct translation. This involves many algorithmic pieces of an RSL specification.

- Some particular structures on a programming language that are necessary to be used, but for which there is no immediate correlation on RSL structures. They include some data structures like *arrays* and *lists*, and special mechanisms like *exceptions*.

- RSL specifications may contain data types whose range of values could be arbitrarily large or infinite — for example, *int*. Similarly for the *real* data type that has a property of arbitrarily precise values. Whether precision and range of values is not a critical aspect, they could be represented by the data types *float* or *double*.

The following are the details of the performed procedure of translation. We expose the reasons of different decisions made under the purpose of providing a rigorous equivalence between the two languages.

Some Translation Details

In our model, modules in RSL correspond to Java classes; although the formal specification consists of a list of modules defined in any order, while Java imposes a particular order for creating and instantiating classes. To build a component, we use the package *specification-classes*. It creates a reference space for all component's classes and represents a code distribution unit. Following we describe some issues distinguished during the translation process:

- **Type equivalence:** In RSL, two types are structurally equivalent if and only if they are the same basic type, or they are produced by the application of the same constructor to structurally equivalent types. Rather, in Java two different type definitions produce two different and not compatible types, even though their structures might be the same.

- **Equality:** both RSL and Java languages supply similar equality operators. They only differ in implementation preserving their meanings.

- **Schema declaration:** There is no correspondence between an RSL scheme and structures in Java. However, the class definition is the closest option when comparing functionality and the possibility of parameterization.

- **Object declaration:** Although RSL is not an object-oriented language, its expressiveness allows us to represent objects, though it does not have the same visibility of a definition (*public/private*).

Some examples of translation are given as follows:

- **Type declaration:** The name of an RSL type corresponds to the name of a Java class, and the state variables on the formal specification represent the variables in the state of Java classes

- **Functions:** Parameters on RSL represent a cartesian product of types. In the formal model, some parameters represent an important aspect, and as such in Java they may represent the object which will receive the corresponding function (in the form of a method) as a message. That is, such parameter is represented as a class containing such function as a method into its interface.

RSL:
```
type
  Actual_Signature ::
    meth_name : G.Method_Name
    a_params : G.Actual_Parameters
```

Java:
```
public class ActualSignature
{
  private String meth_name;
  private Vector a_params;  }
```

- **Structured expressions:** the *let* expression allows introducing local names into an RSL proposition. The translation is in the form of local variables into a method. The RSL *if* expression involves the same definition as in the Java language.

- **Quantified expressions:** RSL quantified expressions are emulated by means of Java conditional sentences *while* and *if*.

RSL:	Java:
value	*public class Parameter*
is_wf_formal_parameters :	*{*
Parameter → Bool	*public boolean is_wf_formal_parameters(); }*

- **Recursion:** both RSL and Java, allow recursive functions.

Documentation of Components

We have used a standardized documentation to components of the tool, since they must support interoperability with other components and also to ease the composition. Thus we have used the specification provided by OMG (2004) (Jacobson, Christeron, & Overgaard; SUN), which exposes a detailed profile to model technologic artifacts according to the development stage. Such profiles are briefly summarized as follows:

- **Component collaboration architecture (CCA):** details how UML diagrams (UML Consortium) (classes, collaboration and activity) could be used to model structure and behavior of components.
- **Entity profile:** describes a set of UML extensions that may help modeling domain concepts as objects, which can also be combined.
- **Business process profile:** specializes the CCA and describes a set of UML extensions to conform business rules for a domain context.
- **Relation profile:** describes extensions in the UML core in order to allow a rigorous specification of relations.

In the following sections, we exemplify the whole documentation of the components comprising the tool support, by means of the OOD-M component.

Design Structure Component

We base the documentation of this component on the *entity profile*, and we use the UML diagrams of classes and collaboration to represent its elements.

This component provides functionality to instantiate objects for composing the representation of a design that is graphically modeled by a user. It also allows to verify the object structure and delete some of the comprising objects. As we have shown at the beginning of this section, the component provides such functionality by means of particular interface access points. Thus, we have

Figure 14. Class diagram of classes from the pattern metamodel component

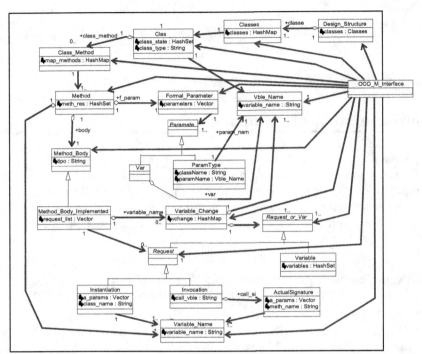

created a Java *interface,* called *OOD_M_Interface*, which allows encapsulating the inner classes comprising the component. Figure 14 shows the interrelation of classes comprising the component.

The *OOD_M_Interface* interface is actually an application of the Facade design pattern (Gamma et al, 1995), and it involves the following responsibilities:

- Providing the glue for classes which are truly responsible of handling external requests.
- Delegating requests from external entities to proper inner objects.
- To hold the instantiated objects inside its structure.
- Implement the logic associated to management of inner objects.

Figure 15 shows the class implementing the interface *OOD_M_Interface*, including the signature of its methods and its state variables. State variables are

Figure 15. Interface of the OOD metamodel component

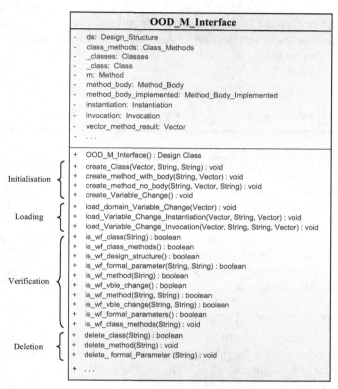

in charge of keeping the component's configuration during an instantiation procedure. The component's services can be classified according to their functionality into four groups as follows:

- **Component initialisation:** Represents actions performed by the constructors methods upon requirements of new instances of the component.

- **Design structure load:** information to be created from the Design_Structure Metamodel, is stored using instances which form the inner structure of the component.

- **Design structure verification:** objects holding information from an instantiated OOD-M structure are verified.

- **Deletion of instantiated objects:** objects that comprise the OOD-M structure may be eliminated either during the load of the structure or after the structure is completely instantiated.

In this section we have seen the internal pieces of the tool support, the design decisions during their construction, and the way these pieces operate on the modeling and verification steps. In the next section, we focus on the design as a process of modeling and verification by means of the application of patterns and the use of the tool support.

Pattern-based Design Process

There are clear benefits of applying patterns to a design concerning the flexibility to face different changes — for example, user requirements, data structures or algorithms, platforms, social environment, and so on (Gamma et al, 1995; Ghezzi, Jazayeri, & Mandrioli, 2002; Prechelt, Unger, Tichy, Brössle, & Votta, 2001). However, the application of patterns as well as modeling a design, does not concern simple tasks. OO designers should be capable of building models with certain quality properties, which have been considered relevant for the project. This lead a developer to analyze, for example, how to make a design easier to be modeled, modified, understood, and so on. We refer here to the well-known design principles, criteria, and heuristics, which indeed useful are not so easily satisfied in a particular model solution.

Nevertheless, a designer would be highly benefited by utilizing a supporting media, which may identify the missing desire aspects. Therefore, the usefulness of our tool relies not only in providing some help to verify a correct pattern usage, but also in assisting on the application of such design fundamentals into the user design solution.

In this section we present some changes that the application of patterns induces to an OO design process. In addition, the presence of the tool support for modeling and verification has been incorporated into such a pattern-based design process. In the following, we make explicit the changes suggested to the design process. After this, we will illustrate such a process by means of a simple but consistent case study, which involves the application of patterns.

A Changed Process

In previous subsections we have described the internal steps which are performed by the tool support to carry out the verification of correctness of a design and patterns. Now, we present the changes realized on the design process in order to include the application of patterns and both phases of verification — design and patterns. Thus, Figure 16 depicts the changed pattern-based design

Figure 16. Pattern-based design process with automatic design&pattern verification

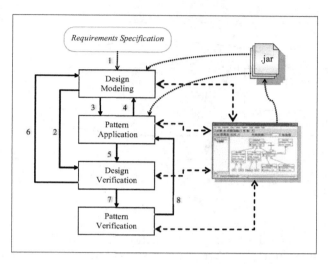

process where modeling and verifications are supported by the automatic tool. We describe both the comprising steps and the sequences of involving actions in the following:

1. This action receives the collection of requirements to create the initial design model. The graphical component of the tool is used.

2. This action is performed after an initial model has been created. It intends to verify the current state of the design model. In this step it is not possible to choose the verification of both design & pattern, since no pattern has been applied yet. Before verifying the design, an *extended Java specification* is exported.

3. This action is performed after the initial step. It intends to apply a pattern. For this, the designer selects a specific pattern and sets their roles on each of the corresponding design elements. The tool includes menu items, tool bars and dialog boxes to perform this step.

4. This action produces a return to the initial step for the addition/update of design elements.

5. Idem action 2, and after the application of a particular pattern. Here the designer may choose to verify only the design or execute the verification of design&pattern.

Figure 17. Modeling and verification cycle in the pattern-based design process

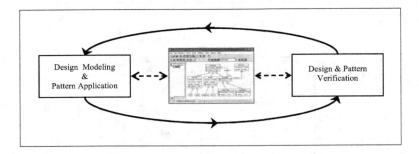

6. This action could be initiated after actions 2 or 5, and produces a return to the initial step. Here an erroneous result is returned from the verification of design. This is done from the internal process of verification located into the tool, and then showed to the designer by means of a dialog box.

7. This action is initiated after action 5 where the designer has chosen the verification of design but also the applied pattern. Since the previous step has been successful (verification of design), the verification of the applied pattern is carried out.

8. This action produces a return to the second step. It returns the results from the verification of an applied pattern. The result, which can be successful or a set of errors, is shown to the designer on a dialog box.

The whole pattern-based design process with the inclusion of automatic verification for design and patterns could be seen as iterative cycles of modeling and verification as Figure 16 and Figure 17 describe. Such cycles are not only meaningful to the achievement of a successful pattern-based design as a resulting product, but also to the learning process that a designer would certainly realize. Initially, the learning process may involve several of those cycles until designers produce the necessary insight into their minds. Nevertheless, we might suppose that the usual phenomenon of "internalization" of every learning process would significantly reduce the number of cycles on a certain interval of time.

In the next section we illustrate this updated process by means of a simple case study.

Case Study

Let us suppose we have to develop a management system for a library. The library contains books and magazines which correspond to printed items. In addition, recorded material is available as video and DVD. All these items can be lent to people in two ways: being accessible only to be managed into the library, or being able to take them outside the library for some days. Such ways of lending library items are dynamically defined according to decisions made by librarians on different moments. In such way, items can sometimes exhibit one or even the two lending forms. Information from borrowers is recorded in order to keep track of destination of items. From this domain description, the software system should provide information to be properly displayed on a user interface. For example, the number of items currently available in the library; those that have been lent inside the library; and those that have been lent to be taken away for few days.

We could start modeling our design by considering only the library items, without taking into account lending procedures on them. Figure 18 shows a possible hierarchy of items classified according to the source of the material (printed/recorded). Objects in this hierarchy should include the number of copies of each library item and the responsibilities to display their stored information.

On a second step, we can focus on the conditions that make an item available to be lent. Here, we could think that the responsibility to manage the information concerning the current number of copies, and the destination of lent items, corresponds particularly to those items.

However, an item can be borrowed in two different ways, so two different responsibilities should be added to the representative classes. Additionally, librarians may dynamically assign one lending way on one time, and then change to the other on another time, or even make the item to be lending on the two ways as well. Hence, such responsibilities should be incorporated to the objects in a dynamic form too, and this make us think about the application of a "pattern."

Figure 18. Initial hierarchy of library items

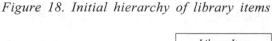
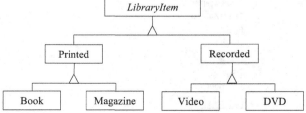

Thus, we start searching the appropriate pattern and we decide that the right choice should be the "decorator" pattern.

Thus, we update the diagram in Figure 18 to include considerations from the previous discussion and also representing borrowers, as shown in Figure 19. Items from this model can be managed to store the available number of copies, and also to dynamically receive a particular condition for being borrowed, which is assigned and changed by librarians.

Since we would like to know whether this pattern has been properly applied, we use our tool to select the use of this pattern and then set their roles on the corresponding design elements. Figure 20 shows menu items or tool bar items that could be used to select the pattern.

Figure 19. Model of library with application of decorator pattern

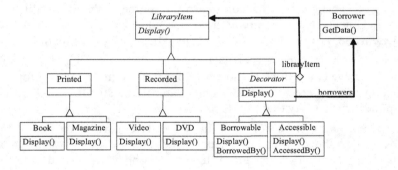

Figure 20. Establishing the use of decorator pattern by means of the tool

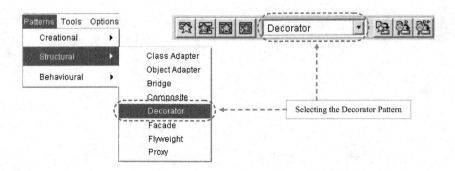

Figure 21. Setting the component role on the LibraryItem class by the tool

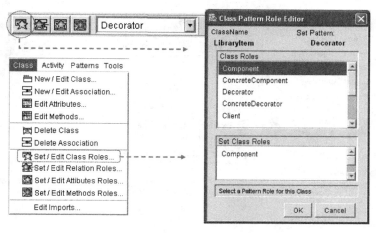

Figure 22. The whole library model displayed by the tool

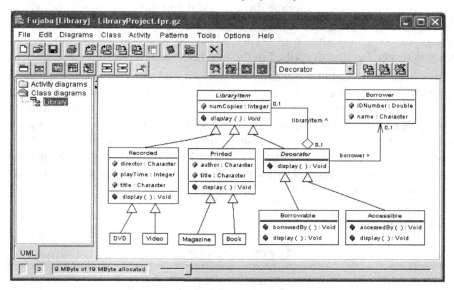

In addition, Figure 21 shows the setting of the component role on the libraryitem class by using menu items and dialog boxes. All pattern's roles are instantiated in a similar way by using the appropriate tool bar or menu items, and the corresponding dialog boxes. Figure 22 shows the display screen displayed to a designer when modeling the current case study.

Figure 23. Initiating the process of verification on the tool

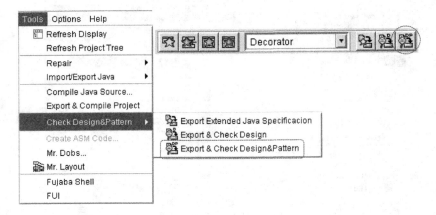

Now, we must check whether the design model and the applied pattern exhibit the expected adequacy. To do so, we select the option to "Export and Check Design&Pattern" (as shown in Figure 23). This selection triggers the whole process of verification described in the previous subsection.

In this case, we have correctly satisfied the required aspects both at the design and at the pattern level, so the two phases of verification produce a successful result, though in case any kind of error is generated during one of such phases, they are explicitly showed to the designer by means of a window message. It helps the designer to understand situations where a variation of a pattern produces a bias from the pattern intent. Even when the selection of the pattern is still a task to be performed by the designer, the accuracy on the pattern usage might be fairly satisfied.

Conclusion

Design patterns are a valuable tool for OO designers. There are a number of pragmatic benefits from using design patterns, and of course, there are also a number of common problems. For example, some design patterns are simply too difficult for the average OO designer to learn. In some cases, the pattern is inherently complex; in other cases, it is given a name and a description that are not obvious. Whatever the cause, pattern understanding is a practical problem when they are adopted by an organization.

In practice, an OO designer needs personal time and personal initiative to become skilful in design patterns. For example, a design pattern may be used in a toy example before it can be used in the real case; a real case may be verified against the application of pattern's properties; and so forth. The main issue here is that every OO designer should learn how to apply design patterns.

Learning processes might be facilitated through improving understanding of semantics behind the patterns. Several reasons to formalize patterns were discussed in the second section; however, current formal notations for characterizing pattern models mainly rely on descriptive concerns — that is, the formal notation suggests a more specific meaning of pattern's elements as modeling building blocks.

Verification of pattern's properties adds another exploiting dimension to formal notations. Patterns can be used to build robust designs with design-level parts that have well-understood trade-offs. Using our supporting tool for the learning process might facilitate pattern understanding, and hence improve the whole design process. By means of a graphical user interface, an OO designer may model a particular design allowing the tool to check properties and different circumstances of application. Thus, designers with regular skills on both OO graphical modeling and design patterns may now take advantage of a rigorous back-end derived from our formal basis for OO design and pattern application. They do not need to have a background on formal languages and still may be benefited by a formally described Metamodel.

Besides, our supporting tool may facilitate learning by allowing experimentation, which identifies semantics of applications according to the formal model behind the tool. It allows us to compare different situations on several different contexts and detect whether a pattern is appropriately used to solve a specific design problem (Reynoso et al, 2002). As a consequence, the design process as a whole is improved by using a reuse technique — patterns — supported by automatic verification of their properties.

Since we are aware of the current running projects using the Fujaba tool (Fujaba Home Page), we expect to move forward to produce a transformation of our deployed product into a *plug-in,* which any current Fujaba's user could download to improve the tool he/she already uses. For identification purposes, the plug-in is named DePMoVe (*Design and Pattern Modeling and Verification*).

Diversity on contexts of use is quite outstanding for experimentation. Naïve OO designers may test different aspects of patterns through systematically using our supporting tool during their training period. Then, trainees will iteratively learn and check new knowledge, which facilitate understanding. Expert OO designers might take advantage of this process too. They could use the tool to improve current designs by experimenting "*what-if*" situations on different alternatives.

Information collected from experiences in the different cases will increase knowledge on the use of patterns, which in turn improve future uses of the tool. Patterns and their variations are stored for future analysis; hence sharing knowledge among OO designers is also possible.

So far, the tool has been used in the context of training students. Results show a time reduction in learning, compared to similar courses without using the tool. Additionally, the number of errors introduced in the design highly decreases. However, we are aware that more empirical evaluation is needed to quantify advantages on the use of the tool. To do so, the tool is currently being checked on academic as well as industrial environments. Firstly, we have grouped designers according to their profile — beginners and advanced — to reduce effects of different backgrounds on the same sample. Beginners designers are those who initiate using patterns, thought they are already skilled in object-oriented practices. Advanced designers are those who regularly use design patterns, but they show some difficulties at dealing with variations of particular patterns. Both groups of designers come from different organizations — academic and industry. For each of them, a domain problem has been selected to be solved by applying patterns. Secondly, domains have been evaluated to select cases where complexity is similar, hence the working domain is considered uniform among the different cases (reducing influences on future conclusions).

Beginners were split into two sub-groups and only one of them is currently using our process and tool (the other group is solving the problem domain by using patterns through traditional learning processes). In a similar way, advanced designers were split into two groups — one of them using our process and the other traditional object-oriented design practices.

Results will be analyzed in terms of learning time for beginners, development time for advanced designers, and number of errors introduced in the design (considering an error as a wrongly use of a pattern).

Experiments and results will be available at http://giisco.uncoma.edu.ar.

Acknowledgments

Our work was developed under the GIISCo/UNComa research projects 04/E032, 04/E048, and 04/E059 (http://giisco.uncoma.edu.ar/); and the UNU/IIST research project "Formalization of GoF patterns using RSL" (http://www.iist.unu.edu/home/Unuiist/newrh/II/1/2/11/page.html).

References

Alagar, V., & Lämmel, R. (2002, October 22-25). Three-tiered specification of micro-architectures. In *Proceedings of the 4th International Conference on Formal Engineering Methods* (LNCS 2495), Shanghai, China. Springer-Verlag.

Aranda, G., Flores, A., Buccella, A., & Reynoso, L. (2002, May 16-17). Tool support for verifying applications using object-oriented patterns. In *Proceedings of the 4th Argentinean Workshop of Researchers on Computer Science* (pp. 253-257). Bahia Blanca, Argentina: RedUNCI.

Aranda, G., & Moore, R. (2000, August). *GoF creational patterns: A formal specification* (Tech. Rep. No. 224). Macau, China: UNU/IIST. Retrieved from http://www.iist.unu.edu

Booch, G. (1994). *Object oriented analysis and design with applications*. Benjamin/Cummings.

Buschmann, F., Meunier, R., Rohnert, H., Sommerland, P., & Stal, M. (1996). *Pattern-oriented software architecture: A system of patterns*. Chichester, UK: John Wiley & Sons Ltd.

Cechich, A., & Moore, R. (1999a, January). *A specification of GoF design patterns* (Tech. Rep. No. 151). Macau, China: UNU/IIST. Retrieved from http://www.iist.unu.edu

Cechich, A., & Moore, R. (1999b, December 7-10). A formal specification of GoF design patterns. In *Proceedings of the Asia Pacific Software Engineering Conference (APSEC '99)* (pp. 248-291), Takamatsu, Japan.

Cooper, J. (2000). W. *Java™ design patterns: A tutorial*. Boston: Addison-Wesley Longman Publishing Co., Inc.

Coplien, J. O. (1996, October). Code patterns. *The Smalltalk Report*. New York: SIGS Publications.

Crossroads Student Magazine. (1998). *FUJABA (from UML to Java and back again)*. Software Engineering Group, University of Paderborn, Germany. Retrieved April 14, 2006, from http://www.uni-paderborn.de/cs/fujaba

Eden, A. H. (1998). Giving the quality a name. *Journal of Object-oriented Programming, 11*(3). Retrieved April 14, 2006, from http://www.edenstudy.org/publications.html

Eden, A. H. (2000, May). *Precise specification of design patterns and tool support in their application*. PhD thesis, Tel Aviv University, Department of Computer Science, Tel Aviv, Israel.

Flanagan, D. (1997). *Java in a nutshell* (2rd ed.). Sebastopol, CA: O'Reilly & Associates, Inc.

Flores, A., & Fillottrani, P. (2003, October 6-10). Evaluation framework for design pattern formal models. In *Proceedings of the IX Argentinean Conference on Computer Science (CACIC '03)*, La Plata, Argentina (pp. 1024-1036). RedUNCI.

Flores, A., & Moore, R. (2001, February 19-22). Analysis and specification of GoF structural patterns. In *Proceedings of the 19th IASTED, International Conference on Applied Informatics (AI2001)*, Innsbruck, Austria (pp. 625-630).

Flores, A., & Moore, R. (2000, August). *GoF structural patterns: A formal specification* (Tech. Rep. No. 207). China: UNU/IIST. Retrieved from http://www.iist.unu.edu

Flores, A., Moore, R., & Reynoso, L. (2001, March 14-15). A Formal model of object-oriented design and GoF design patterns. In *Proceedings of the Formal Methods Europe (FME'01)* (pp. 223-241). Berlin, Germany: Springer Verlag. Retrieved from http://www.iist.unu.edu

Flores, A., Reynoso, L., & Moore, R. (2000, July). *A formal model of object oriented design and GoF design patterns* (Tech. Rep. No. 200). Macau, China: UNU/IIST.

Fowler, M. (1997). *Analysis patterns*. Menlo-Park, CA: Addison-Wesley Longman Publishing Co., Inc.

Fujaba Home Page. University of Paderborn, Software Engineering Group. Retrieved April 14, 2006, from http://wwwcs.uni-paderborn.de/cs/fujaba/

Gamma, E., Helm, R., Johnson, R., & Vlissides, J. (1995). *Design patterns: Elements of reusable object-oriented software*. Boston: Addison-Wesley.

Ghezzi, C., Jazayeri, M., & Mandrioli, D. (2002). *Fundamentals of software engineering* (2nd ed.). Englewood Cliff, NJ: Prentice Hall.

Grand, M. (1997). *Java language Reference* (2nd ed.). Sepastopol, CA: O'Reilly & Associates, Inc.

Grand, M. (1998). *Patterns in Java-Volume 1*. NY: Wiley.

Grand, M. (1998). *Patterns in Java-Volume 2*. NY: Wiley.

Hoang T. T. L., & George, C. (2000, August). *Translation for a subset of RSL into Java* (Tech. Rep. No. 210). Macau, China: UNU/IIST. Retrieved from http://www.iist.unu.edu

Jacobson, I. *Object-oriented software engineering: A use case driven approach..* Boston: Addison-Wesley.

Klein, T., Nickel, U., Niere, J., & Zündorf, A. (2000, September). *From UML to Java and back again* (Tech. Rep. No. TR-RI-00-216). Germany: University of Paderborn.

Lauder, A., & Kent, S. (1998, July 20-24). *Precise visual specification of design patterns*. In E. Jul (Ed.), *Proceedings of the 12th European Conference on Object-Oriented Programming (ECOOP'98)*, Brussels, Belgium (LNCS 1445pp. 230-236). Berlin: Springer-Verlag.

Martin, J., & Odell, J. (1995). *Object oriented methods: A foundation*. Englewood Cliffs, NJ: Prentice Hall.

Meijers, M. (1996, August). *Tool support for object-oriented design patterns*. Master's thesis, Utrecht University, The Netherlands.

Moore, R., Cechich, A., Reynoso, L., Flores, A., & Aranda, G. (2002). Object-oriented design patterns. In H. Dang Van, C. George, T. Janowski, & R. Moore (Eds.), *Specification case studies in RAISE* (pp. 287-314). Springer FACIT (Formal Approaches to Computing and Information Technology) series.

Nickel, U., Niere, J., Wadsack, J., & Zündorf, A. (2000, May 11-12). *Roundtrip engineering with FUJABA*. In *Proceedings of the WSR'00, 2nd Workshop on Software Re-engineering*, Bad Honnef, Germany.

OMG. (2004). *UML profile for enterprise distributed object computing (EDOC)*. Object Management Group. Retrieved from http://www.omg.org

Polo, M., Piattini, M., & Ruiz, F. (2002). *Advances in software maintenance management: Technologies and solutions*. Hershey, PA: Idea Group Inc.

Prechelt, L., Unger, B., Tichy, W. F., Brössler, P., & Votta, L. G. (2001, December). A controlled experiment in maintenance comparing design patterns to simpler solutions. *IEEE Transactions on Software Engineering*, *27*(12), 1134-1144.

Pree, W. (1995). *Design patterns for object-oriented software development*. Boston: Addison-Wesley Longman Publishing Co., Inc.

RAISE Language Group. (1992). *The RAISE specification language* (BCS Practitioner Series). Hemel Hempstead, UK: Prentice Hall International Ltd.

RAISE Method Group. (1995). *The RAISE development method* (BCS Practitioner Series). Hemel Hempstead, UK: Prentice Hall International Ltd.

Reynoso, L., Aranda, G., Buccella, A., & Flores, A. (2002, October). Component-based tool for verifying applications using object-oriented patterns. *Journal of Computer Science and Technology*, *2*(7), 42-48. Retrieved April 14, 2006, from http://journal.info.unlp.edu.ar/default.html

Reynoso, L., & Moore, R. (2000, May). *GoF behavioural patterns: A formal specification* (Tech. Rep. No. 201). Macau, China: UNU/IIST. Retrieved from http://www.iist.unu.edu

Rumbaugh, J., Blaha, M., Premerlani, W., Eddy, F., & Lorensen, W. (1991). *Object-oriented modeling and design*. Englewood Cliffs, NJ: Prentice Hall.

SUN. (n.d.). The source for developers. *Sun Developer Network*. Retrieved April 14, 2006, from http://java.sun.com/

UML Consortium. (n.d.). *UML home page*. Retrieved April 14, 2006, from http://www.rational.com/uml

Chapter VII

From Bad Smells to Refactoring:
Metrics Smoothing the Way

Yania Crespo, Universidad de Valladolid, Spain

Carlos López, Universidad de Burgos, Spain

María Esperanza Manso Martínez, Universidad deValladolid, Spain

Raúl Marticorena, Universidad de Burgos, Spain

Abstract

This chapter presents a study on the relation of refactoring, bad smells, and metrics. The notions of refactoring and bad smells are revised as well as metrics that can be used as guides in the refactoring process. Connection among those metrics, the usual flaws that could be suggested by them, and the required corrective actions to reduce or erase these flaws are analyzed. The usual flaws can be described in terms of bad smells and the corrective actions, in terms of the refactoring operations suggested by each bad smell. Then, we can go from metrics to bad smells and from this, to refactoring. The chapter also describes solutions for tool support in a language independent manner. In this sense, it describes the tool architecture which can be defined as metamodel-centered. A metamodel representing a family of languages is defined as well as framework based solutions for collecting metrics, as well as for a refactoring engine and repository. These solutions allow reusing the effort on a wide family of object-oriented languages. The developed frameworks were instantiated to work on instances of our own metamodel. In addition to this, it also describes how to use the approach and its support, with other metamodels. Finally, a case study on the use of metrics in bad smells detection is presented.

Introduction

One of the key subjects in code refactoring process is: *when* and *where* do we perform refactorings? In Fowler (2000) he proposes a list of clues or symptoms that suggest refactorings. These symptoms or stinks are named "*bad smells*" and their detection must be achieved from "the programmer intuition and experience."

Currently, there are a big number of integrated development environments (Eclipse, NetBeans, Visual Studio .NET, Refactoring Browser, etc.) which include refactoring. These environments contain or allow adding plug-ins for obtaining metrics. The programmer is also able to customize the warning messages and corrections for every metric over the threshold.

However, there are common points between these concepts not connected until now. Although we have metrics, they are not used to determine refactorings. There is not a direct connection among these metrics, the usual flaws that could be suggested by them, and the required corrective actions to reduce or erase these flaws. The usual flaws can be described in terms of bad smells and the corrective actions, in terms of the refactoring operations suggested by each bad smell. Then, we can go from metrics to bad smells and from this to refactoring.

On the other hand, metrics should be implemented for each object-oriented environment/language that we use. Nevertheless, one of the intrinsic properties of most of them, especially in object-oriented metrics, is their language independence.

Therefore, starting from the current state of the question, we can go forward in two directions:

- Use the metrics as bad smells clues, to hint or suggest the suitable refactorings.
- Define a language independent metric collection support. The main issue when defining this support must be to fit solution for reuse in most of integrated development environments or in a multi-language environment.

This complements a language independent approach to software refactoring.

The chapter is organized according to the following structure. First, in the second section the notion of refactoring is revised. Some refactoring catalogs and tools are presented and surveys and taxonomies (classifications) on the theme are briefly described. According to these works, open issues and trends on refactoring are shown. One of these open issues rests in bad smells detection. So, the third section deals with the bad smell notion. Bad smells were defined in a subjective viewpoint. We state here that it is possible to discover their existence, not only from an objective viewpoint, using metrics. The fourth section is devoted to presenting the role of metrics in maintainability and reusability, and then, in refactoring. In the base of this background, the fifth section presents the rationale and requirements for metrics acting as the link from bad smells to refactoring. Work done in this sense is also revised. The requirements presented in these sections are developed in the sixth section. The problems are tackled from a language independent manner. A metamodel based solution is presented, as well as its architecture and modules such as the metric collector and the refactoring engine and repository. Finally, a case study on the use of metrics in bad smells detection is presented. The last section concludes and precedes a large set of references in the topics mentioned in the chapter.

Refactoring

On The Notion of Refactoring

The word *refactoring* was first used by Opdyke (1992), who defined refactoring as a kind of behavior-preserving *program transformation* that raises program editing to a higher level and is not dependent on the semantics of a program. Opdyke also said refactoring designates a special form of program *restructuring*. It is called restructuring to the direct modification of software elements. When restructuring involves a set of related software elements and transforming the way in which they are related, this can be called *reorganizing*. Summarizing Opdyke statements we could say that refactoring are transformations on object-oriented software elements that, restructuring and reorganizing it, preserve behavior.

The introduction of a new term is intended also to make notice that in the scope of object-oriented systems the main purpose when restructuring is not to endow poorly structured systems with structure. In object-oriented systems the main purpose is to refine. This is because some structural information is always present by means of classes, inheritance, and so forth. It is also because of historical reasons. The history of restructuring has included from the very beginning transformation of non-structured ("spaghetti") programs to structured programs, from structured programs to object-oriented programs, and so on. The reader can find in Arnold (1986) a large introduction to the restructuring area from the first stages.

There was also a seminal work, Chikofsky and Cross (1990), which established terminology and definitions such as reverse and forward engineering, reengineering ... and restructuring. Restructuring was defined in that work as the transformation from one representation form to another at the same level, while preserving the subject system's external behavior (functionality and semantics). Authors described that a restructuring transformation is often one of appearance, such as altering code to improve its structure in the traditional sense of structured design. In addition to code transformations, the definition, in its broader meaning, includes other software artifacts such as reshaping data models, design, requirement structures, and so forth.

On the basis of all this we can state that refactoring is an evolution of the old concept of restructuring in the current context of object-oriented software development.

Recent definitions say that refactoring is a disciplined way to clean up code. Or, in a broader sense, that refactoring consists of changing a software system in such a way that does not alter the external behavior of the elements involved (Fowler, 2000). We prefer the last one because it spreads the definition to different software elements instead of focusing just on the program code, in the same line of the previous restructuring definition.

It is also said that the word refactoring has two definitions depending on the context, as a noun form and as a verb. Refactoring as the noun form refers to the transforming operation. Refactoring as the verb form refers to the process of transforming (applying refactorings).

Refactoring, as well as restructuring, is an important issue in software evolution, reengineering (Mens & Tourwé, 2004), reuse (Crespo, 2000), and incremental development (Arévalo et al., 2002). In software evolution, refactorings are used to improve the quality of the software. In reengineering, it is important in order to convert legacy (or deteriorated) code into a better shape. In software reuse activities refactoring means adapting software to be reused in new contexts as well as improving software structure for better reuse. On the other side, any modern development methodology considers some kind of cycle in the process. Maybe the extreme, redundantly speaking, position can be found at *extreme programming* (XP) (Beck, 1999) in which the central idea is organizing the project work concentrating on just one use case at the same time. The software is designed to manage the use case in progress. When moving to consider the next use case, if it does not fit smoothly in the current design, then design is refactored until the use case solution could be reasonably implemented. One of the key aspects of XP is continuous and aggressive refactoring (see also Beck, 2000).

It is clear that refactoring is a particular form of software transformation. This makes evident that not all kind of software transformation is a refactoring. But refactoring can be seen (and it is desirable to be) as previous steps for any other kind of software transformation in order to better prepare software structure for changes.

Recently, examined in Mens and Tourwé (2004) is a list of the distinct activities in which the refactoring process consists:

1.   Identify where the software should be refactored.

2.   Determine which refactoring(s) should be applied to the identified places.

3.   Guarantee that the applied refactoring preserves behavior.

4.   Apply the refactoring.

5.   Assess the effect of the refactoring on quality characteristics of the software or the process.

6.   Maintain the consistency between the refactored elements and the rest of the related software artifacts.

According to the identified activities in the refactoring process, the current state of the art in refactoring is mainly devoted, on one hand, to defining refactoring operations and refactoring catalogs. On the other hand, intense progress is on building tools to automatically support refactoring activities. There is also work on introducing refactoring in the life cycle of development methods as well as incorporating results from other related areas such as: program slicing (Tip, 1995), formal concept analysis (FCA) (Ganter & Wille, 1999), and knowledge management and artificial intelligence techniques, in order to assist refactoring inference tasks.

Most of the work done in refactoring has been dependent on the language which defines the elements target of the transformation. This tendency is justified because refactoring must guarantee that, starting from correct elements, it obtains correct elements. It is necessary to know in a precise way the element structure and its validity rules. Nevertheless, there is a living work line to achieved (some) language independence in the refactoring process. In this sense, in Crespo (2000) it was defined as a model language to analyze and define refactorings. This was also one of the main goals in the FAMOOS project (see Tichelaar et al., 2000a).

This chapter is devoted to link, via metrics and bad smells, activities 1 and 2. It also describes a solution for activity 4 (refactoring application) which includes an inference mechanism (supporting activities 1 and 2 in a smooth way), all this under the notion of *language independent refactoring*.

Undoubtedly, the boom and importance gained by the works on refactoring and software transformation in general have become significant. There are even those who maintain that either with tools or by using the own experience, we should refactor and optimize applications continuously, and this is not only good for applications but also for developers (Deugo, 2000).

Refactoring Catalogs

In Fowler (2000) we found a refactoring catalog which is ordered from low to greater levels. The catalog is arranged into a classification according to the criterion of the kind of elements the refactoring operates with. Each refactoring definition, in the same way (Opdyke, 1992), is structured as:

- Description
- Motivation
- Mechanics
- Examples

Examples are given in Java code, but refactoring definitions are supposed to be valid to any object-oriented language, statically typed, including Java like concepts. Definitions are given using a kind of UML graphical notation.

The main problem in this refactoring catalog is informality of definitions. Operations are described in a free way, as recommended actions to be achieved on source code. The approach is similar to the so called "cook books" as is the case of Gamma et al. (1995) where problem description and solutions are formulated in a non-formal manner.

Nevertheless, Fowler's refactoring catalog is the main reference in this matter and it is maintained and frequently updated in the www.refactoring.com Web site. Table 1 lists refactoring in Fowler's catalog and their classification.

Figure 1 shows an example of a refactoring defined in Fowler's catalog.

In Tichelaar (2001), refactoring definition is tackled with certain language independence. The author worked with a subset of the Fowler's catalog. Each refactoring definition is structured as:

- Description and motivation
- Preconditions

Table 1. Refactorings in Fowler's (2000) catalog

Composing methods	<ul><li>Extract Method</li><li>Inline Method</li><li>Inline Temp</li><li>Replace Temp with Query</li><li>Introduce Explaining Variable</li><li>Split Temporary Variable</li><li>Remove Assignments to Parameters</li><li>Replace Method with Method Object</li><li>Substitute Algorithm</li></ul>
Moving features between objects	<ul><li>Move Field</li><li>Move Method</li><li>Extract Class</li><li>Inline Class</li><li>Hide Delegate</li><li>Remove Middle Man</li><li>Introduce Foreign Method</li><li>Introduce Local Extension</li></ul>
Organizing data	<ul><li>Self Encapsulate Field</li><li>Replace Data Value with Object</li><li>Change Value to Reference</li><li>Change Reference to Value</li><li>Replace Array with Object</li><li>Duplicate Observed Data</li><li>Change Unidirectional Association to Bidirectional</li><li>Change Bidirectional Association to Unidirectional</li><li>Replace Magic Number with Symbolic Constant</li><li>Encapsulate Field</li><li>Encapsulate Collection</li><li>Replace Record with Data Class</li><li>Replace Type Code with Class</li><li>Replace Type Code with State/Strategy</li><li>Replace Type Code with Subclasses</li><li>Replace Subclass with Fields</li></ul>
Simplifying conditional expressions	<ul><li>Decompose Conditional</li><li>Consolidate Conditional Expression</li><li>Consolidate Duplicate Conditional Fragments</li><li>Remove Control Flag</li><li>Replace Nested Conditional with Guard Clauses</li><li>Replace Conditional with Polymorphism</li><li>Introduce Null Object</li><li>Introduce Assertion</li></ul>
Making method calls simpler	<ul><li>Rename Method</li><li>Add Parameter</li><li>Remove Parameter</li><li>Separate Query from Modifier</li><li>Parameterize Method</li><li>Replace Parameter with Explicit Methods</li><li>Preserve Whole Object</li><li>Replace Parameter with Method</li><li>Introduce Parameter Object</li><li>Remove Setting Method</li><li>Hide Method</li><li>Replace Constructor with Factory Method</li><li>Encapsulate Downcast</li><li>Replace Error Code with Exception</li><li>Replace Exception with Test</li></ul>

Table 1. (continued)

Dealing with generalization	• Extract Subclass • Extract Superclass • Extract Interface • Pull Up Constructor Body • Pull Up Field • Pull Up Method • Push Down Field • Push Down Method • Collapse Hierarchy • Form Template Method • Replace Inheritance with Delegation • Replace Delegation with Inheritance
Big refactorings	• Tease Apart Inheritance • Convert Procedural Design to Objects • Separate Domain from Presentation • Extract Hierarchy

Figure 1. Rename method: An example of the Fowler's catalog (adapted from Fowler 2000)

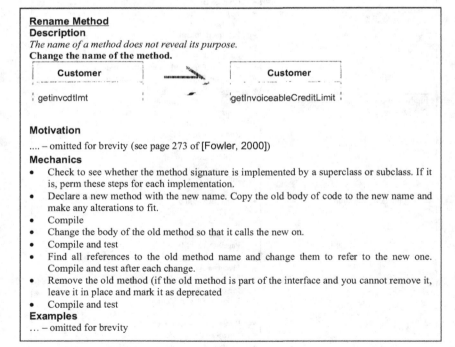

Rename Method
Description
The name of a method does not reveal its purpose.
Change the name of the method.

Customer	Customer
getinvcdtlmt	getInvoiceableCreditLimit

Motivation
.... – omitted for brevity (see page 273 of [Fowler, 2000])

Mechanics
- Check to see whether the method signature is implemented by a superclass or subclass. If it is, perm these steps for each implementation.
- Declare a new method with the new name. Copy the old body of code to the new name and make any alterations to fit.
- Compile
- Change the body of the old method so that it calls the new on.
- Compile and test
- Find all references to the old method name and change them to refer to the new one. Compile and test after each change.
- Remove the old method (if the old method is part of the interface and you cannot remove it, leave it in place and mark it as deprecated
- Compile and test

Examples
... – omitted for brevity

- Preconditions analysis
- Examples
- Related works
- Discussion

When defining preconditions for each refactoring it deals with distinctions between language independent preconditions (general preconditions) and those which are particular to a concrete language. Concrete languages analyzed are Smalltalk and Java. Since both languages lack parametric types and generic classes as well as multiple subclassing, these topics are not taken into account in the analysis.

Figure 2 shows the same refactoring as Figure 1 as is defined in this catalog.

In Marticorena and Crespo (2003) refactorings are defined in a similar way as Fowler (2000) and Tichelaar (2001), using a template. The template is composed by a name, a brief refactoring description, motivation, inputs, preconditions, actions, postconditions. The catalog is devoted to deal with specialization refactoring in a language-independent way. Specialization refactorings stand for removing structural elements from software which make its comprehension difficult, and increases its complexity, while always preserving its external

Figure 2. The Rename method refactoring as in the Tichelaar's catalog

Rename Method (*method, new name*)
Renames *method* and all method definitions with the same signature in the same hierarchy. All invocations to all changed methods are changed to refer to the new name.
...
Preconditions
Language-independent preconditions
1. The subclass hierarchies of the classes highest up in the superclass hierarchies of the class containing *method* do not already contain a method with a signature implied by the *new name* and the parameters of *method*.
Language-dependent preconditions
2. *New name* is a valid method name.
Smalltalk-specific preconditions
3. There exists no method with the same signature as *method* outside of the inheritance hierarchy of the class that contains *method*.
Java-specific preconditions
4. When *method* is a constructor, the refactoring cannot be applied unless in the context of a rename class refactoring.
Precondition discussion
...
Related work
...

behavior. Language independence is achieved by means of defining a metamodel describing a family of programming languages and set of predicate, functions, and edition primitives on the metamodel. Pre-y and post-conditions are defined in terms of these predicate and functions, while actions are defined in terms of edition primitives. Detailed discussion and examples can be found in the sixth section.

One of the current trends in refactoring is the relation of refactoring and design patterns. There are interesting proposals for introducing patterns by transforming source code through refactoring. In this sense, we can find some refactoring catalogs describing refactoring operations to introduce design patterns in code (Kerievsky, 2004; Tokuda, 1999).

Surveys and Taxonomies

As the interest in refactoring grows, revision works on the topic emerge. We can find surveys and taxonomies or classification works. The knowledge collected in refactoring specific taxonomies and classification can benefit also from those developed in related areas such as reengineering (Chikofsky & Cross, 1990) and Evolution (Mens et al., 2003a). There are also interesting points to be taken into account when analyzing refactoring works at surveys on inheritance hierarchies manipulation (Godin et al., 2002; Arévalo et al., 2002) or database schema evolution (Li, 1999).

Specifically on the refactoring topic, we can find (Crespo, 2000; Crespo & Marqués, 2001) a taxonomy (classification) of refactoring operations which also serve as a vehicle for analyzing tendencies and open issues in the area. A very good survey on refactoring can be found in Mens and Tourwé (2004). The survey defines the main activities in the refactoring process and makes a review of the work done to the moment related to each one of these activities.

From the revision of both works, one from the viewpoint of refactoring operations (as a noun) and the other from the viewpoint of refactoring activities (as a verb), we can verify the intense activity in the refactoring field. We also can state that there are a lack of inference mechanisms associated to refactoring operations in order to determine or help to determine when to refactor. We can also discover that, although the majority of the refactoring operations are centered in source code, there are more and more works in the aim of raising the level of abstraction of the refactoring target elements.

Refactoring Support

One of the most important pieces in the refactoring puzzle is automatic support. Without automatic support, time spent in refactoring tasks as well as insecurity on results (because manual refactoring is error prone) is very high. Fowler (2000) includes (technical and practical) criteria for a refactoring tool. Some of these criteria are accuracy, speed, "undo" capabilities, tool integration, and extensibility.

In www.refactoring.com we can found an updated list of refactoring tools. There are refactoring tools as parts of integrated development environments such as IntelliJ, Eclipse, and Together. There are also plug-ins to be connected into other environments such as JRefactor. Refactoring tools are available for a wide variety of programming languages: Java, Delphi, C#, Visual Basic, Smalltalk, and so forth. We have evaluated some of these tools and conclude that they keep a reduced set of refactorings, mainly from the Fowler's catalog, and the refactoring operations as well as the functionalities they offer are basically the same.

Being the same refactoring operations and functionality, there is a lack of reuse, not just from one tool to another, but inside tools themselves. Some tools are related with multilanguage development environments. A rational approach here is to take advantage of working on refactoring from a language-independent point of view. In addition to this, as we mentioned earlier in the section, there is no inference support in these tool to discover or help to discover refactoring opportunities.

Table 2. Bad smells and refactoring relation

Bad Smell	Refactorings
Alternative classes with different interfaces	Rename method, Move method
Comments	Extract method, Introduce assertion
Data class	Move method, Encapsulate field, Encapsulate collection
Data clumps	Extract class, Introduce parameter object, Preserve whole object
Divergent change	Extract class
Duplicate code	Extract method, Extract class, Pull up method, Form template method
Feature envy	Move method, Move field, Extract method
Inappropriate intimacy	Move method, Move field, Change bi-directional association to unidirectional, Replace inheritance with delegation, Hide delegate

Table 2. (continued)

Incomplete library class	Introduce foreign method, introduce local extension
Large class	Extract class, Extract subclass, Extract interface, Replace data value with object
Lazy class	Inline class, Collapse hierarchy
Long method	Extract method, Replace temp with query, Replace method with method object, Decompose conditional
Long parameter list	Replace parameter with method, Introduce parameter object, Preserve whole object
Message chains	Hide delegate
Middle man	Remove middle man, Inline method, Replace delegation with inheritance
Parallel inheritance hierarchies	Move method, move field
Primitive obsession	Replace data value with object, Extract class, Introduce parameter object, Replace array with object, Replace type code with class, Replace type code with subclasses, Replace type code with State/Strategy
Refused bequest	Replace inheritance with delegation
Shotgun surgery	Move method, Move field, Inline class
Speculative generality	Collapse hierarchy, Inline class
Switch statements	Replace conditional with polymorphism, Replace type code with subclasses, Replace type code with State/Strategy, Replace parameter with explicit methods, Introduce null object
Temporary field	Extract class, Introduce null object

Bad Smells

If It Stinks, Change It

In order to help in deciding when to refactor, Fowler (2000) proposes, in a chapter written in conjunction with Kent Beck, a list of situations that "suggest (some times scream for) the possibility of refactoring." They name these situations bad smells. Bad smells are informal descriptions, with a meaningful name. As refactoring is a software change process, they compare the situation with a newborn baby. When do you know that you have to *change* the baby's nappy? That's easy. You smell the baby's rear: *if it stinks, change it.*

They define 22 bad smells. Each bad smells description is accompanied by the refactoring operations that must be applied in order to eliminate or decrease the smell. These bad smells are listed in Table 2.

Also, Brown et al. (1998) describe situations that will lead a project to fail. These situations are named **antipatterns** and they are also described informally according to a template similar to patterns description. Antipatterns describe not just situations in code but even in project organization and management.

Taxonomies

In Mäntylä (2003) a taxonomy for bad smells is defined. The taxonomy intends to make bad smells more understandable and to recognize the relationship between bad smells. It proposes six classes of bad smells: bloaters, object-oriented abusers, change preventers, dispensables, encapsulators, couplers, and others.

- **Bloaters:** represent something in the code that has grown so large that it cannot be effectively handled. The bad smells in the bloaters' category are Long method, Large class, Primitive obsession, Long parameter list and Data clumps.

- **Object-oriented abusers:** represent bad smells describing cases where the solution does not fully exploit the possibilities of OO design. The bad smells in this category are Switch statements, temporary field, Refused bequest, Alternative classes with different interfaces and Parallel inheritance hierarchies.

- **Change preventers:** refer to code structures that considerably hinder the modification of the software. The bad smells in this category are Divergent change and Shotgun surgery.

- **Dispensables:** represent bad smells describing something unnecessary that should be removed from the code. The bad smells in this category are Lazy class, Data class, Duplicate code and Speculative generality.

- **Encapsulators:** deal with data communication mechanisms or encapsulation. Two opposite bad smells belong to this category; decreasing one will cause the other to increase. Bad smells in this category are Message chain and Middle man.

- **Couplers:** refer to bad smells representing high coupling such as: Feature envy and Inappropriate intimacy.

- **Others:** is a class containing the two remaining bad smells: Incomplete library class and Comments which do not fit into any of the five other categories.

Metrics for Refactoring

As we have said before, refactoring, to a large extent, is a way to improve some aspects or attributes of software quality. The quality of software is not a universal concept, but rather "it is very much in the eyes of the beholder" (Fenton & Pfleeger, 1997, p. 337). Software quality is really composed of many attributes, so the quality is modeled through different characteristics and their relationships. There are many quality models such as McCall, Boehm, GQM, ISO, and so forth (Fenton & Pfleeger, 1997), which permit the performance of software quality through metrics, which is not an easy problem. So we need to use software quality metrics to evaluate if refactoring improves the quality or not. Furthermore, the metrics can be used as guides in the refactoring process.

Quality Models and Metrics

Quality Models

The more generalized pattern to design an empirical software quality model is based in three principal elements: factors, criteria and metrics (FCM) (Fenton & Pfleeger, 1997). These elements come from the more external point of view (user) to the more internal point of view (developer). McCall and Boehm define early models to describe quality using this pattern. The ISO 9126 standard (ISO/IEC, 1991), derived from the McCall model, defines the software quality as:

"The totality of features and characteristics of a software product that bear on its ability to satisfy stated or implied needs."

The standard decomposes the software quality into six factors and, any component of software quality depends on one or more of these six attributes. It could be used in refactoring studies, to evaluate the software quality before or after the refactoring, such as used in other areas, for example to qualify legacy software (Etzkorn et al., 2001).

The goal, question, metrics (GQM) (Basili & Rombach, 1988) is a paradigm (GQM) that we can use to measure an external quality attribute (goal), for example, software reusability, identifying questions, and finally analyzing what measurements (metrics) can help us to decide the answer to each question.

In this way the refactoring process could be part of the maintaining or reusing processes, so we have focused on two quality attributes: maintainability and reusability. Table 3 and Figure 3 show these attributes modeled by ISO 9126 standard and REBOOT model, respectively.

Table 3. ISO 9126 standard maintainability model

Analyzability	Attributes of software that bear on the effort needed for diagnosis of deficiencies or causes of failures, or for identification of parts to be modified.
Changeability	Attributes of software that bear on the effort needed for modification, fault removal, or for environmental change.
Stability	Attributes of software that bear on the risk of unexpected effect of modifications.
Testability	Attributes of software that bear on the effort needed for validating the modified software.

The reused based on object-oriented techniques (REBOOT) project (Karlsson, 1995) developed a reusability model using the FCM method (Figure 3), as part of a quality model. Following this model, they found that component reusability was strongly related to reliability, understandability, and portability.

In the OO paradigm there are other approaches to reusability measurement. In Price and Demurjian (1997) we can find a frame which permits us to decide what classes are reusable and what are not, after classifying them. And in Bunge (2000) there is a summary about metrics and models of software reuse.

As we have said before, useful models on reusability and maintainability were designed by the standard ISO 9126. Table 3 shows the ISO 9126 maintainability

Figure 3. Karlsson reusability model

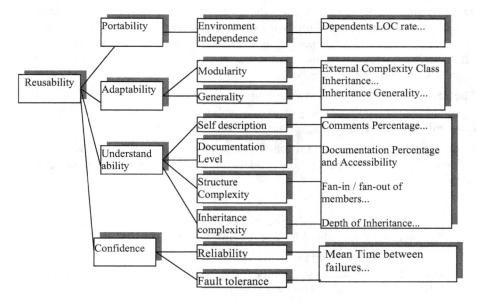

Table 4. Classification of software measures

Entities: Process (Pr), Product (Pd), Resources (Rs)
Internal Attributes of Pr, Pd or Rs: Those that can be measured purely in terms of Pr, Pd or Rs themselves
External Attributes of Pr, Pd or Rs: Those that can be measured only through the behavior of Pr, Pd or Rs.

model. This standard is used, for example, in legacy software to assess the existing software for reusability (Etzkorn et al., 2001) or in maintainability studies (Genero et al., 2005).

Metrics and Validation

Fenton and Pfleeger (1997) propose a classification of software engineering measures based on the element selected (entity) and the characteristic of this element we want to measure (attribute), as shown in Table 4. The principal aim of the quality models is to connect the external software attributes (user's point of view) such as maintainability, reusability, and so forth, with the internal attributes (developer's point of view) such as size, complexity and so forth. But relatively few of the metrics are based on explicit empirical models as is recommended by measurement theory, and an even smaller number of measures has been empirically validated. Thus, they are pending more experimental studies to validate the usefulness of many measures or to validate models. As Basili et al. (1999) suggest: "Experimentation in software engineering is necessary but difficult. It requires a community of researchers that can replicate studies, vary context variables and build models..."

The replication's role in software engineering is presented by Brooks et al. (1994) as a useful tool that will permit us to generalize about the empirical results. In a similar way, the use of meta-analysis is recommended (Pickard et al., 1998).

From the point of view of traditional software development, there are a lot of software metrics and prediction models that have been used in different contexts:

- The lines of code (LOC), the Halstead's software science (Fenton & Pfleeger, 1997) or the McCabe complexity V(G) (McCabe, 1976) are traditional code measures.
- The Albrecht Functional Points (AFP) (Dreger, 1989) to measure the software functionality from early phases.

- Coupling and Cohesion metrics that measure the structural properties of a modular system (Page-Jones, 1988).

- Models to predict costs (COCOMO, PUTNAM etc) or efforts to develop a software product, which use some size metrics (LOC or PFA) as independent variables (Boehm & Papaccio, 1988; Putnam & Myers, 1992).

- Reliability models based on software failures (Musa et al., 1990), and so forth.

Furthermore, the product metrics can be classified depending on the level of granularity: system, program, or module.

Object-Oriented Metrics

The object-oriented (OO) paradigm presents particular characteristics. Many of the traditional metrics can be adapted easily in the new OO context, such as size, coupling, or cohesion. But other metrics have been developed specifically for this paradigm, such as metrics that capture concepts as inheritance or polymorphism. We can use the same metric classification used for traditional metrics (Table 4). In OO paradigm the product metric classification looking at granularity level would be system, class, or method.

Table 5. Chidamber and Kemerer metric suite

Metric	Measure	Meaning and Relations
WMC: Weighted Methods per Class.	ΣW_i, W_i is the method i complexity (for example $V(G)$)	Related with the complexity of a class.
CBO: Coupling Between Object Classes.	Number of other classes that are coupled with the class.	Related with class modularity, reusability and encapsulation. It indicates the complexity of the conceptual functionality.
RFC: Response For a Class.	Number of methods called by local methods, plus number of local methods.	Related with class complexity. It indicates the vulnerability to change propagations of the class.
DIT: Depth of Inheritance Tree.	The length of the maximum path from the class to the root of the inheritance tree.	It measures how many ancestor classes can potentially affect the class. It is related with the properties scope and design complexity.
NOC: Number Of Children.	Number of immediate descendents of the class.	It indicates the generality of a class. It is related with class reusability and complexity.
LCOM: Lack of Cohesion of Methods.	Number of disjoint sets of local methods.	Related with encapsulation and complexity.

The OO metric suites of Chidamber and Kemerer (1994) have been used as a reference in OO contexts (Table 5): WMC, CBO, RFC, DIT, NOC and LCOM, and their definitions are based in the Bunge set of ontological principles (Bunge, 1979). The LCOM metric tries to measure how closely the local methods are related to the local instance variables in the class, but its definition presents problems (Li & Henry, 1993). There are other authors that criticize these metrics (Churcher & Shepperd, 1995). Nevertheless, these measures have been used in many empirical researches. For example:

- Lorentz (Lorenz & Kidd, 1994) proposes several recommendations in design phase, based on analysis of these metrics and other examples appear in Genero et al. (2005).
- The Constantine's Law "A structure is stable if cohesion is strong and coupling low", introduces two factors that have become a base when talking about system structure: cohesion and coupling, measuring in OO by LCOM and CBO (Endres & Rombach, 2003), etc.

Li and Henry (1993) redefine LCOM to improve it, and adding other simple size metrics. These metrics were used in an empirical study to investigate whether metrics could predict maintenance effort. As a result, they conclude that these metrics are indeed useful. Briand (Briand et al., 1996, Briand et al., 1998) defines a unified framework for cohesion and coupling measurement in OO systems. Furthermore, he summarizes the empirical studies that validate these coupling and cohesion measures. Brito et al. (1996) define an interesting bounded metric suite for different granularity levels, together with recommended limits. Further-more, they develop some empirical studies to investigate the relation between these metrics and software quality attributes such as maintainability.

In Genero et al. (2005), there is a good summary of the most relevant metrics that can be applied to UML class diagrams at the conceptual level. This study includes a classification related to the theoretical and the empirical validation of these metrics. Furthermore, it includes new metrics of the system because the majority of the OO metrics are of class and methods granularity level. These metrics have been theoretically and empirically validated as maintainability metrics. From the point of view of the refactoring process, they could be useful, because many of the metrics used in refactoring have been used to evaluate quality factors such as maintainability (Du Bois & Mens, 2003).

Using Metrics in Software Refactoring

We can consider three principal steps into the process of software refactoring: detect when to refactor, identify which refactorings to apply and perform these

Table 6. Predictive metrics in refactoring

	Metrics	Pending Research ways
Evolution-critical (Simon et al., 2001; Du Bois & Mens, 2003)	Quality OO metrics, Chidamber & Kemerer Lorentz & Kidd, and so forth	Metrics as guides to identify the kind of refactoring
Evolution-prone (Lanza, 2001)	Number of times a change has been made in a software element	Tool and Metrics to detect software unstable parts and empirical validation
Evolution-sensitive (Hitz & Montazeri, 1996; Li & Henry, 1993; Chimdaber & Kemerer, 1994)	Coupling metrics (CBO, RFC, etc) Cohesion metrics	Metrics that detect evolution-sensitive parts

Figure 4. Metrics usage in refactoring process

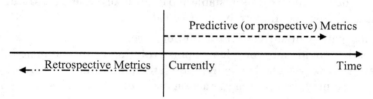

refactorings. If we consider this process in the time (Figure 4) we can use the metrics as guides before refactoring or after the refactoring to evaluate the software improvement. Following this idea, Mens and Demeyer (2001) have classified the metrics depending on their use:

- Predictive metrics that are used before the evolution has occurred, so they are useful to guide the refactoring process
- Retrospective metrics that are used after the evolution process

The predictive metrics can be used to study (Table 6):

- What software parts need to be evolved, *evolution-critical*, that is, parts with lack of quality so refactoring is often appropriate. In this case are the studies of Simon (Simon et al., 2001) and Du Bois (Du Bois & Mens, 2003).

Table 7. Retrospective metrics in refactoring

(Gall et al., 1998)	Coupling metrics used to better estimate maintenance activities.	Find out which metrics detect the kind of evolution that take place.
(Demeyer et al., 2000)	Size and Inheritance metrics that confirm restructuring evolution	
(Du Bois et al., 2004)	The impact of some particular refactoring on a particular class quality metric that measures an internal attribute.	Empirical validation. Study the impact of refactoring on external quality metrics.

- Which parts are likely to be evolved, *evolution-prone*, that is, parts with good quality but with highly volatile software requirements. So, it is necessary to have access to previous software versions. The metrics can help to detect which part is unstable and likely evolves, and there are studies that use a visualization of the metrics values (Lanza, 2001).

- Which parts can suffer from evolution, *evolution-sensitive*, that means parts that could cause problems upon evolution or the estimated cost of changes is very high. Typically, these are parts of the software in which evolution may have a high impact on many other parts (see Table 7).

The retrospective metrics (Table 7) can be used to find out whether quality has improved after the reengineering process, but in the majority of the refactoring studies there is not a quality model. Additionally, one could study the evolution process: what has been changed and how, or to identify where the most substantial changes appear.

Figure 5. Elements of an empirical study

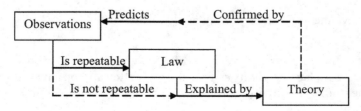

Refactoring and Empirical Studies

The principal methods to do empirical investigation are experiments (controlled experiments), case studies (or quasi-experiments), and surveys. We can work with different levels in the experimentation and systematic methods guiding experiments (Dolado & Fernández, 2000; Juristo & Moreno, 2003). Furthermore, Wohlin et al. (2000) propose the experimentation as a process, a set of guidelines of how to perform experiments to evaluate methods, techniques and tools in software engineering. This process has been used in many empirical studies in software engineering.

As Basili says "Experimentation in software engineering is necessary but difficult. Common wisdom, intuition, speculation, and proofs of concepts are not reliable sources of credible knowledge" (Basili et al., 1999).

Table 8. Refactoring studies summary

	Empirical Study Subject	Empirical Study Method
(Demeyer et al., 2000)	Heuristics based on metrics to conduct refactoring.	Retrospective case studies.
(Du Bois et al., 2004)	Practical guidelines for use of refactoring to improve internal structure (coupling and cohesion).	Case study.
(Mens et al., 2003b)	Tool that links bad smells and refactoring.	Case studies.
(Marinescu, 2001)	Metrics-based approach that detects two well-known design-flaws (bad smells).	An industrial case study.
(Mäntylä, 2004)	Relation between code metrics and subjective evaluations of three bad smells.	Case study.
(Simon et al., 2001)	Tool that use metrics (distance based cohesion) that support the subjective perceptions (bad-smells) and so, they can help to identify special anomalies for certain refactorings.	Case studies.
(Stroulia & Kapoor, 2001)	Lehman's law.	Case study.
(Trifu & Dragos, 2003)	1. Mapping from bad smells to refactoring activities 2. Methodology that, using the mapping, leads to the successful elimination of detected bad-smells.	Pending

The empirical studies in the area of software engineering help to match the ideas with reality, so a new approach is needed if we want to close the gap between theory and practice in this area (Endres & Rombach, 2003). There are three important elements in empirical studies (Figure 5):

- The observations (facts or simply subjective impressions)
- The laws as consequence of repeatable observations; they explain how things occur, not why. So we like to have a theory
- The theories which explain and order our observations

Some of the laws affecting the refactoring area, those about evolution, reuse or maintainability, for example, are Lehman's law or McCabe's hypothesis. So, they are a way to investigate. For example, in Stroulia and Kapoor (2001) we find a study which hypothesis is that refactorings decrease size (LOC and statements), complexity (methods), and coupling (collaborator) of each class (Lehman's law).

Looking at refactoring studies, we have found case studies in the majority of them without empirical validation. All checked documents (Table 8) had pending more empirical validation and extensions of their hypothesis. As a result, there is a long way to search in this area from this point of view. More specifically, there are open lines of research about the links between:

- **Metrics of quality attributes and bad smells:** The hypothesis will try to answer the questions: Which values or range of values of the metrics M_i detect the bad smell S_j?
- **Refactoring and metrics of quality attributes:** Now the questions to answer are: When we do the refactoring R_j? How must we change the quality attribute metrics M_i? and Which is the direction of the change?

Metrics as the Link from Bad Smells to Refactoring

Rationale

We have formerly stated in the chapter that one of the key subjects in the code refactoring process is *when* and *where* do we accomplish refactoring? As we have explained previously in the third section, in Fowler (2000), he proposes a list of clues or symptoms that suggest refactorings be named "Bad Smells." It is stated that bad smells detection must be achieved from "the programmer intuition and experience." We claim that the use of metrics as signs of software flaws, lead to "Bad Smell" detection based on an objective point of view.

Modern integrated development environments include refactoring capabilities (see the second section) and also contain or allow adding plug-ins for obtaining metrics. Although we have metrics, they are not used to determine refactorings (see the first and third sections). On the other hand, metrics must be implemented for each object-oriented environment/language that we use. Nevertheless, one of the intrinsic properties of most of them, especially object-oriented metrics, is their language independence: for example, number of methods, number of attributes, depth of inheritance tree, and so forth (Hitz & Montazeri, 1996).

Therefore, current proposals can be improved. The next improvement must bring the use of metrics as bad smells clues to hint or suggest the suitable refactorings. Due, on one side, to the independence of metrics from source language and, on other side, to the current trend on language independent refactoring support, solutions in this sense must be conditioned to satisfy language independence to a large extent.

Requirements

From this approach, it seems necessary to enumerate the different requirements which allow us to link metrics and refactoring in a natural way.

Metric Collector

Most of the current solutions about metric calculation are proposed to work on a particular language. They usually use particular syntax knowledge as solution, such as abstract syntax trees (AST) (Dudziak & Wloka, 2002). Although it is a correct solution, there is an outstanding issue to be taken into account. Most of the metrics, especially object-oriented metrics, are language independent.

Even if it seems to be worth the trouble, in practice, it does not take advantage of this opportunity. The same definition and implementation effort is achieved from the scratch to obtain metrics, for each development environment and programming language.

One of the possible solutions to this problem consists in abstracting object-oriented languages statements into a metamodel. Metamodels must describe commonalities as well as variations of the abstract syntax (concepts) of a family of languages.

In addition to this, a wide set of metamodels can be defined, depending, for instance, on the kind of languages gathered in the family each metamodel describes. In order to bring a global solution, frameworks appear as a suitable foundation. Frameworks as sets of abstract and concrete classes defining an easily extensible behavior (Fayad et al., 1999) allow supporting, on one side, a solution to different metamodels, and on the other side, allow us to reuse and extend the metric support with classical and new metrics. We will explain later (see the sixth section) an OO detailed design of such a framework as well as a particular implementation and instantiation to our own metamodel. Instructions for adapting the solution to deal with different metamodels are also given.

Metric Collection Using Frameworks on a Metamodel

MOOSE (an extensible language-independent environment for reengineering object-oriented systems) includes a metric engine for the computation and storage of metric measurements. These metrics are used to assess the size and, in some cases, the quality and complexity of software. The current implementation of the metrics engine includes language-independent as well as language-specific metrics. The language-independent metrics are computed based on the core FAMIX metamodel (see the sixth section).

Other tools have been developed on the FAMIX metamodel. By example, CodeCrawler supports reverse engineering through the combination of metrics and visualization. Through simple visualizations which make extensive use of metrics, it enables the user to gain insights in large systems in a short time (Tichelaar, 2001).

However, the metric engine is an additional module or subsystem in MOOSE architecture (see http://www.iam.unibe.ch/~scg/Research/Moose/description.html). There is not implication from metrics to refactoring or any similar inference engine, so metric calculation is isolated from the refactoring process.

Although Lanza and Ducasse (2002) propose the need of a metamodel for the design of independent language object-oriented metrics, there is not a clear description of the metric engine design so it is not evident to extend the current solution with new metrics.

Metric Collection Using Logic Metaprogramming

Another solution for reasoning about code is using logic metaprogramming (Muñoz, 2003). Authors use SOUL as Logic Metaprogramming language on top of Smalltalk, which used with the library LiCoR, allows to reason over Smalltalk code at a high level of abstraction. In this work, even if most of the logic predicates are language independent, some of them describe language specific relation.

In order to apply the proposed refactorings, they integrate their framework with the refactoring browser which provides a number of useful but rather primitive refactoring implementations.

Authors also use a set of rules that describe basic characteristics and relationships between classes, methods, interfaces, variables, symbols, and other code entities. All of them are language independent but the meta level interface (MLI) implementation is language dependent. The solution also provides logic queries that compute object-oriented metrics. They completely cover eight bad smells and partially, five of them. They do not deal with bad smells that are too fuzzy to be defined in automated means, smells related to maintenance, smells that need static typing information and smells that need runtime information. The process is similar in establishing a threshold for each bad smell.

Although this proposal suggests refactoring from heuristics and metrics, its solution is only applicable for an object-oriented language, Smalltalk. Therefore, this solution, in its current state, is not directly reusable due to the use of the base language as repository. This means that their "Prolog" is reasoning about the real Smalltalk code base, and not about an imported logic representation of the code.

If you want to reuse this architecture, you must implement all the LiCoR predicates for a new base language. For example, a Java migration is available at http://prog2.vub.ac.be:8080/ which includes the NewLiCoR library.

Metamodel for a Family of Languages

Solutions to these problems are based on metamodels. The metamodel must collect the basic elements of any object-oriented language: classes, attributes, methods, client-provider relations between classes, inheritance, and genericity. In particular, it would be necessary to include information about flow-control instructions, assignment instruction, and expressions. All these instructions are needed to calculate metrics like V(G) (McCabe, 1976), WMC (Chimdaber & Kemerer, 1994), and so forth.

The UML metamodel (OMG, 2004) does not contain information about instructions. Although Actions are included in version 1.5, they are not a "de facto" standard yet. This information must be contained in order to be a suitable metamodel. As we will present in the sixth section, evaluating new versions of UML metamodel as a suitable solution is future work.

We defined in previous works (López & Crespo, 2003; López et al., 2003) a metamodel for abstracting a family of languages, in the same line of other similar metamodels such as FAMIX (Demeyer et al., 1999). On the basis of this, we propose a solution based on frameworks to collect metrics with language independence. Metric analysis is used to infer refactoring opportunities in the line of bad smells detection.

The relation between metrics and bad smells is studied in Mäntylä (2004). Starting from the results presented in that work, we establish what metrics should be used to point out bad smells. Refactoring a big scale project for which we have source codes available but not experience about the project domain, brings us some problems: Where do we begin to refactor? How much time do we need to detect bad smells? Are we applying an objective process? Metrics could be an answer to all of these problems.

We establish several stages detecting bad smells:

- Metric analysis detecting those over thresholds.
- Combining data mining techniques to manage the large amount of data.
- Software evolution studies.
- Other "stinks" using heuristics

Metrics Analysis

Each defined metric usually has an associated threshold. Although the definition of each threshold is language dependent, it could be a good sign to reveal the bad smells existence.

Usually, we establish a minimum and maximum value for a metric. All the values out of this threshold could be marked as suspects. If we can contribute with a metric automatic collector, the process is simplified.

Data Mining Techniques

The problem using metrics is the large amount of data that we must manage. Taking a medium size project, we can find more than a hundred classes, each one of them with an approximate number of ten or 20 metrics associated. If we repeat this with methods, the numbers become greater still.

Obviously, if we try to manage this amount of data in a manual way to find bad smells, it turns almost impossible. However, we can use data mining tools and techniques to help us to detect bad smells. For example, the use of clustering techniques helps to group classes with similar features. This avoids inspecting all the classes with a great saving of time. This kind of solution has been used successfully by Xing and Stroulia (2004) in detection of class co-evolution.

Evolution Studies

Metrics can be used together with software evolution studies. Using different versions and studying the changes in metric values, we could be able to infer a kind of bad smells which can be classified as "dynamically identifiable" such as divergent changes, shotgun surgery and parallel hierarchy.

In this case, we will need several versions of a system to calculate metrics of each version and compare the differences among the values. From these comparisons, there are works (Gîrba et al., 2004; Ratiu, 2003) detecting those "bad smells" though the concept of "evolution matrix." Trying to identify the "dynamically identifiable" bad smells without snapshots of the system evolution, could be quite difficult.

Other "Stinks" Using Heuristics

Although the use of metrics, data mining, and evolution studies are all objective methods, there are always other problems not directly detected with well-known metrics. Wake (2003) claims that many bad smells are detected not only using metrics but other symptoms, such as name convention, comment lines, and so forth. Currently, we find many tools and studies that allow detecting these other signs. However, as usual, they are language dependent.

Language Independent Bad Smell Detection and Correction

A Metamodel Based Solution

As we previously stated (see the fifth section), there are integrated development environments (Eclipse, IntelliJ Idea, Together-J, JBuilder, Visual Studio VS.NET, etc.) that incorporate refactoring tools. Refactoring definition in a language independent way offers a solution to the reuse possibilities in the development of refactoring tools when they are adapted to new source languages. In this solution, the effort of defining refactorings in a general way guarantees a recovery of the initial effort and its future application in new languages. Some approaches to the problem of language independence are based on metamodel solutions.

FAMIX is defined as a metamodel storing information (see the fifth section) with the aim of integrating several CASE environments (Tichelaar, 2001; Tichelaar et al., 2000b). One of these CASE environments was a refactoring assistant tool denominated MOOSE (Ducasse et al., 2000). Trying to cover in the metamodel

Figure 6. MOON CORE model

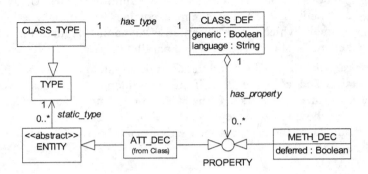

statically typed languages as well as dynamically typed, FAMIX does not consider advanced inheritance and genericity features.

The FAMIX core model (see http://www.iam.unibe.ch/~famoos/FAMIX/ Famix20/Html/famix20.html) specifies the entities and relations that can (and should) be extracted immediately from source code. The core model consists of the main OO entities, namely Class, Method, Attribute and InheritanceDefinition. For reengineering purposes, it needs another two entities, the associations: Invocation and Access. An Invocation represents the definition of a Method calling another Method, and an Access represents a Method accessing an Attribute. These abstrac-

Figure 7. MOON method description

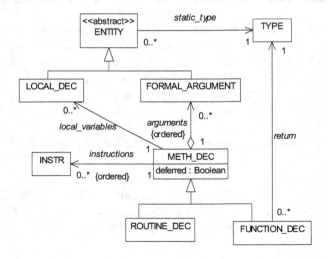

tions are needed for reengineering tasks such as dependency analysis, metrics computation, and reengineering operations.

Another work in the problem of language independence is based on the definition of a model language named MOON (minimal object-oriented notation) (Crespo, 2000; Crespo et al., 2001; López & Crespo, 2003). MOON, like FAMIX, represents the necessary abstract constructions in the refactoring definition and analysis. The MOON abstractions are common to a family of programming languages: object-oriented programming languages (OOPL), statically typed with or without genericity. The model language is the base for a metamodel-centered solution to the reusability in development and adaptation of refactoring tools.

The MOON definition includes an abstract and concrete syntax for a language and a metamodel to store classes, relationships, variants on the type system, a set of correctness rules to govern inheritance, and the type system in general. The main difference with FAMIX is the type system. Figure 6 shows the core of MOON metamodel. Entity represents anything in source code that has a Type (self reference, super reference, local variable, method formal argument, class attribute, and function result). Figure 7 presents the method body description: local variables, formal arguments, and instructions. The instructions are classified in the following way: creation, assignment, call, and compound instructions.

Figure 8 outlines the MOON metamodel classes related with genericity and their semantics rules expressed in OCL (object constraint language) (OMG, 2004).

One of the principal abstractions in the model is the type concept. Types are classified into formal parameters (FORMAL_PAR) and types derived from class definitions (CLASS_TYPE). Non-generic class definitions lead to a 1-1 association between class (CLASS_DEF) and type (CLASS_TYPE). When class definition is generic, it is said that is the "determining class" of a potentially infinite set of types (Crespo, 2000). Each generic instantiation corresponds to a different type (CLASS_TYPE). A generic class definition contains a list of formal parameters. MOON model language supports three variants regarding bounds of formal parameter. Since the first two variants are structurally the same, in terms of the framework, we have two kind of bounds in genericity: on the one hand, we have bounds by subtyping (Cardelli, 1984; Cardelli & Wegner, 1985) or by conformance (Meyer, 1997) (variant S) and on the other hand, by *where clauses* (Liskov, 1977; Liskov et al., 1995) (variant W). Both variants, S and W, intend to constraint the features that can be used by entities typed with formal parameters, in order to guarantee type correctness in generic instantiations. They determine a set of valid substitutions for the formal parameters.

The kind of generic bounding named *where clauses* associates a method signature set to the formal parameter that must be defined by any type that is intended to be used as real parameter. In general, if a formal parameter is not

Figure 8. MOON type system

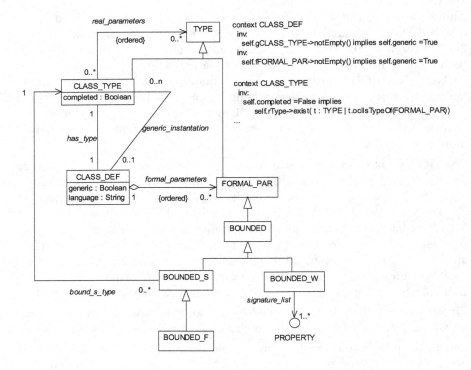

bounded, the type of the real parameter in a substitution will be bounded to the universal type Object.

Within the set of types obtained from the generic instantiations, we distinguish two subgroups: complete (or completely instantiated) types, and noncomplete (or noncompletely instantiated) types:

- Complete types, coming from complete generic instantiations (completed = true), are those whose set of real parameters does not contain any formal parameter (FORMAL_PAR), that is, the set of real parameters remains fixed.
- Non-complete types, coming from noncomplete generic instantiations, (completed= false) are those whose set of real parameters contains at least one formal parameter (FORMAL_PAR), that is, the set of real parameters remains variable depending on the context.

Figure 9. Language independent refactoring framework

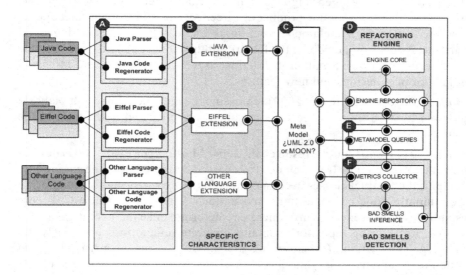

Types derived from noncomplete generic instantiations are necessarily contained within generic classes, so they use a formal parameter in the instantiation. Whether a type is a formal parameter or is a type derived from noncomplete generic instantiations, it has a local scope in the definition of the class that contains it. Types derived from complete generic instantiations have a global scope.

A Refactoring Framework Based on the MOON Metamodel

There is also a MOON-based framework to define and execute refactoring in a language independent way. Figure 9 shows the main modules that compose the framework architecture. We present a brief description of them.

Module A (Crespo, 2000) is responsible for picking up source code information and transforming in metamodel extension instances, as well as for retrieving source code from metamodel instances. Each supported language has its parser and its code regenerator.

Module B (López et al., 2003) stores the particular features of the concrete languages. They are represented as different extension points from the metamodel core (JAVA EXTENSION, EIFFEL EXTENSION, etc.). In an ideal case, if the metamodel can represent all the features of a language family, a projection of its abstractions as metamodel instances could be enough. Thus, parsing source code written in a statically typed language with or without genericity and with multiple or single inheritance could produce a direct instantiation of the metamodel classes. Although a metamodel can represent commonalities and general variants, it does not include all the features of the language families. Then, it is necessary to deal with common abstractions as well as variability and extension points for peculiarities and new features.

Module C (López & Crespo, 2003) represents the metamodel itself. It makes it possible to store source code information. The metamodel is the base of the solution.

Module D (Crespo, 2000; Crespo et al., 2004; Marticorena et al., 2003) defines the refactoring engine. It is composed of a core and a repository. The engine core contains the abstract classes necessary to define the refactorings by composing their inputs, pre-, postconditions and actions. The engine framework core establishes how to execute any concrete refactoring, once their components are known. Refactoring repository contains concrete refactorings previously defined. All the actions (transforming metamodel instances), predicates, and concrete functions (querying metamodel instances) are extensions of the common abstractions defined within the engine core. In order to define new concrete refactoring operation, it is necessary to introduce, in the worst case, new predicates, functions, and actions or, in the best case, can be defined by reusing the ones already defined in the repository. Usually a mixed solution applies.

Module E isolates the queries on metamodel elements. These queries are necessary in refactoring repository, as in metrics collector. So this module is reused, avoiding duplicated code in modules D and F.

Module F (Crespo et al., 2005) is composed of two submodules: metrics collector and bad smells inference. It is responsible from detecting bad smells using metrics. To eliminate the detected bad smells, it is possible to suggest a refactoring set. Fowler (2000) has studied relations between bad smells and refactoring.

Future: A UML Based Metamodel

In the future, framework can evolve to fit for a standard metamodel. UML (OMG, 2004) is currently embraced as "the" standard in object-oriented modeling languages. The recent work of OMG on the meta object facility (MOF) is the most noteworthy example. The progress in CASE technology has reached a high stage of maturity. Indeed, the consensus on a common notation helps both tool vendors and program designers to concentrate on more relevant issues.

Figure 10. MOF 2.0 features and classifiers

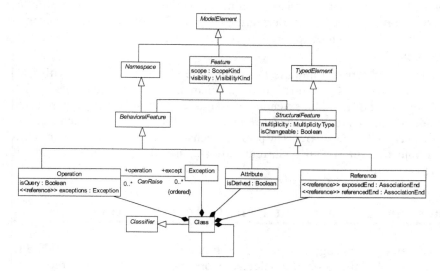

Figure 10 outlines the core modeling concepts of the MOF, including classes and its features. Many of these concepts are the same as those that are used in UML models.

One of the most relevant issues is the notion of round-trip engineering: the seamless integration between design diagrams and source code, between modeling and implementation. With round-trip engineering, a programmer generates code from a design diagram, changes that code in a separate development environment and recreates the adapted design diagram back from the source code. Object-oriented development processes, with their emphasis on iterative development, undoubtedly make round-trip engineering a relevant issue.

A second related issue that has become quite relevant is the tool interoperability. While many of the early CASE tools tried to cover the whole development process, practice has shown that such a generic approach has trouble competing with a series of concrete specialized tools. Consequently, CASE tools are becoming more and more open, permitting developers to assemble their favorite development environment from different tools purchased from different vendors yet co-operating via a single interoperability standard.

Regarded the requirements for a metamodel of languages in the refactoring context, a question is missing: can the method body (instruction, local variable…) be stored with UML? Action concept, defined in UML 2.0 (OMG, 2004), is the fundamental unit of behavior specification. An action takes a set of inputs and converts then into a set of outputs. Basics actions include those that perform operations calls, signals send, and direct behavior invocation. Actions could store method body information and can become metamodel candidates as the module C framework (see Figure 9). Furthermore, UML 2.0 includes mechanisms for template, which provide support for a generic type available from programming language.

Dependencies between module B and module C could be solved with UML profiles (OMG, 2004). The profiles are mechanisms that allow metaclasses from existing metamodels to be extended to adapt them for different purposes. This includes the ability to tailor the UML metamodel for different language features such as Java, C#, C++, Eiffel. The profile mechanism is consistent with the OMG meta object facility (MOF). Currently, this approach was only explored with some case studies.

Language Independent Refactoring Definition

In the trend of language independence, it is always necessary to validate the refactoring definition on the selected representation. More concretely, the repository or metamodel plays a basic role, because all the refactoring elements must work on the available information. Next, we analyze two different approaches that define refactoring with language independence on a metamodel.

The MOOSE Approach

Ducasse et al. (2000) define a language independent support for refactoring. Using a refactoring template, they present a template with name, short description, preconditions, precondition analysis, related work, and discussion (see the second section).

Analyzing fifteen refactorings, they give a non-formal description for each one of them. The discussion about language independence is reduced to Java and Smalltalk. They separate the language independent preconditions and language dependant preconditions.

From this theoretical work, they implement the MOOSE refactoring engine that provides code transformation support (see Figure 11). The analysis performed by the refactoring engine, that is, checking preconditions, and determining what pieces of code need to be changed is completely based on the Moose Repository, and thus on the information available in FAMIX metamodel and its language extensions.

The refactoring analysis module checks that preconditions are fulfilled. The engine uses the gathered information to trigger the actual code transformers. Code transformers work directly on the source code, so they are language

Figure 11. Partial architecture of MOOSE refactoring engine

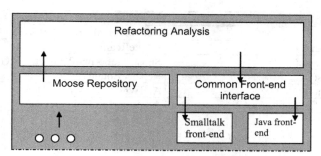

specific. They cannot work on the level of the model, because it does not contain enough information to regenerate source code. Instead they use source anchor information in the model to determine where a specific transformation must take place.

Although the precondition analysis is reusable and language independent, the transformations on the source code are language dependant, and therefore are not reusable. The metamodel and extensions are well-defined but the refactoring engine design is not shown from a point of view of reuse. The sixth section presents how we solve this problem.

Refactoring Definition on the MOON Metamodel

As was introduced in the second section, we accomplished the definition of refactorings on the model language according to a template (Fowler, 2000; Tokuda & Batory, 2001). The template is composed by a name, a brief description, motivation, inputs, preconditions, actions, and postconditions. The preconditions and postconditions are defined on the basis of a set of logical predicates and functions — see the sixth section. Concrete actions which transform classes are presented below — see the sixth section. Precondition, function, action and postcondition definitions should be expressed on the basis of the information represented in the metamodel. If some feature depends on a concrete language peculiarity, then hot spots in the framework are analyzed and extended if possible. In other case, they are classified as "not possible to be defined." Once this process is finished, we can discover which refactoring operations can be performed with language independence. Later on in the section, the set of definable predicates, functions, and actions analyzed to describe some refactoring operations are presented.

Table 9. Action set

Simple Transformations	Transformations on Generic Classes
AddAttribut(a,C)	DeleteFormalParameter(C,G)
AddMethod(m,C)	DeleteRealParameter(C,G,B)
RemoveAttribute(a,C)	SubstituteFormalParameter(C,G,T)
RemoveClass(C)	ReplaceBoundType(C,G,T)
RemoveMethod(m,C)	AddWhereClause(C,G,W)
RemoveRedefineClause(m,C)	AddSignatureInWhereClause(C,G,F)

Predicate and Function Definitions

In the refactoring definition, we establish a basic set of predicates and functions that gather most of the concepts handled in the MOON model language and the associated metamodel. They allow expressing the conditions to be fulfilled as pre- or postconditions in refactoring execution.

The definition of these functions and predicates is semiformal (not specified in a language with precise semantics) and based on query functions on the model language syntax (queries on the metamodel). The complete definition of all the predicates and functions can be consulted in Marticorena and Crespo (2003). Predicates and functions have been classified in the following categories:

- **Basics:** on languages that support the concept of "class".
- **Inheritance relations:** express the inheritance relations between classes.
- **Client relations:** express the use relations.
- **Types and generic instantiations:** describe the parametric types, completely and non-completely instantiated.
- **Generic parameters:** describe information on the generic parameters.
- **Bounds:** describe the different bounded types according to the three variants supported by MOON.

Action Definitions

Actions operate on the syntax of MOON code, whose grammar is defined in previous works (Crespo, 2000; Crespo et al., 2001). Depending on the abstraction they transform, we are able to classify actions into several categories. One example of this is shown in Table 9: actions that modify classes in general and actions focused on manipulate generic classes.

Table 10. Example of refactoring moving member variable to subclasses

Description	move the attribute to the direct descendants
Motivation	the attribute is only used by some of the direct descendants
Inputs	attribute (a) and class (C)
Precondition	1. The attribute must not be referenced by other classes or the C class itself. *ReferenceAttribute (C,a)* $= \varnothing$
	2. Direct subclasses do not contain an attribute with the same name (in languages with name hiding) $\forall D \in DDesc(C), \neg \exists b \in Attributes(D) / IsEqualName(a,b)$
Actions	1. *RemoveAttribute(C,a)*
	2. $\forall D \in DDesc(C) \Rightarrow AddAttribute(D,a)$
Postconditions	1. The current attribute does not belong to C class. $a \notin Attributes(C)$
	2. The attribute is essential/intrinsic property in all of the direct descendants of C class. $\forall D \in DDesc(C) / a \in EP(D)$

Figure 12. Refactoring engine architecture

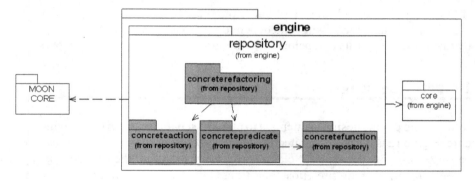

In actions listed in Table 9, *C* and *B* represent classes, *m* methods, *a* attributes, *G* formal generic parameters, *T* types, *W* where clauses and *F* method signatures. The complete definition of actions on the MOON grammar can be consulted in Marticorena and Crespo (2003).

Refactoring Definition Using the Template: An Example

A set of refactorings has been implemented following this template. Next, we present an example, using it. In this case, we have taken one of the refactorings named "moving member variable to subclasses" (Opdyke, 1992). The refactoring moves an attribute from a class to the direct descendants because it does not use this attribute, but their direct descendants do.

Table 10 shows all the elements of the refactoring. The complete definition of the rest of refactoring operations is available in Marticorena and Crespo (2003).

From the study of predicates and functions, when accomplishing the definition of several refactorings, we classify them in three groups:

- **Generals:** the basic predicates and functions on which they are defined must be completely included in the model language, and could be incorporated in the framework core that supports the metamodel (and the model language).
- **Language dependent:** the predicates and functions can be defined, although their implementations will have to be deferred to the concrete extensions of the framework when they are instantiated to a particular programming language.
- **No verifiable:** the predicates and functions cannot be verified through the model language (metamodel).

If refactoring preconditions and functions can be classified as "language independent," and even "language dependent," refactoring could be supported by the framework or its extensions, and therefore, it would be smoothly reused.

Refactoring Engine

Refactoring engine design is intended to manage separation from the metamodel core. Figure 12 is the basic architecture of the refactoring engine. The engine.core package contains the abstract classes necessary to define the refactorings by composing their inputs, pre-, postconditions and actions. The engine framework core establishes how to execute any concrete refactoring, once their components are known.

Method isValid():boolean, in pre- and postconditions, encapsulates queries to the class repository which captures the structure of the software system being refactored. Method run() in actions, encapsulates insert, delete, and modify operations on the same structure. Queries and operations are based in the metamodel.

In Figure 12, an association between predicates and functions occurs to represent how some predicates lean on functions in order to be evaluated. This improves the degree of reusability in predicate definitions, since they can share the same functions.

The refactoring engine structure (according to the solution of the Template Method design pattern) allows establishing common refactoring execution environments. The outline of the run() method of the class Refactoring, is shown in Listing 1. In order to be able to guarantee the correct execution of the refactoring, a hierarchy of exceptions is designed to be thrown in case of pre- and postconditions violations. Pre- and postconditions guarantee the external behavior.

Listing 1 run method

```
public void run() throws
    PreconditionException, PostconditionException {
try{
        validatePreconditions();
        runActions();
        validatePostconditions();
}
catch (PostconditionException postconditionEx) {
// Policy of organized panic.
undoActions();
throw postconditionEx;
} // catch
} // run (Template Method PD)
```

All associated preconditions are checked calling abstract method isValid():boolean from validatePreconditions(). Concrete preconditions define the body of the validation. Later, these preconditions can be reused i when defining another refactoring. Just in the case that all the preconditions are correctly validated, the method does not throw an exception. The structure of validatePostconditions() method is just like the previous validatePreconditions() method, but working on the postcondition set.

Regarding the methods related to the actions of the Refactoring class, runActions() and undoActions(), the structure is similar to the method validatePreconditions varying the hook methods defined in the class Action, run() and undo(),and without throwing any exception.

Refactoring Repository

The repository stores all the necessary specific information for refactoring definition shown in the sixth section, through extensions of the classes in core package. The repository structure is organized storing each element involved in a concrete refactoring definition to be reused in an independent manner. The main refactoring repository has three repositories of smaller levels: to store concrete predicates, other for concrete actions, and other for concrete functions as is shown in Figure 12. Concrete refactorings definitions are based on the associations between concrete predicates, functions, and actions; their constructors instantiate the different elements.

Engine Framework Extension

A process of engine.core extension is performed for each one of the refactorings. The elements (predicates, functions, and actions) are implemented through classes and are stored in different repositories.

By means of this process, the definition of new refactorings from the elements already stored is allowed, increasing reusability. The general functionality is defined in the package engine.core. The algorithm in class refactoring (package engine.repository) executes, by dynamic binding, the concrete hot spots extensions.

Figure 14 shows an example of the extension process of the classes of the engine.core package. The refactoring moving member variable to subclasses, already analyzed earlier is selected to illustrate it.

Then, when defining other refactoring as, for example, create member variable (Opdyke, 1992) reuse is achieved by choosing already defined elements from the repository. In this refactoring, we can reuse the definition of predicates (IsEqualName), functions, (Attributes) and action (AddAttribute) (see Figure 14), coming from previous refactoring definition efforts. This iterative process leads to complete new refactorings reusing the elements in the engine.repository package.

Figure 14. Concrete repositories: An example

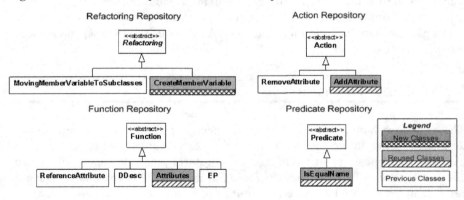

The Metrics Collector Module

In this section, we show the metric calculation support in the aim of obtaining an assisted refactoring process. In order to bring a global solution, frameworks appear as a suitable foundation. A framework design that allows it to support, on one side, a solution to different metamodels, and on the other side, to reuse and extend the metric support with classical and new metrics is presented. We will explain an OO detailed design of such a framework as well as a particular implementation and instantiation to our own metamodel. Instructions for adapting the solution to deal with different metamodels are also given.

Metamodel Traversal

To avoid modifications on every class representing metamodel instances which contain information to be collected when measuring, we apply the visitor (Gamma et al., 1995) design pattern. The aim of this design pattern is to avoid including a new method in all the elements each time we need to make a new operation with all of them. In this particular case, the necessity emerges from measuring different element properties. This is also important in a metamodel solution based in order to preserve the metamodel definition.

The pattern indicates that accept methods must be introduced in each element to visit. In a metamodel with unique hierarchy, this is reduced to introduce an accept method in the root of hierarchy. On the other side, we define a Visitor interface which must include visit methods for each one of the measurable elements (see Figure 15).

Figure 15. Collection traversal with visitor and strategy

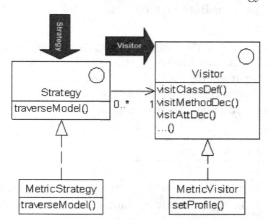

The traversal algorithm is defined independently of the visitor, allowing the use of a strategy (Gamma et al., 1995) design pattern. We choose dynamically the concrete algorithm to access each metamodel instance.

Runnable Metric Hierarchy

Metrics have been classified in several ways. As related earlier, in Lamb and Abounader (1997) we find different taxonomies more or less complex. Particularly, we only focus in the granularity level: system, class, and methods.

Metrics related on attributes are linked to classes as containers. For example, metric NOA (number of attributes, also known as NOF — number of fields —) (Lorenz & Kidd,1994) measures the number of encapsulated attributes in the class context.

Depending on the information the metamodel describes, some metrics could have problems being defined. Metamodels, as abstractions in general, lose some information from the elements they describe. In our metamodel, the loss is reduced to branching instructions (conditional and loop sentences). They are stored without semantic content.

This does not allow us to define metrics related with McCabe ciclomatic complexity (McCabe, 1976) in a language-independent way. However, we calculate those using key words stored in concrete extensions (with language dependence). Their executions are still supported by the framework.

The framework inheritance hierarchy for metrics is presented in Figure 16. Metric abstract class plays the **template method** (Gamma et al., 1995) role. Before running it, it is checked (check method) to verify that the metric is related with the type element to measure. If it is possible, the metric is calculated through run method. While checks are defined in the framework core, concrete executions are defined in the framework extension, following the **command** (Gamma et al., 1995) design pattern. Both methods, check and run, build the template method calculate.

To collect the metrics, we use the **collecting parameters** design pattern defined in Beck (1997). A MetricResult (see Figure 17) implements the pattern. The object collects the measures each time the calculate method is called on an object which implements the IMetric interface. This solution is similar to a blackboard where everyone writes their results.

Profiles: Metric Customization

Metrics suggest certain problems for their application and interpretation. We observe that, depending on the context, minimum and maximum values can

Figure 16. Metric core hierarchy

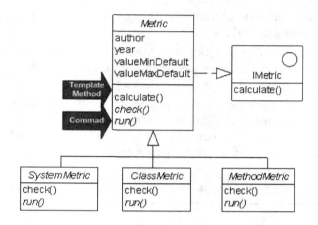

Figure 17. Metric profiles

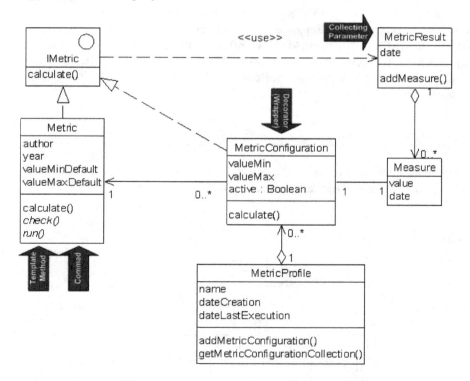

change. Therefore, the framework must support the customization of these values. Initially, metrics are instantiated with recommended default values. These values are subjective and must be fitted by means of empiric observation, tuning and adjusting the values.

With this aim, we define a wrapper class MetricConfiguration (see Figure 17), that allows us to change the initial metric definition, rewriting the default values and adjusting the metrics to a particular context or domain.

By means of a configuration profile in MetricProfile class (see Figure 17), programmers can define different profiles. They can tune the values, on the basis of previous observations or depending on the domain. We do not focus, by the moment, on aspects related to profile persistence and recovery.

Metric Calculation

Bringing together all the pieces, the metric calculation process begin visiting the elements, and obtaining the measures, following a concrete strategy. It uses a visit method for each one of the metamodel elements to be visited. A metric profile is linked to the visitor.

On each element we apply metric as pre-configured in the current profile. Results for each metamodel object are collected as a measure that allows navigability to the metric using MetricConfiguration class, on one side, and to the object where the metric has been calculated, on the other side. Measures are grouped in which we name a MetricResult to allow the result analysis and later presentation.

Framework Instantiation: An Example

We have implemented some metrics such as DIT (depth inheritance tree), NOC (number of children) (Hitz & Montazeri, 1996), and so forth.

Figure 18. Framework extension with concrete metrics

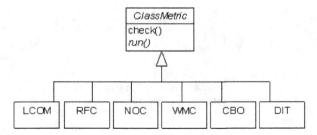

Both metrics are defined as class metrics, so we can define them as extensions of ClassMetric class (see Figure 18). Body of method run is redefined using the information extracted from the metamodel and represented as instances of Measure. The entry point to calculate the metric value is, in this case, a class of the analyzed code. From this class, we navigate through its inheritance relations to determine its deep and number of children.

To run on a particular example, all the effort rests on the framework. The programmer must simply include these metrics in a profile to apply. The implementation of the metamodel and the metric framework has been validated in Java, but the open design allows it to be implemented in any other object-oriented language. The main benefit of this approach is the reuse of the framework. We have a tool to obtain metrics for a wide set of object-oriented languages so many as parsers from language to metamodel. The tool is implemented on the MOON metamodel and parsers for Java and Eiffel are available. Nevertheless, as we said before, the metamodel can be smoothly replaced by other metamodels.

Improvements to the current version of the framework could be:

- Include the observer (Gamma et al., 1995) to update and recalculate only metrics associated to modified elements.
- Include additional filters to point out that certain metrics are not suited to certain kind of elements. By example, in those languages that define constructors, the NOP (number of parameter) (Page-Jones, 1988) metric could be relaxed in its maximum values.
- Add a graphical representation tier to help in the measures interpretation.

Detecting Bad Smells and Applying Refactoring: Case Study

From the work (Mäntylä, 2004) where the relation between metrics and bad smells is not closed, we establish a particular case study to show the bad smells detection usefulness based on metrics, in the aim to propose refactorings.

Refactoring a big scale system from which we have source codes, but not experience about the project, creates a problem: *where* do we begin to refactor? Next, we present a case study with an open source project. We do not know anything about this project; however, using metrics we are able to propose refactorings.

We choose the open source project JFreeChart (www.jfree.org). It is a library of Java classes to draw graphics. The metrics results are calculated on the last version (1.0.0-pre2). The case studied is constrained to bad smells that can be found with widely accepted metrics and language independence (according to solutions presented former in this section).

We take four bad smells: Data Class and Lazy Class in the Dispensable category (Mäntylä, 2004), parallel inheritance hierarchy in the vhange preventers category, and finally, switch statements in the object-oriented abusers category. The goal is to determine which classes in this library present these symptoms.

The case study focuses on class and method metrics. We have selected size metrics as NOA, NOM, and so forth (Lorenz & Kidd, 1994), and other object-oriented metrics as (Chimdaber & Kemerer, 1994): WMC, NOC, DIT, LCOM, CBO, and RFC. Also, we use method metrics as V(G) (McCabe, 1976), LOC (Lines Of Code) and NBD (Nested Block Depth) (Lorenz & Kidd, 1994).

Bad Smell: Data Class

This bad smell appears in classes with a high number of attributes (NOA) and methods (NOM), usually get and set methods. Their complexity and cohesion are low.

Using this filter, taking the five classes with higher values using clustering techniques, we are able to detect: AbstractRenderer, ChartPanel, PiePlot, XYPlot and CategoryPlot. If we observe their codes, all of them are classes with a big number of accessor (get) and mutator (set) methods, and their complexities are low.

Refactoring to be applied (Fowler, 2000) (See the third section): *Move Method* to add more functionality to these classes.

Bad Smell: Lazy Class

Lazy classes are classes with a low number of attributes (NOA) and methods (NOM). Their complexities are low. Their DIT values are also low, so they do not add any functionality directly or indirectly by inheritance. Cohesion among methods is usually low.

Using this filter we obtain:

- If we set a DIT value of 1:
  - We find classes merely functional, without state, which do not accomplish any tasks (i.e., CountourPlotUtilities, DataSetReader).
  - Some of the selected classes by this filter also implement the Factory Method design pattern (Gamma et al., 1995) (i.e., ChartFactory).

- DIT higher values are in classes with low functionality. The class names begin with Default which suggests a default behavior (i.e., Default-KeyedValues2DDataSet, DefaultKeyedValuesDataSet).

All these classes, although they have been discovered with different filters, are grouped into the same set (cluster). Their role in the system is to provide low functionality so they should be refactored.

Refactorings to be applied (Fowler, 2000) (See the third section): *Move Method*, *Remove Class*, *Collapse Hierarchy* and *Inline Class* to increase or decrease the class complexity.

Bad Smell: Switch Statements

Applying V(G) metric, we find the executeQuery method in JDBCXYDataset class with a value of V(G) = 54. Usually, this value should not be greater than 10. We find also two other values over threshold: LOC = 153 and NBD = 7. Inspecting the source code of this method, we observe three switch control statements, with 12, 3, and 13 case clauses. The remainder of the methods in classes maintains the metrics in the recommended thresholds.

Refactorings to be applied (see the third section): *Replace Conditionals with Polymorphism* and *Replace Type Code with Subclass* or *Replace Type Code with State/Strategy*. Besides, we must apply *Extract Method* refactoring to reduce the complexity of long methods and high density of statements.

Bad Smell: Parallel Inheritance Hierarchy

We establish the use of the two metrics (DIT and NOC) to detect this bad smell. Depending on the depth of the inheritance tree and the number of children, we use these values as indicators of parallel inheritance hierarchies' existence. More concretely, we choose classes with a number of children greater than 1, so the inheritance hierarchies are obviously complex. Collecting the metric values and applying clustering techniques with the Weka tool (http://www.cs.waikato.ac.nz/~ml/index.html), we found four clusters (see Table 11). Studying the different mean values and standard deviation for each cluster, we only focus on classes taking into account the mean values of DIT and NOC. We are looking for classes at the top of the inheritance hierarchy (DIT between 1 and 3) with a medium number of children (NOC greater than 4 in this case).

The rest of the clusters contain classes with high depth and without children (Cluster 0), very deep with few children (Cluster 1), or low deep with few children (Cluster 2). These three last clusters do not seem suitable in order to find

Table 11. JFreeChart — 1.0.0_pre2 — clusters

Cluster	Num.Classes	%	Mean DIT	St.Dev	Mean NOC	St.Dev
0	410	65%	2.8592	0.5164	0	1.4839
1	64	10%	5.1989	0.7940	0.1642	0.3704
2	128	20%	1.0478	0.2198	0.0921	0.3133
3	**27**	**4%**	**1.9991**	**0.9162**	**4.0688**	**3.4295**

parallel hierarchies. Therefore, we take Cluster 3 with its 27 classes. To find parallel inheritance hierarchies we establish that classes must have values of DIT and NOC very similar. Also we added the criterion that class names must have similar prefixes as Fowler (2000) suggests. By means of this process, we have detected three parallel hierarchies. We show the root classes and their metric values:

Hierarchy 1:

- Tick $(DIT=1, NOC=2)$
- TickUnit $(DIT=1, NOC=2)$

Hierarchy 2:

- AbstractCategoryItemLabelGenerator $(DIT=1, NOC=4)$
- AbstractPieItemLabelGenerator $(DIT=1, NOC=2)$
- AbstractXYItemLabelGenerator $(DIT=1, NOC=2)$

Hierarchy 3:

- RenderederState $(DIT=1, NOC=3)$
- Plot $(DIT=1, NOC=12)$

Hierarchy 1 does not need any explanation about the metric values. In Hierarchy 2, the NOC value includes two inner classes that must not be considered to find the bad smell. In Hierarchy 3, similarity has been obtained by similar prefixes. Besides, the other nine child classes of Plot have not descendants; the other three classes have an association one to one with descendants of the RendererState class.

Through this process, we point out a set of parallel inheritance hierarchies that follow a similar pattern. They must be observed manually by the programmer to decide the suitable refactoring set to apply.

Refactorings to be applied (see the third section): *Move Method* and *Move Field*.

Conclusion

Metrics and quality models must be considered as inseparable from refactoring processes. One of the most important goals of refactoring is to improve software quality. Recent refactoring studies start to mention the ISO 9126 quality model.

Refactoring inference, as well as refactoring opportunities detection, is one of the main tasks in the refactoring activities. This is also a key open issue. It is important in order to make the most of a refactoring tool power and to make efficient use of it in software development.

The notion of bad smell appears as an organized way of relating, on the one hand, situations where something is not going well with, on the other hand, the suitable refactoring operations to make things correct. Bad smells definitions are subjective and informal. They are not directly usable in decision support tools to point out refactoring opportunities.

Nevertheless, if we connect the subjective description of refactoring-prone situations with objective criteria given by metrics, we can use these (metrics) as a bridge between the bad smells definitions and automation of inference mechanisms in refactoring tools.

In this chapter we have relied on the notions of refactoring, bad smells and metrics for refactoring and evolution processes. It was presented how to link both bad smells and refactoring through metrics in a smooth way. The rationale for it, as well as the requirements for tool support, was discussed. Different solutions to the problem were described. In particular, a language independent solution was presented. It was shown that the use of frameworks in metrics collection, refactoring inference, and execution enable a rapid construction and validation of tools supporting these features for different languages.

Taking a metamodel (of a family of languages) as the solution cornerstone, we give a complete support to the whole process from source code with flaws to refactored code. Refactoring inference is supported by a bad smell detection module, tightly integrated with a metric collector and a refactoring repository, as we have described. One of the main goals achieved with the described solution is the continuous reuse of previous developed elements.

The case study sets a process of refactoring detection based on metrics. Obviously, the number of case studies must be increased to validate the accuracy in bad smell detection due to the subjective starting point in their detection. But improving and tuning of this iterative process must lead to a precise determination of refactorings to be applied.

Open Issues and Trends

Refactoring definitions evolve continuously. New catalogs appear including advanced aspects such as dealing with genericity (recently included in some mainstream languages) and design patterns.

At the moment the majority of the available refactoring operations are focused on source code. Nevertheless, a lot of them can be adapted to apply to other software artifacts (UML diagrams — activity, sequence, state, etc.) from different stages of software processes development. It is expected new refactoring will come out, focused on these and other software artifacts.

On the other hand, metrics usage in refactoring process and tool support must evolve to be part of a quality model such as the former mentioned ISO 9126. Another possibility lies in flexible tools allowing configuring the link metrics-quality model. Each quality aspect that refactoring is supposed to improve, must be associated with a metric set.

The solution to the problem of language independent refactoring inference and execution we have presented in this chapter is prepared to assimilate these progresses. Furthermore, there remains a lot of work to do in the construction of extensions for each supported language, facing their particular features and measuring the reuse and language independence rate reached as well as the precision and correction of refactoring results. As future work, it remains also to add new metrics into the tool support and carry on empirical validation of links "metrics-bad smells" and "refactoring-quality improving."

Relevant open issues in this matter are behavior preserving verification and dealing with side effects of refactoring in unit tests.

We have mentioned in several sections the existent relation between the concepts involved in this chapter and design patterns. Although the relation has been briefly pointed, recent works have begun to relate patterns directly with metrics, bad smells, and refactoring. This is an important open issue to be taken into account.

In order to complement the aspects mentioned here, in Mens and van Deursen (2003) can be found a statement of emerging trends and open problems in refactoring.

References

Arnold, R. (Ed.). (1986). An introduction to software restructuring. *Tutorial on Software Restructuring*. Washington, DC: Society Press (IEEE).

Arévalo, G., Black, A., Crespo, Y., Dao, M., Ernst, E., Grogono, P., Huchard, M., & Sakkinen, M. (2002). *The inheritance workshop* (LNCS 2548). Malaga, Spain: Springer.

Basili, V. & Rombach, H. (1988). The tame project: Towards improvement-oriented software environments. *IEEE Transactions on Software Engineering, 14*(6), 758-773.

Basili, V., Shull, F., & Lanubile, F. (1999). Building knowledge trough families of experiments. *IEEE Transactions on Software Engineering, 25*(4), 456-73.

Beck, K. (1997). *Smalltalk: Best practice patterns*. Upper Saddle River, NJ: Prentice-Hall.

Beck, K. (1999). Extreme programming explained: Embrace change. Upper Saddle River, NJ: Addison-Wesley.

Beck, K. (2000). *Extreme programming and reuse*. Keynote Presentation at the 6th International Conference on Software Reuse (ICSR'2000).

Boehm, B. & Papaccio, P. (1988). Understanding and controlling software costs. *IEEE Transactions on Software Engineering, 14*(10), 1463-1477.

Briand, L., Daly, J., & Wüst, J. (1996). *A unified framework for coupling measurement in object-oriented systems* (Technical Report 14). Kaiserslautern, Germany: ISERN.

Briand, L., Daly, J., & Wüst, J. (1998). A unified framework for cohesion measurement in object-oriented systems. *Empirical Software Engineering, 3*, 65-117. Boston: Kluwer Academic Press Publishers.

Brito e Abreu, F. & Melo, W. (1996). Evaluating the impact of object-oriented design on software quality. In *Proceedings of the IEEE Symposium on Software Metrics* (pp. 90-99). Berlin, Germany: IEEE Computer Society.

Brooks, A., Daly, J., Miller, J., Roper, M., & Wood, M. (1994). *Replications role in experimental computer science* (Tech. Rep. No. RR/172/94). Glasgow, UK: EFoCS.

Brown, W., Malveau, R., Brown, W., McCormick, H., & Mowbray, T. (1998). *AntiPatterns: Refactoring software, architectures, and projects in crisis*. New York: John Wiley & Sons.

Bunge, M. (1979). *Treatise on basic philosophy: Ontology II, the World of Systems*. Boston: Riedel.

Bunge, M. (2000). *Medición para la gestión en la Ingeniería del Software.* Ra-MA. Madrid, Spain: Editorial Ra-Ma.

Cardelli, L. (1984). A semantics of multiple inheritance. In *Semantics of Data Types* (LNCS 173, pp. 51-68).

Cardelli, L., & Wegner, P. (1985). On understanding types, data abstraction and polymorphism. *Computing Surveys, 17*(4), 471-523.

Chikofsky, E., & Cross, J. I. (1990). Reverse engineering and design recovery: a taxonomy. *IEEE Software, 7*(1).

Chimdaber, S., & Kemerer, C. (1994). A metrics suite for object oriented design. *IEEE Transactions On Software Engineering, 20,* 476-493.

Churcher, N., & Shepperd, M. (1995). "Comments on a metrics suite for object oriented design". *JIEEE Transactions on Software Engineeering, 21*(3), 263-265.

Crespo, Y. (2000). *Incremento del potencial de reutilización del software mediante refactorizaciones.* PhD thesis, Universidad de Valladolid. Available at http://giro.infor.uva.es/docpub/crespo-phd.ps

Crespo, Y., Cardeñoso, V., & Marqués, J. (2001). Un lenguaje modelo para la definición y análisis de refactorizaciones. In *Actas PROLE'01*, Almagro, España. Available at http://giro.infor.uva.es/docpub/crespo-prole2001.pdf

Crespo, Y., López, C., & Marticorena, R. (2004). Un framework para la reutilización de la definición de refactorizaciones. In *Actas JISBD'04*, Málaga, Spain.

Crespo, Y., López, C., & Marticorena, R. (2005). Soporte de métricas con independencia del lenguaje para la inferencia de refactorizaciones. In *Actas JISBD'05*, Granada, Spain.

Crespo, Y. & Marqués, J. (2001). Definición de un marco de trabajo para el análisis de refactorizaciones de software. In *Actas JISBD'01*, Almagro, España.

Demeyer, S., Ducasse, S., & Nierstrasz, O. (2000). Finding refactorings via change metrics. In *OOPSLA'2000* (pp. 166-177). Minneapolis, MN: ACM Press.

Demeyer, S., Tichelaar, S., & Steyaert, P. (1999). *FAMIX 2.0 — The FAMOOS information exchange model.* Technical report, Institute of Computer Science and Applied Mathematic. University of Bern.

Deugo, D. (2000). Refactoring and optimization. *Java Report, 5*(1), 6.

Dolado, J. J., & Fernández, L. (2000). *Medición para la gestión en la Ingeniería del Software.* Madrid, España: RAMA.

Dreger, J. (1989). *Function point analysis.* Prentice Hall.

Du Bois, B., & Mens, T. (2003). Describing the impact of refactoring on internal program quality. In *International Workshop on Evolution of Large-scale Industrial Software Applications* (pp. 37-48). Brussel: Vrije Universiteit.

Du Bois, B., Verelst, J., & Demeyer, S. (2004). Refactoring — Improving coupling and cohesion of existing code. In 11th *IEEE Working Conference on Reverse Engineering* (pp. 144-151).

Ducasse, S., Lanza, M., & Tichelaar, S. (2000). MOOSE: an extensible language-independent environment for reengineering object-oriented systems. In *Proceedings of the Second International Symposium on Constructing Software Engineering Tools (CoSET 2000)*.

Dudziak, T., & Wloka, J. (2002). *Tool-supported discovery and refactoring of structural weaknesses in code*. PhD thesis, Technical University of Berlin, Department of Software Engineering.

Endres, A., & Rombach, D. (2003). *A handbook of software and Systems Engineering. Empirical observations laws and theories*. Pearson Addison Wesley.

Etzkorn, L., Hughes, W., & Davis, C. (2001). *Automated reusability quality analysis of OO legacy software*. Information and Software Technology, *43*, 295-308.

Fayad, M., Schmidt, G., & Johnson, R. (1999). *Building applications frameworks: Object-oriented foundations of framework design*. Danvers, MA: Wiley Computer Publishing.

Fenton, N., & Pfleeger, S. (Eds.). (1997). *Software metrics. A rigorous and practical approach*. Boston: PWS Publishing Company.

Fowler, M. (2000). *Refactoring. Improving the design of existing code*. Upper Saddle River, NJ: Addison Wesley.

Gall, H., Hajek, K., & Jazayeri, M. (1998). Detection of logical coupling based on product release history. In *Proceedings of International Conference on Software Maintenance (ICSM98)*.

Gamma, E., Helm, R., Johnson, R., & Vlissides, J.(1995). *Design patterns. Elements of reusable object-oriented software*. Reading, MA: Addison Wesley.

Ganter, B., & Wille, R. (1999). *Formal concept analysis: Mathematical foundations*. Secaucus, NJ: Springer-Verlag.

Genero, M., Piattini, M., & Calero, C., (Eds.) (2005). *Metrics for software conceptual models*. UK: Imperial College Press.

Gîrba, T., Ducasse, S., Marinescu, R., & Ratiu, D. (2004). Identifying entities that change together. In *The 9th IEEE Workshop on Empirical Studies of Software Maintenance*. Chicago, IL: IEEE CS Press.

Godin, R., Huchard, M., Roume, C., & Valtchev, P. (2002). Inheritance and automation: where are we now? In Black, A., Ernst, E., Grogono, P., & Sakkinen, M., (Eds.), *Proceedings of the Inheritance Workshop at ECOOP 2002*. Helsinki, Finland: Jyväskylä University.

Hitz, M., & Montazeri, B. (1996). Chidamber and Kemerer's metrics suite: A measurement theory perspective. *Software Engineering, 22*(4), 267-271.

ISO/IEC. (1991). ISO/IEC 9126: Information technology—Software product evaluation—Quality characteristics and guidelines for their use. Retrieved from http://www.cse.dcu.ie/essiscope/sm2/9126ref.html

Juristo, N., & Moreno, A. (2003). *Basics of software enginnering experimentation*. Boston: Kluwer Academic Publisher.

Karlsson, E. (1995). *Software reuse. A holistic approach*. Chichester, UK: John Wiley & Son Ltd.

Kerievsky, J. (2004). *Refactoring to patterns*. Boston: Addison-Wesley Professional.

Lamb, D., & Abounader, J. (1997). *Data model for object-oriented design metrics*. Technical report, Department of Computing and Information Science. Queens's University.

Lanza, M. (2001). The evolution matrix: recovering software evolution using software visualization techniques. In *Proceedings of International Workshop on Principles of Software Evolution (IWPSE2001)*.

Lanza, M., & Ducasse, S. (2002). Beyond language independent object-oriented metrics: Model independent metrics. In *QAOOSE 2002*, pp. 77-84.

Li, W., & Henry, S. (1993). Object oriented metrics that predict maintainability. *Journal of Systems and Software, 23*, 111-122.

Li, X. (1999). A survey of schema evolution in object-oriented databases. In Chen, J., Lu, J., & Meyer, B., (Eds.), *Proceedings of TOOLS 31st, Asia'99*. IEEE CS Press.

Liskov, B. (1977). Programming methodology group progress report. Technical report, Laboratory for Computer Science Progress Report XIV. Cambridge, MA: MIT Laboratory for Computer Science.

Liskov, B., Curtis, D., Day, M., & Ghemawat, S. (1995). *Theta reference manual*. Programming Methodology group Memo 88. Cambridge, MA: MIT Laboratory for Computer.

López, C. & Crespo, Y. (2003). *Definición de un soporte estructural para abordar el problema de la indepedencia del lenguaje en la definición de refactorizaciones* (Tech. Rep. No. DI-2003-03). Departamento de Informática, Universidad de Valladolid. Retrieved from http://giro.infor.uva.es/docpub/lopeznozal-tr2003-03.pdf

López, C., Marticorena, R., & Crespo, Y. (2003). Hacia una solución basada en frameworks para la definición de refactorizaciones con independencia del lenguaje. In *Actas JISBD '03*, Alicante, España.

Lorenz, M. & Kidd, J. (1994). *Object-oriented software metrics: A practical guide*. Upper Saddle River, NJ: Prentice-Hall, Inc.

Mäntylä, M. (2004). Developing new approaches for software design quality improvement based on subjective evaluations. In *Proceedings of ICSE'04*, (pp. 48-50). Edinburgh, UK: IEEE Computer Society.

Mäntylä, M., Vanhanen, J., & Lassenius, C. (2004). Bad smells — humans as code critics. In *Proceedings of ICSM* (pp. 399-408). Edinburgh, UK: IEEE Computer Society.

Marinescu, R. (2001). Detecting design flaws via metrics in object-oriented systems. In *Proceedings of the TOOLS USA 39*, Santa Barbara, CA.

Marinescu, R. (2002). *Measurement and quality in object-oriented design*. PhD thesis, Faculty of Automatics and Computer Science of the Politehnica University of Timişoara.

Marticorena, R. & Crespo, Y. (2003). *Refactorizaciones de especialización sobre el lenguaje modelo MOON* (Tech. Rep. No. DI-2003-02). Departamento de Informática, Universidad de Valladolid. Retrieved from http://giro.infor.uv a.es/docpub/marticorena-tr2003-02.pdf

Marticorena, R., López, C., & Crespo, Y. (2003). Refactorizaciones de especialización en cuanto a genericidad. Definición para una familia de lenguajes y soporte basado en frameworks. In *Actas PROLE '03*, Alicante, España.

McCabe, T. (1976). A complexity measure. *IEEE Transactions on Software Engineering*, *2*, 308-320.

Mens, T., Buckley, J., Zenger, M., & Rashid, A. (2003a). Towards a taxonomy of software evolution. In *Proceedings of the Workshop on Unanticipated Software Evolution*.Technical report, University Warsaw, Poland.

Mens, T. & Demeyer, S. (2001). Evolution metrics. In *Proceedings of IWPSE*. New York: ACM Press.

Mens, T. & Tourwé, T. (2004). A survey of software refactoring. *IEEE Trans. Softw. Eng., 30*(2), 126-139.

Mens, T., Tourwé, T., & Muñoz, F. (2003b). Beyond the Refactoring Browser: Advanced Tool Support for Software Refactoring. In *Proceedings of the International Workshop on Principles of Software Evolution*.

Mens, T. & van Deursen, A. (2003). Refactoring: Emerging trends and open problems. In *Proceedings of the 1st International Workshop on*

REFaCtoring: Achievements, Challenges, Effects (REFACE03). University of Waterloo, Canada.

Meyer, B. (1997). *Object-oriented software construction* (2nd ed.). Upper Saddle River, NJ: McGraw Hill.

Muñoz, F. (2003). *A logic meta-programming framework for supporting the refactoring process.* PhD thesis, Vrije Universiteit Brussel, Belgium.

Musa, J., Iannino, A., & Okumoto, K. (1990). *Software reliability.* New York: McGraw Hill.

Mäntylä, M. (2003). *Bad smells in software — A taxonomy and an empirical study.* PhD thesis, Helsinki University of Technology.

OMG (2004). *Unified modeling language: Superstructure version 2.0.* Retrieved May 10, 2006, from http://www.uml.org

Opdyke, W. (1992). *Refactoring object-oriented frameworks* (Tech. Rep. No. UIUCDCS-R-92-1759). PhD thesis, Department of Computer Science, University of Illinois at Urbana-Champaign.

Page-Jones, M. (1988). *The practical guide to structured systems design* (2nd ed.). Upper Saddle River, NJ: Yourdon Press.

Pickard, L., Kitchenham, B., & Jones, P. (1998). *Use of meta-analysis in software engineering* (Tech. Rep. No. TR98-06). Department of Computer Science, University of Keele Staffordshire.

Price, M. & Demurjian, S. (1997). Analyzing and measuring reusability in object oriented designs. In *Proceedings of 1997 OOPSLA Conference*, Atlanta, GA.

Putnam, H. & Myers, W. (1992). *Measures for excellence.* Upper Saddle River, NJ: Yourdon Press Computing Series.

Ratiu, D. (2003). *Time-based detection strategies.* PhD thesis, Faculty of Automatics and Computer Science of the Polithecnica University of Timiçoara.

Simon, F., Steinbrückner, F., & Lewerentz, C. (2001). Metrics based refactoring. In *Proceedings of CSMR*, Lisbon, Portugal (pp. 30-38).

Stroulia, E. & Kapoor, R. V. (2001). Metrics of refactoring-based development: An experience report. In *The 7th International Conference on Object-Oriented Information Systems (OOIS'2001)* (pp. 113-122). Calgary, Canada: Springer.

Tichelaar, S. (2001). *Modeling object-oriented software for reverse engineering and refactoring.* PhD thesis, University of Bern.

Tichelaar, S., Ducasse, S., Demeyer, S., & Nierstrasz, O. (2000a). A meta-model for language-independent refactoring. In *Proceedings ISPSE 2000* (pp. 157-167). Kanazawa, Japan: IEEE.

Tichelaar, S., Ducasse, S., Demeyer, S., & Nierstrasz, O. (2000b). A meta-model for language-independent refactoring. In *Proceedings ISPSE 2000* (pp.157-167). IEEE.

Tip, F. (1995). A survey of program slicing techniques. *Journal of Programming Languages*, *3*(3), 121-189.

Tokuda, L. (1999). *Evolving object-oriented designs with refactorings.* PhD thesis, University of Texas in Austin, Department of Computer Sciences.

Tokuda, L. & Batory, D. (2001). Evolving object-oriented designs with refactorings. *Journal of Automated Software Engineering, 8,* 89-120. This is an enlarged version of ASE Conference paper, October 1999.

Tourwé, T. & Mens, T. (2003). Identifying refactoring opportunities using logic meta programming. In *Proceedings of 7th European Conference on Software Maintenance and Reengineering*, Benvento, Italy (pp. 91-100). IEEE Computer Society.

Trifu, A. & Dragos, I. (2003). Strategy based elimination of design flaws in object-oriented systems. In *Proceedings of ECOOP Workshop on Reengineering*, Darmstadt, Germany.

van Emden, E. & Moonen, L. (2002). Java quality assurance by detecting code smells. In *Proceedings of the 9th Working Conference on Reverse Engineering*. Richmond, VA: IEEE Computer Society Press.

Wake, W. (2003). *Refactoring workbook.* Boston: Addison-Wesley.

Wohlin, C., Runeson, P., Höst, M., Ohlsson, M., Regnell, B., & Wesslén, A. (2000). *Experimentation in software engineering. An introduction.* Norwell, MA: Kluwer Academic Publisher.

Xing, Z. & Stroulia, E. (2004, June 20-24). Data-mining in support of detecting class co-evolution. In *The 16th International Conference on Software Engineering and Knowledge Engineering*, Banff, Alberta, Canada (pp. 123-128).

Chapter VIII

Heuristics and Metrics for OO Refactoring:
A Consolidation and Appraisal of Current Issues

Steve Counsell, Brunel University, UK

Youssef Hassoun, University of London, UK

Deepak Advani, University of London, UK

Abstract

Refactoring, as a software engineering discipline, has emerged over recent years to become an important aspect of maintaining software. Refactoring refers to the restructuring of software according to specific mechanics and principles. While in theory there is no doubt of the benefits of refactoring in terms of reduced complexity and increased comprehensibility of software, there are numerous empirical aspects of refactoring which have yet to be addressed and many research questions which remain unanswered. In this chapter, we look at some of the issues which determine when to refactor (i.e., the heuristics of refactoring) and, from a metrics perspective, open issues with measuring the refactoring process. We thus point to emerging trends in the refactoring arena, some of the problems, controversies, and future challenges the refactoring community faces. We hence investigate future ideas and research potential in this area.

Introduction

One of the key software engineering disciplines to emerge over recent years is that of refactoring (Foote & Opdyke, 1995; Fowler, 1999; Hitz & Montazeri, 1996; Opdyke, 1992). Broadly speaking, refactoring can be defined as a change made to software in order to improve its structure. The potential benefits of undertaking refactoring include reduced complexity and increased comprehensibility of the code. Improved comprehensibility makes maintenance of that software relatively easy and thus provides both short-term and long-term benefits. In the seminal text on the area, Fowler (1999) suggests that the process of refactoring is the reversal of software decay and, in this sense, any refactoring effort is worthwhile. Ironically, Fowler also suggests that one reason why developers do not tend to undertake refactoring is because the perceived benefits are too "long term." Despite the attention that refactoring has recently received, a number of open refactoring issues have yet to be tackled and, as such, are open research concerns. In this chapter, we look at refactoring from two perspectives.

This first perspective relates to the heuristics by which refactoring decisions can be made. Given that a software system is in need of restructuring effort (i.e., it is showing signs of deteriorating reliability), IS project staff are faced with a number of competing choices. To illustrate the dilemma, consider the question of whether completion of a large number of small refactorings is more beneficial than completion of a small number of large refactorings. A good example of the former type of refactoring would be a simple "rename method," where the name of a method is changed to makes its purpose more obvious. This type of refactoring is easily done. An example of the latter, more involved refactoring, would be an "extract class" refactoring where a single class is divided to become two. This type of refactoring may be more problematic because of the dependencies of the original class features.

As well as the decision as to "what" to refactor, we also look at the equally important decision as to "when" we should refactor. Throughout all of our analysis, we need to bear in mind that refactoring offers only a very small subset of the possible changes a system may undergo at any point in its lifetime. We return to this theme later on.

Combined with the need to choose refactorings and the timing of those refactorings, the need to be able to measure the refactoring process is also important. Software metrics (Fenton, 1996) provide a mechanism by which this can be achieved. A metric can defined as any quantifiable or qualitative value assigned to an attribute of a software artefact. The second perspective thus relates to the type of metric applicable for determining firstly, whether a refactoring is feasible, which of competing refactorings are most beneficial and how the effects of carrying out refactoring have impacted on the software *after* it has been completed. In terms of "when" to refactor, a metrics program implemented by an organization may provide information on the most appropriate timing of certain refactorings according to metric indicators as, for example, a rapid and unexplained rise in change requests.

For both perspectives investigated, there are a large number of issues which could possibly influence their role in the refactoring process. For example, most refactorings can at best only be achieved through a semi-automated process. For example, the decision on how to split one class into two can only be made by a developer (and aided by tool support once that decision has been made). Some metrics are subject to certain threats to their validity and are thus are largely inappropriate for judging the effect of a refactoring; the lines of code (LOC) metric is a good example of such a metric because of the unclear definition of exactly what a line of code is (Rosenberg, 1997). In our analysis, we need to consider these issues.

The objectives of the chapter are three-fold. Firstly, to highlight the current open issues in the refactoring field. In particular, some of the associated problems that may hamper or influence any refactoring decision. Secondly, to highlight the role that software metrics of different types can play in the refactoring process and the interplay between refactoring mechanics and the measurement of refactoring. Throughout this chapter we appeal to a number of previous empirical studies to inform and support our ideas and opinions. A final objective of the chapter is to identify potential future research possibilities and concerns considering some of the problems and issues outlined.

The strategy we adopt for our analysis is as follows. We believe strongly that past and ongoing empirical evidence from a range of different systems provides the best mechanism for analyzing and achieving the goals of the chapter. Those goals are firstly, to distill from current empirical thinking (studies and metrics) the elements which impact on the theoretical and practical aspects of refactoring; secondly, to present that evidence in a relevant, interesting and meaningful way. Finally, to propose a set of heuristics from that evidence which we feel will be of value to refactoring practitioners, project managers, and researchers alike. We also feel that the results will be of interest to the wider software engineering community in terms of informing our understanding of change patterns and trends.

The chapter is arranged as follows. In the next section, we describe background and related work in the field of refactoring and discuss our viewpoint in a broad sense. Next, we focus on the "what" aspects of refactoring, drawing on previous empirical studies in the area to decide what refactorings to apply. We then look at the "when" of refactoring; when should we apply refactorings? Next, we summarize the heuristics presented in the chapter (in particular, those in previous sections) and then we describe some future research directions in the refactoring field. Finally, we draw some conclusions.

Background

We view three interrelated areas as particularly relevant to our analysis; theory and the mechanics of refactoring, practical application and motivation of empirical studies of refactoring and finally, work in the metrics field. By "mechanics" of refactoring we mean the prescribed steps that need to be applied to complete a refactoring (Fowler, 1999).

Refactoring Theory and Mechanics

There are a number of works relevant specifically to refactoring that have contributed to the field and which could be said to be seminal. In terms of early work in the area, the main text and from which we will draw significantly in this chapter is that of Fowler (1999). In this text, Fowler describes the mechanics of 72 different refactorings and assorted "bad smells" in code. Bad smells in code have a special significance to the work in this chapter. According to Fowler, the key indicator of when refactoring is overdue is when code starts to "smell." An example of a bad smell is an inordinately long method and is thus an obvious candidate for splitting in two.

In the same text, Fowler categorizes the 72 refactorings according to four areas. These are whether a refactoring: makes method calls simpler, organizes data, moves features amongst objects, or deals with generalization. The Ph.D. work of Opdyke (1992), work by Johnson and Foote (1988) and Foote and Opdyke (1995) has also been instrumental in promoting refactoring as a discipline and demonstrating the viability of the refactoring approach. As well as investigating the "what" and "when" of refactoring, we also illustrate potential areas for novel empirical research to build on these foundations.

Most of the early refactoring literature focused on Java and Smalltalk as the target languages. The unique features of object-oriented (OO) languages (e.g., encapsulation and inheritance) make refactoring a particularly interesting challenge for the developer. For example, encapsulation issues and the need to conform to sound OO principles means that there is frequently a need to apply relatively *simple* refactorings. For example, the "encapsulate field" refactoring modifies the declaration of a field from public to private. The motivation according to Fowler (1998) is that:

One of the principal tenets of object-orientation is encapsulation, or data hiding. This says that you should never make your data public. (p. 206)

In the next section, we provide evidence that shows developers (for the C++ language) do not seem to attach importance to getting encapsulation "right"; the key (and worrying) point is that refactoring may require the breaking down of "bad developer habits."

In terms of the OO inheritance feature, there are a number of challenges for the developer. For example, ensuring that methods and fields are declared and used in the most appropriate place of an inheritance hierarchy. The "pull up field" refactoring for example requires that a field in a subclass is moved up to its superclass. According to Fowler, the motivation for this refactoring is that "two subclasses have the same field". In this case, the field in question should be moved to the superclass to avoid duplication of that field. This is a relatively simple refactoring related to inheritance. A less simple refactoring is the "pull up method" refactoring, where two identical methods are moved from subclasses to their superclass (again to avoid duplication of behaviour). Both the mechanics and testing effort required is significantly greater for the latter type of refactoring.

Empirical Studies

The benefits of refactoring are therefore clear in terms of qualitative (subjective) values. In terms of empirical studies, recent work by Najjar, Counsell, Loizou, and Mannock (2003) has shown that refactoring can deliver both quantitative and qualitative benefits; the refactoring "replacing constructors with factory methods" of Kerievsky (2002) was analyzed. The mechanics of the refactoring require a class to have its multiple constructors converted to normal methods, thus eliminating the code "bloat" which tends to occur around constructors. The moved methods thus have new, more meaningful names. Results showed quantitative benefits in terms of reduced lines of code due to the removal of duplicated assignments in the constructors as well as potential qualitative benefits in terms of improved class comprehension.

In Najjar, Counsell, and Loizou (2005), the problems associated with a simple refactoring such as the encapsulate field (EF) was studied. To investigate the EF refactoring, samples of classes were chosen from five different Java systems and the potential for applying the mechanics of the refactoring investigated. Results showed certain potential for applying the refactoring *per se*. In other words, no shortage of opportunity was found for applying the refactoring; public attributes were found in a number of classes in each system. However, three features exhibited by the five systems suggest that applying the EF refactoring is not as straightforward or applicable as it first seems. Firstly, the number of dependent classes requiring changes as a result of applying the refactoring may prohibit the refactoring; secondly, the large number of classes with zero attributes would seem to render the refactoring almost redundant. Finally, the features of the inheritance hierarchy in each system pose a dilemma with the use of the *protected* declaration (as opposed to private). A final finding was the practical trade-off and applicability of the EF refactoring when considering different application domains. Some of the systems studied were more amenable to the EF refactoring than others.

Recent work by Advani, Hassoun, and Counsell (2005b) describes the results of an empirical study of the trends across multiple versions of open source Java software. A specially developed software tool extracted data related to each of fifteen refactorings from multiple versions of seven Java systems according to specific criteria. Results showed that, firstly, the large majority of refactorings identified in each system were the simpler, less involved refactorings. Very few refactorings related to structural change involving an inheritance relationship were found. Secondly, and surprisingly, no pattern in terms of refactorings across different versions of the software was found. Results thus suggested that developers tend to carry out simple "core" refactorings at the method and field level, but not as part of larger structural changes to the code (i.e., at the class level). The research in the same paper highlights an important refactoring issue. It is unlikely that we will be able to identify whether those "core" refactorings were done in a conscious effort by the developer to refactor, or as simply run-of-the-mill changes as part of the usual maintenance process. In other words, the question, "do developers refactor without realising it?" needs to be addressed. This then raises the question as to whether refactoring is subsumed by usual changes typically made by developers. Despite these issues, we feel that identification of the major refactoring categories is a starting point for understanding the types of change typically made by developers and the interrelationships between changes typically made by developers. The same paper identified refactorings according to specific rules and heuristics. Developing heuristics for undertaking refactorings based on system change data has also been investigated by Demeyer, Ducasse, and Nierstrasz (2000).

Strategy Used for Empirical Studies

The empirical studies described as part of this chapter and from which we draw data were all undertaken over the past seven years. For each study, there was at least one underlying objective and/or hypothesis; as we describe each study, we point out what these were. This chapter represents an interleaving and distillation of these studies in a purely refactoring context. For one or two studies, the hypotheses were not stated from the outset. For example, it is difficult to reason about when most refactorings are likely to occur. On the other hand, hypotheses about cohesion and how human subjects would rate class cohesion are far easier to compose.

Many of the metrics used in the studies were collected manually and, wherever possible, collected automatically using tailored software. For example, the study described in the fourth section used human subjects as a basis and data from that study could only be collected from hand-written scripts. Data such as number of class attributes and methods, on the other hand, can easily be collected automatically. Where data was collected automatically, it was always verified afterwards through human inspection.

The threats to the validity of each study were also considered. For example, we tried to choose systems for each study that gave as wide a cross-section of application types as possible. We also tried to choose systems which were industrial-sized and which were developed by professional software engineers. Of course, we can never study too many systems and so many of results need to be supported by other studies in other research using other systems to build up a knowledge base in the area concerned. We have also provided evidence from both Java and C++ systems as a way of reflecting trends in different OO languages. Finally, we have included a variety of statistical techniques in this chapter; we chose different techniques for different studies as a way of highlighting the salient features we were trying to demonstrate.

Automation and Metrics

In terms of related work on automating the search for refactoring trends, research by Tokuda and Batory (2001) has shown that three types of design evolution, including that of hot-spot identification, are possible. A key result of their work was the automatic (as opposed to hand-coded) refactoring of fourteen thousand lines of code. Finally, the principles of refactoring are not limited to object-oriented languages. Other languages have also been the subject of refactoring effort including that of visual basic (Arsenovski, 2004).

A central feature of our analysis is the use of metrics to quantitatively capture the features of the system under study. Many metrics have been proposed and used for analyzing object-oriented and procedurally-based software both theoretically and empirically (Bieman & Ott., 1994; Briand, Devanbu, & Melo, 1997; Chidamber & Kemerer, 1994; Hitz & Montazeri, 1996). In most previous studies, we have used simple counts of the number of the class feature "number of attributes." Metrics play a central role in allowing us to measure features of systems at different levels of abstraction whether at the class or method level).

In all the studies previously mentioned and studies we draw on in this chapter, metrics play a part.

Finally, as well as the need to understand "what" and "when" to refactor, it is also important to point to one other key motivation for our analysis of refactoring in this chapter. An earlier investigation by some of the authors to identify suitable candidates for refactoring failed for one simple reason. It highlighted obvious candidates for refactoring according to obvious criteria such as large numbers of class methods and attributes. Inspection of the same classes revealed very few opportunities for refactoring, because classes with large numbers of features often have those features for a good reason. For example, we found one class with several hundred attributes, a class called PageAttribute.MediaType. This class contained an attribute for each type of paper and other form of media (e.g., A4, A3, etc.). Refactoring this class would have been counterproductive in terms of benefits obtained, even it though it was identified according to specific refactorings and bad smells therein (e.g., large method, large class, and primitive obsession (Fowler, 1999). In the next section, we investigate the issue of "what" should be refactored and in the section following that the question of "when" refactoring should be done. We use results from previous empirical studies to support our arguments.

The "What" of Refactoring

One of the most fruitful research areas in recent years has been that of an empirical study. Carrying out empirical studies helps us to understand more in a quantitative and qualitative sense about how systems and the people using those behave (Bieman, Straw, Wang, Munger, & Alexander, 2003; Briand, Bunse & Daly, 2001; Counsell, Swift & Mendes, 2002; Harrison, Counsell & Nithi, 2000; Ostrand, Weyuker, & Bell, 2004). A multitude of empirical studies have thus been carried out covering all aspects of software engineering and related computer science fields. A particularly interesting area of empirical studies have been those which shed light on or which show how well stated theory stands up in practice. In this section we describe empirical experiences from which we can learn about rules and heuristics of what to refactor. In particular, we highlight some of the problems associated with refactoring observed through some of these empirical studies. More specifically, we highlight separately the empirical reality or refactoring and the applicability of refactorings thereof.

To facilitate an understanding of code features which the empirical studies try to evaluate, the following is a definition of a class APoint that models the operations of two coordinates x and y and two further attributes a and z. The class has a single attribute of each type of declaration (public, private and protected) and inherits from a class called BasePoint. It has a single constructor called APoint and a single method CalcDistance. It is coupled to BasePoint through inheritance and to MathType via the return type in the method CalcDistance. We could also say that this class is reasonably cohesive because the methods are meaningful, operate on the same data and are named meaningfully. Although a simple class, the features demonstrate some of the major elements which empirical studies in later sections tackle in an empirical sense.

```
public class APoint extends BasePoint {
    public int x, y;
    private int a;
    protected int z;

    // constructor
    public APoint (int a, int x, int y, int z) {
        this.a = a;
        this.x = x;
        this.y = y;
        this.z = z;
    }

    public MathType CalcDistance() {
        return((x* y * a) + z);
    }

}
```

In the next section we investigate how the empirical reality is often different to the perceived reality with evidence to support the claims. We look at each study from a refactoring perspective.

The Empirical Reality

The applicability of certain refactorings relies, to a large extent, on the features of the application in question being present in that application. In the study where we replaced multiple constructors with a catchall constructor (Najjar, Counsell, Loizou, & Mannock, 2003), the study would have been impossible had every class had just a single constructor. The "what" to refactor is therefore dependent on the features of the refactoring being present in the systems under consideration. In subsequent sections, we use the terms "attribute" and "field" interchangeably.

Zero Attribute Classes

Figure 1 shows one of the results from the analysis of the "encapsulate field" refactoring (Fowler, 1999). The purpose of the study from which the data is taken was to empirically investigate the potential for simple refactorings. We wanted to show that even perceived trivial refactorings posed certain problems. Figure 1 shows the percentage of classes with zero attributes in samples taken from five Java systems.

One of the key impediments to this refactoring was thus the high percentage of zero-attribute classes found from the samples taken from each system. The applications ranged from a graph drawing package with the lowest proportion of zero-attribute classes (System 1) to the Swing class library (System 5) with the largest.

Table 1 shows summary data for the largest of the five systems investigated in the same research. It also shows the number of public features from the same sample. It shows that 52 of the classes from the sample size of 63 had zero attributes. Only 11 classes had more than one public attribute. Opportunities for the encapsulate field refactoring are thus limited to those 11 classes. The study thus cast doubt on the viability of even simple refactorings such as EF.

Figure 1. Five systems and the percentage of zero-attribute classes

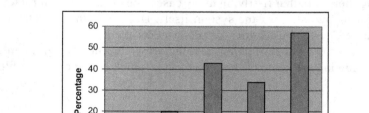

Table 1. Summary data for the Swing library

Sample Size	63
Classes with >= 1 public attr.	11
Classes with zero attributes	14
Classes with zero public attrs.	52
Max number of public attrs.	80

Another feature of the systems investigated in Najjar, Counsell, and Loizou (2005) is the existence of certain *key* classes (Counsell, Swift & Tucker, 2005). One obstacle to a decision as to what to refactor is the existence of certain class features which on the face of it, are excellent candidates for refactoring. One key indicator of a class which suggests it needs refactoring is a class with a large number of attributes. However, inspection of the class revealed it to require each of those attributes as part of its essential functionality. The other problem with key classes is that they tend to have a large number of dependent classes. The purpose and underlying hypothesis of the investigation in Najjar et al. (2005) was to establish the problems associated with dependent classes; we believe that the larger the number of dependent classes, the harder it is, generally speaking, to refactor.

Inspection of the samples of classes chosen from System 3 (another library system) showed it to comprise a class called StrictMath, with 112 attributes and 38 methods. Equally, System 1 (GraphDraw) has a class called GraphCanvas with 66 attributes and 63 methods.

Table 3 shows the summary data for the Swing system and shows that one class has 14 dependent classes. The important point about key classes is that while they may be eminently suitable for refactoring, the problem of dependent classes renders the process as problematic.

The conclusions we can draw from the data in Tables 1 and 2 relevant to the refactoring theme are that firstly, in many cases, the decision about refactoring is made for us by nature of the system itself. Deciding what to refactor is a decision aided partly by features of the systems themselves. If there are no attributes, then the number of potential refactorings is reduced significantly. In fact, the following are some of the refactorings which become impossible as a result:

- **Encapsulate field:** The declaration of a field is changed from public to private.
- **Move field:** "A field is, or will be, used by another class more than the class on which it is defined."

Table 2. Summary of dependencies for the Swing library

Sample Size	63
Median no. of dependencies	1
Max. no. of dependencies	14
Mean no. of dependencies	2.73

- **Rename field:** A field is renamed to make its purpose more obvious.

- **Push Down field:** "A field is used only by some subclasses." The field is moved to those subclasses.

- **Pull Up field:** "Two subclasses have the same field." In this case, the field in question should be moved to the superclass.

Secondly, the problem is more acute that the five refactorings above would suggest. The first three refactorings of the five listed are often part of larger refactorings (we will return to this principle in detail later). For example, the move field is part of the mechanics of the move method refactoring; if there are no attributes, then this is likely to make the move method process simpler. Absence of class features eliminates one refactoring and thus makes others simpler. Finally, in the existence of certain *key* classes may present a false impression of refactoring potential.

Ease of Automation

In a previous study described in Advani, Hassoun, and Counsell (2005b), we automatically extracted data about refactorings from seven Java systems of different types using a software tool (Advani, Hassoun, & Counsell, 2005a). The purpose of the study was to investigate the potential for identifying refactorings automatically using a tool and some of what we perceived was common, popular refactorings. To do this, we developed rules for extracting refactoring data from the source code. For example, to detect whether the "Move Field" refactoring had taken place in the transition from one release to the next, the tool checked whether:

1. A field (name, type) that appeared in a class type (belonging to older version) appeared to be missing, that is, dropped from the corresponding type of a later version.

2.   The field (name, type) did not appear in any superclass or subclass of the original type.

3.   A similar field (name, type) appeared to have been added to another type (belonging to later version).

The mechanics of this refactoring are quite straightforward, and, therefore, we could easily automate it. According to Fowler, moving state and behaviour between classes is the essence of refactoring. However, certain refactorings can only be achieved through manual means and at best a tool can only assist. Consider the case of the "substitute algorithm" (SA) refactoring. The SA refactoring substitutes an algorithm for one which is clearer. The example given by Fowler is a series of "if" statements which can simply be replaced with a loop and an array. In the same way that the EF refactoring was relatively straight-forward, the SA requires only that the code is changed and then run against a set of tests to ensure that the change has worked. However, changing code to meet the same requirements cannot be achieved by an automated process alone. There needs to be a manual component to the process.

In previous work (Counsell, Hassoun, Johnson, Mannock, & Mendes, 2003), it has been shown that the majority of the changes made to a Java Library system were to "if" conditions (yet interestingly not to "while" or "for" loops). The changes made to a set of fifty-two Java library classes over a three year period were investigated. The research attempted to support the hypothesis that certain types of changes made to Java code fall into distinct trends and, furthermore, are likely to be made at a high level of abstraction (i.e., at the method signature and parameter level).

Table 3 shows the distribution of changes categorized as part of the study in Counsell et al. (2003). The 67 additions or modifications to "if" statements were attributable to just fourteen classes. The maximum value in this table denotes the greatest number of changes of that type found for any single class. It shows that 32 new methods were added over the period to the classes studied. Interestingly, these 32 new methods were accounted for by only seven classes of the 52.

The problem from a refactoring point of view comes from two sources. Firstly, it is impossible for a tool to decide whether one section of code is functionally the same as another section of code unless it knows about the semantics of what each section of code does. Syntactically, we can make a wide range of observations about two sections of code. However, it would be virtually impossible to trace an instance of an SA refactoring (whether manually or automatically). This is particularly true if the change to the algorithm was complex in nature. In other words, and very much a topical refactoring issue, is that the most popular refactorings in the study described seem to be those which we cannot automate very easily. Secondly, the SA algorithm is likely to

Table 3. Categorization of changes made to 52 Java classes

Change Type	Total	Distribution	Max.	Mean
New method added	32	7	14	0.62
Method call added	45	9	32	0.85
Parameter in method call added or modified	32	19	9	0.62
Method signature modified	51	26	14	0.98
"If" added or modified	67	14	11	1.26

incorporate other refactorings; for example, the add parameter refactoring which may mask the SA refactoring even further. The lesson in terms of heuristics and relevant to the chapter is therefore that for convenience and speed (since developer time and resources are valuable and limited), refactorings which can be supported by a tool are likely to be a better investment of a developer's time. Some refactorings have no mechanics and this in turn make those refactorings difficult to apply.

The Role of Inheritance

Inheritance is claimed to be a fundamental principle of the OO paradigm. It is supposed to bring benefits in terms of reuse and inheritance hierarchy models information in a way which is easily understood and maintained. Despite the potential benefits of using inheritance, a number of studies have shown that the claims about ease of maintenance can be questioned (Briand et al., 2001; Counsell, Loizou, et al., 2002a).

In another recent study by the authors, it has been observed that the number of refactorings related to the category "dealing with generalization" were a very small part of the total overall number of refactorings. A tool was used to extract refactoring information from multiple versions of seven Java systems. The purpose of the study was to identify trends in core refactorings across a wide range of systems. Table 4 illustrates the number of refactorings extracted across the seven systems and *n* versions categorised according to the "dealing with generalization" type identified by Fowler.

It also shows the totals for that refactoring/version in the final row. Between versions 3-4, only 41 of the 236 refactorings were attributed to this category. Only 6 occurrences of the extract subclass were found in all versions of the systems (looking across the row). Clearly, the lack of inheritance-based refactorings is evident from Table 4. The large number of zero values suggests that across versions, inheritance-based refactorings are not common. The

Table 4. Inheritance-based refactorings across multiple versions of seven Java systems

Refactoring Type	1-2	2-3	3-4	4-5	5-6	6-7	7-8	8-9	9-10
Push Down Method	0	0	1	0	1	0	0	0	4
Extract Subclass	0	2	3	0	1	0	0	0	0
Pull Up Field	0	1	7	0	2	4	0	0	0
Extract Superclass	0	2	10	0	8	1	0	0	2
Push Down Field	0	16	3	0	7	0	0	0	0
Pull Up Method	0	9	17	0	24	5	0	0	10
Total	89	151	23 6	8	67	61	17	7	51

worrying trend is that the result suggests that developers avoid complex refactorings in favour of simpler refactorings (which accounted for the majority of the values in the final row of Table 4).

Evidence of the limited role that inheritance can play in the determination of refactorings can be found in Table 5. It shows that for the same five systems analyzed in Najjar et al. (2005), a high proportion of classes (except those for the drawing tool) are leaf classes, that is, have no subclasses. This feature should make the classes at leaves easier to refactor since, in theory they have less dependencies than classes with their own subclasses.

This would certainly apply to the encapsulate field refactoring where there are no subclasses dependent on the field in question. The same however could not be said of any refactoring which requires parts of the class to be moved — the methods of the class may use inherited features and this may cause problems.

The key lesson in terms of the chapter is that in certain circumstances, some refactorings may be trivial and easily completed. The same situation may however make other refactorings prohibitively expensive in terms of developer

Table 5. Location of Java classes in the inheritance hierarchy

System	Leaf Classes	% of Total
Drawing Tool	5	2.45
Framework	34	20.06
Java Library	44	38.72
Compiler	73	32.59
Swing	577	54.59

time and effort. Generally speaking, it seems that inheritance refactorings are so involved that they are avoided by developers. In the next section, we discuss the related issues of coupling and cohesion.

Cohesion and Coupling

We have seen already that one of the key impediments to refactoring for even a simple refactoring is the role that dependencies between classes plays. An accepted software engineering principle is that developers should try to make classes as cohesive as possible and that those classes should contain minimal coupling (Pressman, 2005). In the metrics community, cohesion is often associated with ease of comprehension. If a class is cohesive, then in theory it should be easy to understand. If a class is uncohesive then the purpose of the class is not obvious and it is difficult to understand what the purpose of that class is.

The best known of the cohesion metrics is that proposed by Chidamber and Kemerer (C&K) — the lack of cohesion of the methods of a class LCOM (Chidamber et al., 1994). The LCOM metric views a class as cohesive if the instance variables are distributed in such a way that all methods use all instance variables. Equally, a class is viewed as uncohesive if the use of instance variables amongst the methods of a class are disjoint. Various other metrics have been proposed to measure cohesion, but, as of yet, there is no general consensus on cohesion metric. In other words, we have no accepted way of measuring the benefit of a refactoring such as "extract class" whose purpose is to remove code from one class to make the source class more cohesive.

In terms of other related work, a number of attempts have been made to capture cohesion through software metrics. As well as the C&K LCOM metric, the cohesion amongst the methods of a class metric (CAMC) by Bansiya, Etzkorn, Davis, and Li (1999) based on the overlap of parameters used by a class was found to correlate with LCOM and the views of three developers on what constituted cohesion. Hitz and Montazeri (1996) also propose metrics for measuring cohesion (as well as coupling). Bieman and Ott (1994) demonstrated the measurement of functional cohesion in C software. Finally, Briand et al. (1998) propose a framework for measurement of OO cohesion and conclude that many of the cohesion metrics proposed are in most cases not validated theoretically and even fewer validated empirically.

In terms of refactoring, high cohesion would seem to be a synonym for high comprehensibility. If a class is cohesive, then the class will be easier to understand and modify. We note that any measure of cohesion based on the attributes of a class cannot be assessed if the class has no attributes. In this chapter, we adopt the stance that coupling is a far better indicator of comprehensibility than any measure of cohesion. High coupling will make refactorings more difficult to apply. Lower coupling will make them easier to apply. This brings into question the whole issue of the coupling and cohesion interplay.

As part of an earlier study into OO (C++) cohesion, the correlation between coupling given by the number of associations metric (NAS) metric and a component of a metric called normalised hamming distance (NHD) metric was analyzed. The NAS represents the number of couplings of a class and can be counted as the number of lines emerging from a class on a UML class diagram. The NHD is based around the inter-relationship between the parameters of the methods of a class in a similar vein to the CAMC metric. The purpose of the study was to investigate the hypothesis that, in an OO sense, cohesion and coupling were so interrelated that one could be substituted for another.

Table 6 shows the strong relationship between the key component of our cohesion metric P (number of unique object "P"arameters in the class as a whole) and NAS metric; the results are a summary of the results from the study in Counsell, Swift, et al. (2002). Correlation at the 1% level is asterisked by the value in each case. We thus adopt the stance that firstly, coupling has a strong relationship with cohesion (where method parameters are assumed to be a key component of class cohesion). Secondly, that unlike coupling, cohesion is a subjective issue and cannot be measured objectively.

Reduced coupling has also been a claim of certain refactorings. For example, the motivation behind the "move field" refactoring is that "a field is, or will be, used by another class more than the class on which it is defined. It therefore makes sense to move that field to the class which needs to most and eliminate the coupling. Various metrics have been defined to measure coupling (Briand et al., 1997; Chidamber et al., 1994). The difficulty arises when the decision as to what represents too much coupling has to be made. For certain applications, a high level of coupling may be necessary. There is also the problem that certain types of coupling are more of a feature in some applications than others. A GUI-based system (with a high dependence on inheritance) lends itself well to a structure incorporating frames, panels and dialog boxes, all of which share certain generic properties. Although some amount of work has been done on finding an optimal level of coupling (El Emam, Benlarbi, Goel, Melo, Lounis & Rai, 2002), further empirical studies need to be carried out before a consensus can be reached.

When making refactoring decisions, we therefore suggest that coupling should be the prime determinant of which refactorings to carry out. We should choose refactorings which can be measured in reduced levels of coupling rather than aiming for high cohesion. Furthermore, in assessing the post-impact of any refactoring, coupling not cohesion should be used where possible. We accept that many refactorings involve no coupling issues and for these refactorings, the decision amongst competing refactorings may require subjective judgements.

Table 6. Pearson, Kendall and Spearman's correlation coefficients (NAS vs. P)

System	Pearson's	Kendall's	Spearman's
Framework	0.59*	0.61*	0.69*
Compiler	0.41	0.28	0.30
Graph Editor	0.83*	0.62*	0.79*

Another point in terms of the overall chapter is that we should always look for refactorings which provide quantifiable benefits. In the next section, we address the issue of when to refactor; that is, we have looked at "what" to refactor, but the "when" is equally important.

The "When" of Refactoring

The decision as to when to refactor is as important a decision as to what to refactor. Fowler suggests that rather than being one large concerted effort, refactoring should be done in little bursts. He also suggests that a developer does not decide to refactor; the developer refactors because he/she wants to achieve something else and doing that "something else" requires that they refactor first. Similarly, Beck (2000) urges developers to refactor when the system tells them to, not through speculation alone. Very little research has empirically tackled the issue of when we should refactor.

To support the arguments about when to refactor, we return to the study of the seven open source Java systems analyzed in Advani et al. (2005b). The first question which arises is whether there any patterns within the systems studied as to "when" refactoring is carried out. Figure 2 shows that for the Antlr system, the majority of refactorings happen at versions 2-3 and 3-4. It is noticeable that some refactorings (particularly inheritance-based refactorings) are few and far between. Figure 3 for the same system shows the same trend for the HSQLDB system and similarly for the JasperReports system in Figure 4. In each of the figures, there seems to be a trend of refactoring being undertaken at earlier stages of the system's life rather than at later versions.

Figure 5 shows the cumulative values of refactorings across time for all seven systems studied. It supports the results for the individual systems and shows that

Figure 2. Refactorings for the Antlr system across five versions

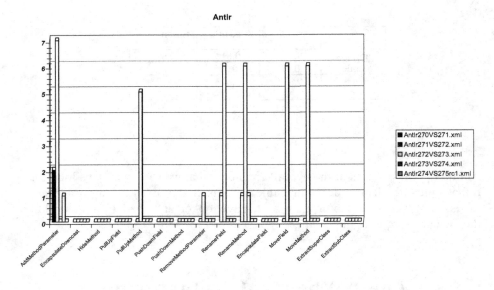

Figure 3. Refactorings for the HSQLDB system across four versions

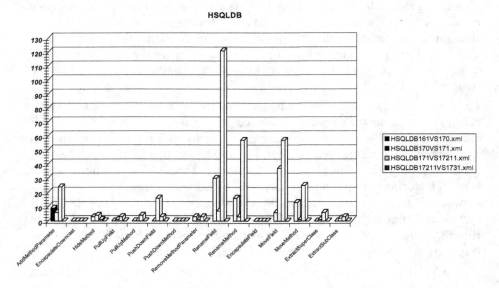

Figure 4. Refactorings for the JasperReports system across four versions

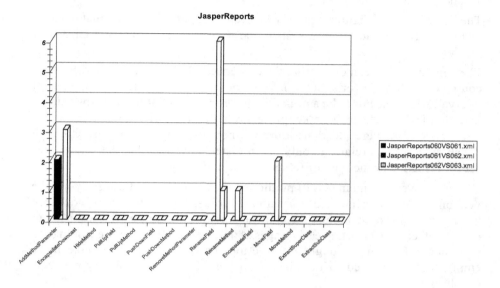

Figure 5. Refactorings across versions of the seven systems

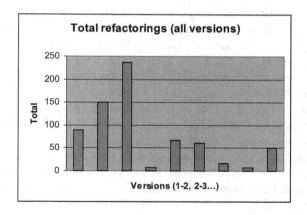

the bulk of refactorings tend to occur not at the earliest stages of a system, but around versions 2-3 and 3-4.

The evidence from Figures 2, 3, and 4 therefore supports the view that in terms of the need for refactoring, a system starts to degrade or decay after 3 or 4 versions.

The conclusion we can draw from the evidence in Figures 2, 3, 4, and 5 is that contrary to what Fowler states would be the best time to refactor (at constant intervals), there seems to be a peak around versions 3-4 for the systems studied in terms of when refactoring takes place. From Figure 5, it is also noticeable that after version 3-4, there is a dramatic drop in the number of refactorings. Although the study described relates to only seven systems, we feel that the results give useful evidence of the type of refactoring trends in systems.

Of course, we have no means of predicting the trend in refactoring beyond the versions studied, and it would be as unreasonable to suggest that there would not be any more peaks. Although the empirical evidence suggests that we need to devote refactoring efforts at early stages of the system's lifetime, we would urge consistent refactoring throughout the period of a system's life. Of course, more empirical studies need to be undertaken before we can draw any concrete conclusions.

Monitoring Growth

One of the key benefits of carrying out refactoring is reduced class complexity. For example, the motivation behind the "extract class" refactoring is that a class should be split into two classes because it is becoming too large to understand easily. In other words, the class is becoming too complex. One current issue is therefore that as a result of carrying out refactoring, we may well attain improved comprehension, but the difficulty arises when we try to measure that benefit. One conclusion is thus that if a class has zero attributes, then it affects the number of refactorings which can be carried out and also the means by which we can measure the outcome of any refactoring. One of the other key potential benefits of refactoring is a reduction post-refactoring in the number of lines of code. However, the lines of code added to a class together with the number of changes that have been applied to a class may give a good indication of the potential for refactoring.

A previous study by Bieman et al. (2003) investigated the hypothesis that large, object-oriented classes were more susceptible to change than smaller classes. The measure of change used in the study was the frequency with which the features of a class had been changed over a specific period of time. From a refactoring perspective, the frequency of class change in terms of its versions is of real value. However, since for any relatively simple refactoring, multiple classes may be changed without any net increase in class (and hence overall system) size, we contest that including number of added lines of code in the assessment gives a better impression of which classes are most volatile and hence more suitable candidates for refactoring.

We thus support the view that refactoring should be applied to classes with a high growth rate as well as a high change frequency. To support our investigation, data relating to changes from 161 Java classes were used as an empirical basis. Our results supported the conclusion of Bieman et al. (2003) relating to the change-proneness of large classes. Finally, we believe refactoring effort is most economically applied to classes which have both a high number of versions and a large increase in added lines of code over their lifetime. The "when" to refactor should be informed by sudden changes to the system.

A high frequency of changes made to an object-oriented class may suggest that the class was poorly written and hence required a large amount of maintenance effort applied to it. In a refactoring sense, frequency of change takes on a different meaning. It is thus likely that refactoring will not significantly increase the number of physical lines of code in the system since most refactorings require either modifications to current code or corresponding deletions for each insertion required by the refactoring. The extract class refactoring is one example where code is removed from one class to become a class in its own right without any significant net increase in system size. In the recent study by Bieman et al., number of class changes was used as the measure of change-proneness for five C++ systems. While we believe that there is merit in using number of changes as a measure of class volatility, we believe that classes which have had a large number of changes made to them (i.e., have many versions) and which have had significant numbers of lines of code added to them are better potential candidates for refactoring. A previous study by some of the authors collected the change data and growth in class size from one hundred and sixty one Java classes. It was found that much more information about the growth f the system could be gleaned by using both number of changes and changes in the lines of code in those classes. Basing the choice of classes for refactoring on alarming increases in class size supports the dictum of Beck which urges developers to refactor when the system tells them to, not through speculation alone.

Experimental Evidence

The obvious experimental means of establishing whether comprehension has improved is to carry out a formal experiment using developers, but any experiment is subject to certain threats to validity. For example, the level of

Table 7. Summary data for an empirical cohesion study

Position	Class Name	NCL	Position (Inexp,)	NMC
1.	ApplnDialog	0	7	5
2.	Alert	0	5	7
3.	Dialog	2	8	4
4.	CycleItem	0	2	14
5.	Arc	29	10	5
6.	Bitmap	0	3	22
7.	BagItem	3	1	11
8.	Assoc	3	4	11
9.	ArcList	47	9	9
10.	DDGNodePtrList	54	5	9

experience of the subjects used may influence the results. The measurement of experience is also itself subject to a range of criticisms.

Often, a refactoring is accompanied by a reduction in the number of lines of code. This was a feature of the refactoring undertaken as part of Najjar et al. (2003). The "replace constructors with factory methods refactoring" removed duplicate lines in constructors which had arisen due to code "bloat" (Fowler, 1999). However, the lines of code (LOC) metric has been subject to a range of criticisms (Rosenberg, 1997) and so any refactoring which reduces the number of LOC is subject to the same criticism.

Table 7 illustrates the role that size and, in this case, comment lines can have on the perception of cohesion by subjects taking part in a controlled experiment (Counsell et al., 2005). Twenty-four subjects with varying levels of experience were asked to rate on a scale 1-10 how cohesive they thought a set of ten C++ classes (10 represents the most cohesive class, and 1 the least cohesive). The 24 subjects were each given a set of the ten C++ class header files being analyzed. The ten classes were chosen at random from two industrial-sized C++ systems. The only restriction placed on the choice of these classes was that there had to be a relatively broad range of class size and make-up, but at the same time not too wide a range as to bias the outcome of the study.

Table 7 shows the "Position" of the classes in terms of the rating of cohesion by experienced subjects. Class ApplnDialog was thus rated the least cohesive and class ArcList the most cohesive. The Number of Comment Lines (NCL) in the class is followed by the position rated by subjects without experience. For example, class ApplnDialog was ranked the seventh most cohesive class. Class BagItem was rated most cohesive by subjects without experience. The number of methods in the class (NMC) also included in the table is a measure of the size of the class.

Table 7 also shows that classes with relatively larger numbers of comment lines were generally considered by the experienced subjects to be cohesive. The same is true of the inexperienced group. Clearly, the top two classes in terms of comment lines were ranked relatively highly in terms of their cohesion values (by the inexperienced group). This would seem to indicate that comment lines are an aid to the assessment of cohesion. However, in saying this, an allied factor (or even the critical factor) may be the low NAS values found for those classes.

In other words, on the one hand, size and growth are important in our determination of when to refactor, but there may be features which do not contribute to size necessarily, but yet are crucial to the mechanics of most refactorings (i.e., coupling). In the next section we describe a previous analysis carried out to see if, in an empirical sense, one refactoring triggers other refactorings.

A Dependency Analysis

As part of our refactoring research, we developed a dependency diagram which showed the inter-relationships between the 72 refactorings originally stated by Fowler. The diagram was developed by hand using Fowler's text as a basis. As a result of producing this graph, it becomes possible to see the likely implications of undertaking a specific refactoring in terms of how many other potential refactorings either *must* be carried out or *may* be carried out at the same time. In terms of the question about "when" and "what" to refactor, we must accept the possibility that one refactoring may embrace *n* other refactorings, and this would be an important consideration in the choice of both what and when to refactor.

For example, for the "Encapsulate Field" refactoring, Fowler (1998) himself suggests that one possible implication of the refactoring is that once he had completed encapsulate field he would look for methods that use the new methods (i.e., accessors needed for the encapsulated field) "to see whether they fancy packing their bags and moving to the new object with a quick Move Method" (p. 206).

The encapsulate field refactoring thus has only one possible "dependency." From a developer's point of view, the encapsulate field is an attractive and relatively easy refactoring to complete. The "add parameter" refactoring falls into the same category as the encapsulate field refactoring. It does not need to use any other refactorings. The only other refactoring that it may consider using is the "introduce parameter object" refactoring where groups of parameters which naturally go together are replaced by an object.

The extract subclass refactoring, on the other hand, requires the use of six (possible) other refactorings, two of which are mandatory. It has to use "push

Table 8. Breakdown of related refactorings from study in Advani et al. (2005b)

Refactoring Type	1-2	2-3	3-4	4-5	5-6	6-7	7-8	8-9	9-10
Pull Up Field	0	1	7	0	2	4	0	0	0
Extract Superclass	0	2	10	0	8	1	0	0	2
Extract Subclass	0	2	3	0	1	0	0	0	0
Pull Up Method	0	9	17	0	24	5	0	0	10
Rename Method	19	15	71	6	16	21	1	2	16
Rename Field	31	22	137	0	2	5	1	1	10

down method" and "push down field" as part of its mechanics. It *may* (under certain conditions) also need to use the "rename method," "self encapsulate field," "replace constructor with factory method," and "replace conditional with polymorphism" refactorings. The extract superclass refactoring requires a similar number of refactorings to be considered. In fact, for most of the refactorings involving a restructuring of the inheritance hierarchy, the mechanics are lengthy (requiring many steps and testing along the way).

Connections Between Refactorings

One explanation for the result found in Advani et al. (2005b) (i.e., the high values for simple refactorings and the low values for more "complex" refactorings) could be attributed to the relative effort required in terms of activities required to complete the refactoring. The testing effort of more complex refactorings has also to be considered; the more changes made as part of the refactoring then other things remaining equal, the more testing would be required.

In terms of whether refactorings are somehow linked, we can see from Table 8 that when the extract superclass refactoring is evident, the pull up method is also a feature for those versions. The mechanics of the extract superclass refactoring insist that pull up method is part of that refactoring. Equally, there seems to be evidence of pull up field for the same refactoring, also a part of the extract superclass refactoring. Rename field and method also seem to feature when extract superclass is carried out; rename method (but not rename field) play an important role in the extract superclass refactoring. The rename field refactoring is not specified in Fowler's text. This is interesting since it suggests that may be some effects of refactoring which aren't covered by the refactoring according to Fowler.

Extract subclass also requires use of the rename method refactoring, which may explain the high numbers for that refactoring. To try and explain the high numbers of rename field refactoring, one theory may be that developers automatically change the name of fields when methods are "pulled up" (in keeping with the corresponding change of method name). A conclusion that we can draw is that there may well be relationships between some of the fifteen refactorings in line with the mechanics specified by (Fowler, 1999). However, we suggest that most of the simple refactorings were not as part of any larger refactoring, based on the very low number of "larger" refactorings. When considering refactoring, we have to understand the implications of carrying out what may appear to be a straightforward refactoring. In the next section, we summarize and distill the heuristics that the previous two sections have presented.

Summary of Heuristics

In the third and fourth sections, we identified a number of experiments and empirical studies as a means of demonstrating firstly, what should be refactored and secondly, when refactoring should be undertaken. A number of key indicators were identified as a result, most based on data from those studies. In this section, we summarize and distill the heuristics and metrics identified in the third and fourth sections. We begin by proposing six heuristics which we feel could be applied in a refactoring sense.

Heuristics

The first heuristic that we propose is *Look at the trends in class features and class dependencies of your system before you attempt any refactoring.* Many systems have evolved to contain very few of the features that lend themselves to refactoring. For example, the relatively low number of attributes, severely restricting the possibility of refactorings related to attributes. The same can be said of key classes, that is, those classes which have many dependencies. Care should be exercised in any refactoring because of the potential for mistakes.

The second heuristic that we propose is *Accept that automation is realistic for a relatively small subset of refactorings. Many of the more complex refactorings can only be achieved manually with tool support.* The example which we used was that of the Substitute Algorithm refactoring. Identifying what code has been changed and how is best undertaken manually. Tools can help, but only as support.

The third heuristic that we propose is *Within an inheritance hierarchy, dependencies of descendent class should be a prime consideration in making any refactoring decision.* Many of the relatively simple refactorings proposed by Fowler are complicated by the need to account for affected classes in the inheritance hierarchy.

The fourth heuristic that we propose is *Coupling (rather than cohesion) should be the feature of a class we aim to optimise.* Cohesion is a subjective concept and for any refactoring, we should try to eliminate where possible any subjectivity.

The fifth heuristic that we propose is *Consistent effort should be applied to the refactoring process whenever possible; growth of the system should also be monitored.* Despite the fact that empirical evidence suggests a surge in refactorings at version 3-4 of a system, we would encourage a smooth and consistent use of refactoring techniques.

Finally, we propose that: *When considering any refactoring, we need to appreciate that other refactorings may also be necessary due to a dependency between refactorings.* There is some empirical evidence of a nesting of refactorings; this may have implications for the cost both in time and financially of making a refactoring change.

Metrics

From the analysis of the different empirical studies, and in the same sense that we proposed heuristics for refactoring, we can propose six metrics which would provide the refactorer with an indication of "what" to refactor and "when" to refactor. These can be summarized as:

1. The number of attributes (public, private and protected)
2. The number of methods (public, private and protected)
3. Number of descendents of a class in the inheritance hierarchy
4. Number of classes to which a particular class is coupled
5. Changes in LOC to classes
6. Changes in "the number of changes" applied to a class

Interestingly, the set of six metrics include both product metrics, aimed at the static program code (metrics 1-4) and process metrics, aimed at what happens to the program over its lifetime (metrics 5-6). We note also that the metrics should be used in combination and not in isolation. For example, metrics 1 and 2 are very often related in terms of refactoring mechanics. Metric 4 includes inheritance coupling (metric 3), and as we suggested in the fourth section, metrics 5 and 6 should both be used to target classes growing at a relatively higher rate than other classes. Finally, the existence of key classes (the third section) embraces and requires the monitoring of all six metrics. (It is noteworthy that metrics 2-4 have corresponding equivalents in the C&K set of metrics and metric 1 is used in the computation of the LCOM metric, also of C&K.) In the next section, we point to future directions in the refactoring sense.

Future Directions

Some of the issues outlined in previous sections have tended to cast doubt on the viability of certain refactorings. Some have shown how quantitative and qualitative benefits can accrue from undertaking refactorings. Some of the issues have shown that we should focus on the coupling levels of the classes as a mechanism for deciding whether to refactor or not. The first area which the refactoring area could benefit from is a series of tools to guide the refactoring process. These tools should indicate the quantitative and qualitative effects of carrying out that refactoring in terms of other refactorings also applicable; simulating the effect and mechanics would provide the developer with valuable information about the structure and state of the application being considered. Software metrics could be used at each stage of the refactoring mechanics to inform any such decision. This may help in the quest for "what" to refactor. The metrics which guide this process would need to be chosen carefully, however.

In terms of when to refactor, we would envisage that useful future research would be to investigate the key indicators which would help the development staff to know that refactoring is overdue. For example, if a subset of classes appears to require a disproportionate amount of maintenance effort then this should be a warning signal to the development staff.

In terms of *whether* to refactor (are the costs outweighed by the benefits?), a significant piece of research, already started by the authors, and a relatively short-term future direction would be to identify the relationships between the different refactorings (including those herein) and the occurrence of faults. In other words, is there a correlation between, let us say, the changes made to method signatures and consequent occurrence of faults directly related to that change? This research could lead to a refactoring order which states the relative possibility of faults arising should a particular refactoring be made. On the other hand, it may also indicate typical areas for refactoring effort to be directed and invested.

A further future direction would be use of appropriate intelligent data analysis techniques for simplifying computationally difficult problems. Identification of many of the more complex refactorings, for example, the Substitute Algorithm refactoring (third section) are very difficult to automate; they would require some form of heuristic search to be tackled effectively. Future research could investigate the potential for applying the different algorithms in a refactoring sense. Such techniques may also be able to provide predictive features for estimating the likely impact of undertaking a single or combination of refactorings. Use of simulation techniques may also be a fruitful research topic in this context for demonstrating the benefits of refactoring. Software metrics could play a key role in this sense.

This chapter has used a series of ongoing experiments and empirical studies as a basis of many of its claims. Finally, an important direction which the empirical research community should take in the future is thus to build up a body of experimental knowledge from which we can learn about refactoring (in general), the possibilities for applying new refactorings and the dissemination of information about refactoring. This knowledge should form a freely-available repository of data and other resources to inform the process of what and when to refactor.

Conclusion

In this chapter, we have tried to show how empirical studies have informed our understanding of refactoring. More empirical studies of various types need to be undertaken to build up a body of knowledge about refactoring before any conclusions can be drawn. We have also not included in this chapter any discussion about the role and relationship that refactoring has with the occurrence of faults. In other words, does *not* undertaking certain types of refactoring cause faults to arise? Equally, does refactoring uncover faults through the extra testing necessary as part of the refactoring mechanics?

In this chapter, we have also hypothesized on a number of occasions that developer habits may cause systems to deteriorate such that refactoring is then necessary. Future research directions may also include an analysis of developer habits as a good indication of where systems are beginning to decay. We have also described some of the current open issues in the field of refactoring. We have investigated the features of refactoring and looked at the area from two perspectives. Firstly, we attempted to answer the question of "what" to refactor and looked at a number of issues from an empirical viewpoint which either lend themselves or do not lend themselves to refactoring. We have also investigated the question of "when" to refactor. Secondly, we have shown that empirical evidence suggests that refactoring is done in bursts towards the start of the system's lifetime, rather than as Fowler suggests that refactoring needs constant and consistent effort.

Finally, the question which we haven't been able to answer in this chapter is the relationship between refactorings as we've described them and the wide range of other changes made to software as part of the run-of-the-mill maintenance process. This could be an interesting area of potential research, not least because of the discussion on the link between certain refactorings in the previous section.

The key conclusions from this chapter are that we need a good understanding of the features and trends in systems at different levels of detail before we should attempt refactoring. The decision on which refactorings to carry out also needs to be planned carefully since they will require significant effort both in their mechanics and subsequent testing effort. We also feel that development staff should "listen" to the system and use metrics to provide information on what is happening to a system and hence inform the refactoring process. Ultimately, we would want to minimize the amount of time developers spend carrying out maintenance. Although refactoring takes time and effort, the general consensus is that effort expended in the short-term will provide real benefits in the long-term.

References

Advani, D., Hassoun, Y., & Counsell, S. (2005a). *Heurac: A heuristic-based tool for extracting refactoring data from open-source software versions* (Tech. Rep. No. BBKCS-05-03-01). SCSIS-Birkbeck, University of London.

Advani, D., Hassoun, Y., & Counsell, S. (2005b). *Refactoring trends across N versions of N Java open source systems: An empirical study* (Tech. Rep. No. BBKCS-05-03-02). SCSIS-Birkbeck, University of London.

Arsenovski, D. (2004). Refactoring — elixir of youth for legacy VB code. Retrieved April 15, 2006, from *http://www.codeproject.com/vb/net/ Refactoring_elixir.asp*

Bansiya, J., Etzkorn, L., Davis, C., & Li, W. (1999, January) A class cohesion metric for object-oriented designs. *Journal of Object-Oriented Programming,* 47-52.

Beck, K. (2000). *Extreme programming explained: Embrace change.* Boston: Addison-Wesley.

Bieman, J., Straw, G., Wang, H., Munger, P. W., & Alexander, R. (2003, September 3-5). Design patterns and change proneness: An examination of five evolving systems. In *Proceedings of the 9th International Software Metrics Symposium (Metrics 2003)*, Sydney, Australia (pp. 40-49).

Bieman, J., & Ott., L. (1994). Measuring functional cohesion. *IEEE Transactions on Software Engineering, 20*(8), 644-657.

Briand, L., Bunse, C., & Daly, J. (2001). A controlled experiment for evaluating quality guidelines on the maintainability of object-oriented designs. *IEEE Transactions on Software Engineering, 27*(6), 513-530.

Briand, L., Daly, J., & Wust, J. (1998). A unified framework for cohesion measurement in object-oriented systems. *Empirical Software Engineering Journal, 3*(1), 65-117.

Briand, L., Devanbu, P., & Melo, W. (1997, May 17-23). An investigation into coupling measures for C++. In *Proceedings of the 19th International Conference on Software Engineering (ICSE 97)*, Boston (pp. 412-421).

Chidamber, S. R., & Kemerer, C. F. (1994). A metrics suite for object-oriented design. *IEEE Transactions on Software Engineering, 20*(6), 467-493.

Counsell, S., Hassoun, Y., Johnson, R., Mannock, K., & Mendes, E. (2003, June16-18). Trends in Java code changes: The key identification of refactorings. In *Proceedings of the ACM 2nd International Conference on the Principles and Practice of Programming in Java*, Kilkenny, Ireland (pp. 45-48).

Counsell, S., Loizou, G., Najjar, R., & Mannock, K. (2002a). On the relationship between encapsulation, inheritance and friends in C++ software. In *Proceedings of the International Conference on Software System Engineering and Its Applications (ICSSEA'02)*, Paris.

Counsell, S., Swift, S., & Mendes, E. (2002b). Comprehension of object-oriented software cohesion: The empirical quagmire. In *Proceedings of the IEEE International Workshop on Program Comprehension* (pp. 27-29), Paris, France.

Counsell, S., Swift, S., & Tucker, A. (2005). *Subject perceptions of object-oriented cohesion: An empirical study* (Tech. Rep. No. BBKCS-05-03-03). SCSIS-Birkbeck, University of London.

Demeyer, S., Ducasse, S., & Nierstrasz, O. (2000, Ocotober 15-19). Finding refactorings via change metrics. In *Proceedings of the ACM Conference on Object-oriented Programming Systems Languages and Applications (OOPSLA)*, Minneapolis, MN (pp. 166-177).

El Emam, K., Benlarbi, S., Goel, N., Melo, W., Lounis, H., & Rai, S. N. (2002). The optimal class size for object-oriented software. *IEEE Transactions on Software Engineering, 28*(5), 494-509.

Fenton, N., & Pfleeger, S. (1996). *Software metrics: A rigorous and practical approach.* London: Thomson International Publishing.

Foote, B., & Opdyke, W. (1995). Life cycle and refactoring patterns that support evolution and reuse. In J. O. Coplien & D. C. Schmidt (Eds.), *Pattern languages of programs.* Boston: Addison-Wesley.

Fowler, M. (1999). *Refactoring (improving the design of existing code).* Addison-Wesley.

Harrison, R., Counsell, S., & Nithi, R. (2000). Experimental assessment of the effect of inheritance on the maintainability of object-oriented systems. *Journal of Systems and Software, 52,* 173-179.

Hitz, M., & Montazeri, B. (1996). Chidamber and Kemerer's metrics suite: A measurement theory perspective. *IEEE Transactions on Software Engineering, 11*(4), 267-271.

Johnson, R., & Foote, B. (1998, June-July). Designing reusable classes. *Journal of Object-Oriented Programming, 1*(2), 22-35.

Kerievsky, J. (2002). Refactoring to patterns, industrial logic. Retrieved April 15, 2006, from *http://www.industriallogic.com*

Najjar, R., Counsell, S., & Loizou, G. (2005). *Encapsulation and the vagaries of a simple refactoring: An empirical study* (Tech. Rep. No. BBKCS-05-03-02). SCSIS-Birkbeck, University of London.

Najjar, R., Counsell, S., Loizou, G., & Mannock, K. (2003, March 26-28). The role of constructors in the context of refactoring object-oriented software. In *Proceedings of the Seventh European Conference on Software Maintenance and Reengineering (CSMR '03),* Benevento, Italy (pp. 111-129).

Opdyke, W. (1992). *Refactoring object-oriented frameworks.* PhD thesis, University of Illinois.

Ostrand, T., Weyuker, E., & Bell, R. (2004, July 11-14). Where the bugs are. In *Proceedings of the ACM SIGSOFT International Symposium on Software Testing and Analysis* (pp. 86-96), Boston.

Pressman, R. (2005). *Software engineering: A practitioner's approach* (6th ed.). Maidenhead, UK: McGraw-Hill.

Rosenberg, J. (1997, November 5-7). Some misconceptions about lines of code. In *Proceedings of the 4th IEEE International Software Metrics Symposium,* Albuquerque, New Mexico (pp. 137-142).

Tokuda, L., & Batory, D. (2001). Evolving object-oriented designs with refactorings. *Automated Software Engineering, 8,* 89-120.

Chapter IX

A Survey of Object-Oriented Design Quality Improvement

Juan José Olmedilla, Almira Lab, Spain

Abstract

The use of object-oriented (OO) architecture knowledge such as patterns, heuristics, principles, refactorings and bad smells improve the quality of designs, as Garzás and Piattini (2005) state in their study; according to it, the application of those elements impact on the quality of an OO design and can serve as basis to establish some kind of software design improvement (SDI) method. But how can we measure the level of improvement? Is there a set of accepted internal attributes to measure the quality of a design? Furthermore, if such a set exists will it be possible to use a measurement model to guide the SDI in the same way software processimprovement models (Humphrey, 1989; Paulk, Curtis, Chrissis, & Weber, 1993) are guided by process metrics (Fenton & Pfleeger, 1998)? Since (Chidamber & Kemerer, 1991) several OO metrics suites have been proposed to measure OO properties, such as encapsulation, cohesion, coupling and abstraction, both in designs and in code, in this chapter we review the literature to find out to which high level quality properties are mapped and if an OO design evaluation model has been formally proposed or even is possible.

Introduction

In the last two decades there has been a growing interest and effort put after the idea of improving the quality of the software processes (Humphrey, 1989). This increasing trend had it origin in the application of statistical process control techniques (Oakland, 1990) from the manufacturing industry to our sector, thus creating a new discipline that has been called software process improvement (SPI) (Humphrey, Snyder & Willis, 1991). This discipline aids organisations to improve their software producing processes by, firstly, identifying all the broad areas of the process, their goals and the activities and sub-activities needed to achieve them and secondly by establishing a path through which the process can be incrementally improved, this path is a set of quality levels, each of them defined by the areas and their associated goals to be accomplished. Fundamental to the SPI are the associated metrics (Fenton & Pfleeger, 1998) that are the tool by which the organisation can tell at each moment where it is in the path, each of the aforementioned goals has an associated set of metrics that help to tell if it has been achieved and to what extent. Although there are alternative SPI models and methods, like CMMI (Paulk et al., 1993) or SPICE (ISO/IEC, 1999), an organisation can always adhere to a concrete definition of process quality and a way to measure it and improve it.

However the product arena does not seem to be so established in terms of quality improvement models. A fundamental question that managers and developers often face is when it is worth to improve a software product by reengineering it or on the contrary start it all over from scratch. Fowler (2000) states that

There are times when the existing code is such a mess that although you could refactor it, it would be easier to start from the beginning ... I admit that I don't really have good guidelines for it. (p. 66)

In this case Fowler was talking about the refactoring technique but something similar can be said about other OO design knowledge elements. There is plenty of knowledge, more or less formalised, about identifying situations in which to apply an specific design improvement (Brown, Malveau, Brown, McCormick & Mowbray, 1998; Fowler, 2000; Gamma, Helm, Johnson & Vlissides, 1995; Riel, 1996), but is there a formal method to know which design transformations should be applied first or are more important? Is it possible to establish which design transformations, pattern applications, refactorings, and so forth, are more important in a certain quality level?

An organisation or a project could be interested in attaining only a moderate quality level that is acceptable for the time being and it is foreseeable that will consume only a limited amount of resources. Such an organisation could be interested in a guide that tells what quality indicators are really crucial to that quality level, to what extent, in terms of a measurable quantity, how to measure them and which design transformation affect the properties object of the measurements.

First of all it would be necessary to define what is design quality, by identifying what general properties or high level indicators comprise it; second, to organise those indicators in sets that constitute an incremental ladder of quality, so that depending on the situations, the (non-functional requirements and the resources a designer can choose the target level for his or her design; thirdly, choose the metrics that help in the assessment of the goals accomplishment; and finally, define the OO knowledge elements that apply in each case. We are talking here about something that we could call an *OO design maturity model* that would help designers to assess and improve a design before having to implement it.

Product quality has been defined in ISO 9126 (ISO/IEC, 2001) by external and internal attributes that describe the quality of the final software product and its intermediate subproducts, such as design; according to that, design quality should be measured through internal attributes that will predict, somehow, the final outcome of the external attributes. Some authors (Bansiya & Davis, 2002; Basili, Briand & Melo, 1996) have proposed numerical relations between some internal quality attributes and general OO properties, such as coupling or cohesion, for which there are already defined metrics. Other authors (Miller, Hsia & Kung) have proposed directly to measure the levels of accomplishment of certain OO knowledge elements like design principles, using some of the existing OO metrics and map them to internal quality attributes. If the first approach was used then it would be necessary to establish how much each OO knowledge element impacts each OO property or, at least, know what design transformations are directed to which properties and re-measure after applying them and repeat the process until the level of quality is reached (see Figure 1). This chapter will review the state of the art to see whether there is an accepted set of internal quality properties as high level indicators or goals for the assessment of OO micro architecture design quality and if there are already assessment models that map metrics, OO properties and these high level indicators. A secondary objective of the review is the identification of what role the OO knowledge

Figure 1. Measurement and improvement model for object-oriented design

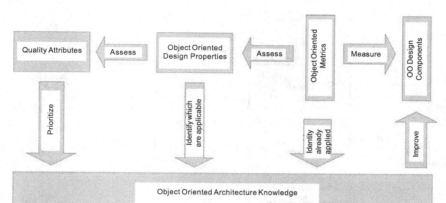

elements play in the assessment. There might be evaluation models based on the detection of the elements in the design so that they will not only be part of the improvement model but also of the appraisal. The sources of review will be journals, transactions, conference proceedings, and other periodicals published in the main areas of knowledge affected by this study which are object orientation design, metrics, and software maintenance.

In the next section a background on software product quality and OO metrics and OO knowledge will be presented, the method followed to perform the review will be explained one section later and the results exposed along with critical comments on the most relevant studies, and conclusions will be drawn in the closing section.

Background

Software Product Quality

Quality can be measured at a process or product level, although there are obvious relationships among them, as Figure 2 illustrates. There are other quality aspects besides those two but are not of interest to us. ISO/IEC has issued two standards that refer to software product and process quality respectively, ISO 14598 (ISO/IEC, 1999) and ISO 9126. As is usual with these kind of standards the authors do not give an explicit assessment methodology nor do they give guidelines to

Figure 2. Quality in the software lifecycle

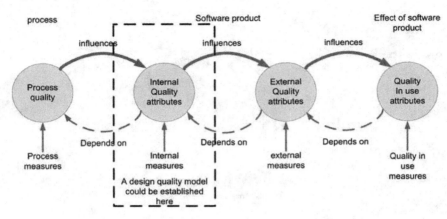

achieve quality through specific software processes or development methodologies. Rather they simply put in places what is understood by quality, in terms of attributes that must be measured, in each of the cases. The CMMI model connects with ISO 14598 in being a classification of maturity levels in the software process and giving a set of specific guidelines to assess and evaluate the quality of a software process.

ISO 9126 states that software product quality can be evaluated by measuring internal attributes, or by measuring external attributes; the former are obtained through metrics defined on intermediate products, such as design, and the latter are based on the behavior of the final executing code. It also takes in account "quality in use" which deals with the perspective of behavioral quality of the finished product in a speciûc environment under a user's perspective. In both cases, internal and external, quality is defined as a set of six characteristics:

- **Functionality:** The capability of the software product to provide functions which meet stated and implied needs when the software is used under specified conditions.

- **Reliability:** The capability of the software product to maintain a specified level of performance when used under specified conditions.

- **Usability:** The capability of the software product to be understood, learned, used, and attractive to the user, when used under specified condition.

- **Efficiency:** The capability of the software product to provide appropriate performance, relative to the amount of resources used, under stated conditions.

Figure 3. ISO 9126 Quality characteristics and sub-characteristics

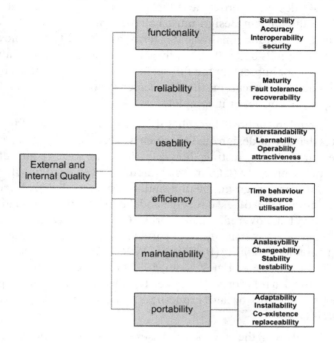

- **Maintainability:** The capability of the software product to be modified. Modifications may include corrections, improvements or adaptation of the software to changes in environment, and in requirements and functional specifications.

- **Portability:** The capability of the software product to be transferred from one environment to another.

These characteristics are general for any kind of software product and being object-oriented or structured does not affect the choice of characteristics, although it will affect the way to measure them. These characteristics are further divided in subcharacteristics as shown in Figure 3. But we are centered in the design quality in early stages of the development cycle and certain attributes in that list, apparently, should not be addressed yet. Let us see which of them are addressable at the design stage and which are not:

- The correct coverage of all user requirements should be addressed in previous phases of the life cycle, such as analysis, and verified during testing; therefore, it is logical to suppose that the quality of a design should not be measured by the functionality attribute, as defined in ISO 9126. In fact the OO design improvement techniques always state that to apply them, first the current design must behave "mostly" correctly (Fowler, 2000) (in terms of functionality and in terms of reliability). But how can we decide if a design is better than another, for the same requirements? If one of them does not implement the full set of requirements as described in the corresponding specifications then the design is not "worse" than the other, it is simply not correct or incomplete.

- Again we tend to suppose that reliability should not be one of the internal attributes that define design quality, given that reliability has been traditionally measured during testing; however, McCabe (1976) introduced the cyclomatic complexity (CC) metric which has been used to calculate, for a given, software program, the minimum set of tests that are necessary to ensure a certain level of test coverage and therefore a prediction of the ratio of defects yet uncovered. Later works (Chidamber & Kemerer, 1991) created equivalent metrics for OO software and there are certain studies that try to predict reliability (Basili et al., 1996; Briand, Wust, Daly, & Victor Porter, 2000; Brito e Abreu & Melo, 1996) from design. These and other works[1] establish a relationship between the complexity, as an OO property, and the defect density or fault prone-ness, which we interpret as synonyms for reliability.

- Usability deals with the way the final user feels about the finished product. No evidence was found in the sense of establishing usability as an internal attribute for design quality. Understandability is mentioned in the literature (Bansiya & Davis, 2002; Deligiannis, Shepperd, Roumeliotis, & Stamelos, 2003; Dumke & Kuhrau, 1994) as a desired property to have in a design. However, it is more than arguable that it refers to the ISO 9126 sub-characteristic of usability, and it must be understood as "analysability." However, other voices (Fowler, 2000) claim that the "user" of a design is not the same as the user of the ûnal product. He or she could be the developer that has to implement the specified design, or that same designer (or other) in the future when a new feature has to be introduced in the system or the design must be modified for whatever reason, the latter case is already contained under "maintainability," but the former is not so clear.

- Efficiency is divided into "time behavior" and "resource utilisation" which has made this attribute a clear measuring target in the testing phases; however, there are proposals, mostly in the real-time systems area, to measure efficiency, usually addressed as "performance," early in the design stage. This could be a good candidate quality attribute for a higher level of design quality and not for a basic one. Making an OO design more understandable by, for instance, introducing patterns, introduces indirections which in turn penalises performance, so it looks like they are opposite. However if a design is more understandable thanks to being decomposed in more entities, that allows a better isolation and identification of those spots where most of the performance issues tend to be (Fowler, 2000).

- Maintainability is a clear focus of most of the OO knowledge dedicated to improve designs as we will see, this is intuitive since most design efforts in OO paradigm are centred around ideas such as data hiding, encapsulation and abstraction which enhance a better understand ability (analysability) through domain concept representation, separation of components in testable units, and so forth.

- Portability looks completely out of the scope of the design stage since the design must remain conceptually separated from the actual implementation environment. In any case, we have not found sufficient evidence to support that this attribute is important, quality wise, during early design phases.

In Bansiya & Davis (2002), a set of six design quality attributes are derived from ISO 9126 quality characteristics, although they are not taken exactly but rather adapted to the particularity of design. Two are discarded as not measurable in design, two are changed for equivalent ones, and two are added from general concepts present in software design literature.

These quality attributes are abstract concepts and, therefore, not directly observable, so we need some properties that can be observed and quantified and that are particular of object-oriented design. In many of the OO metrics suites the speciûc metrics are implicitly mapped to general design properties as cohesion, coupling, encapsulation, complexity, and inheritance, although not all of them are specific to OO design and could be applied to modular design as well. Measurements are proposed in different works for those properties and in some cases there is an explicit mapping from the former to the latter, as in Bansiya & Davis (2002) where each design property is measured by a single metric. In Miller et al. (1999), 11 properties were chosen. In fact, object-oriented design principles, which according to Garzás and Piattini (2005) are part of the OO architecture knowledge, as we previously said, and five measurements, all of them at class level, are used to assess their degree of fulfillment. On the contrary, Bansiya and Davis (2002) choose not only classes but also class attributes, methods, and packages.

A very sound set of object-oriented design properties could be:

- Design size
- Hierarchies
- Abstraction

Table 1. Measurable entities in design and their attributes

Entity	Attribute
Association	Size
Attribute	Position
Class	Abstractness
	Behavior
	Comments
	Effort
	Interaction
	Interface
	Performance
	Position
	Reuse
	Size
	Structure
Hierarchy	Structure
Link	Arity
Method	Abstractness
	Effort
	Interaction
	Interface
	Performance
	Position
	Reuse
	Size
	Structure
Package	Abstractness
	Interaction
	Size
	Structure
Parameter	Size
Scenario	Size
System	Behavior
	Change
	Comments
	Dynamics
	Effort
	Interface
	Performance
	Requirements
	Reuse
	Size
	Structure
Use case	Interface
	Size
	structure

- Encapsulation
- Coupling
- Cohesion
- Composition
- Inheritance
- Polymorphism
- Messaging
- Complexity

But these quality attributes and OO design properties must be measured on specific components or entities of the design (see Figure 1), thus it is important to define what a design is or what components are in a design susceptible to be measured. Purao and Vaishnavi (2003) survey product metrics for OO systems and propose a framework and a formalism, according to which, the product goes through different "states" during the development process and in each of them different components that he calls "entities," are produced or modified. In his work, Purao, reviewed all the different metrics suites to see what entities where measured in each state and gathered an extensive set of which we only recall here those in the design state, along with the their attributes (see Table 1).

Object-Oriented Metrics

We are going to present a summary of the most important object-oriented metrics and identify which OO properties they can measure.

Chidamber and Kemerer's Metrics Suite

Chidamber and Kemerer (C&K henceforth) first proposed in 1991 a suite of six metrics. All except one were applied to the class entity and measured complexity, coupling, cohesion, inheritance, and messaging (see Table 2).

Henderson-Sellers Metrics

Another important suite was given by Henderson-Sellers, Constantine, and Graham (1996) but it was related to coupling and cohesion. Only AID (average

Table 2. Metrics of the C&K suite

Metric	Definition	Properties
Weighted methods per class (WMC)	Consider a class C_1 with methods $M_1, M_2, ..., M_n$. Let $c_1, c_2, ..., c_n$ be the static complexity of the methods. Then: $WMC = \sum_{i=1}^{n} c_i$ The static complexity can be measured in many ways, one of them being CC(McCabe, 1976).	Complexity
Depth of inheritance tree (DIT)	The DIT metric of a class A is its depth in the inheritance tree. If A is involved in a multiple inheritance the maximum length to the root of the tree will be the DIT.	Inheritance
Number of children (NOC)	NOC of a class is the number of immediate subclasses subordinated to a class in the class hierarchy.	Inheritance
Coupling between object classes (CBO)	CBO for a class is a count of the number of other classes to which is coupled. One class is coupled to another if it uses its methods or instance variables, excluding inheritance related couples.	Coupling
Response for a class (RFC)	$RFC = \|RS\|$ where RS is the response set for the class, given by $RS = \{M\} \bigcup_{all\ i} \{R_i\}$ where $\{R_i\} =$ set of methods called by method i and $\{M\}$ is the set of all methods in the class. The response set of a class is the set of all methods that can potentially be executed in response to a message received by an object of that class.	Messaging
Lack of cohesion in methods (LCOM)	Consider a Class C_i with n methods $M_1, M_2, ..., M_n$. Let $\{I_j\}$ be the set of instance variables used by method M_i. There are n such sets $\{I_1\}, ..., \{I_n\}$. Let $P = \{(I_i, I_j) \| I_i \cap I_j = \varnothing\}$ and $Q = \{(I_i, I_j) \| I_i \cap I_j \neq \varnothing\}$. If all n sets $\{I_1\}, ..., \{I_n\}$ are $\varnothing$ then let $P = \varnothing . LCOM = \|P\| - \|Q\|$, if $\|P\| > \|Q\|$ or 0 otherwise.	Cohesion

Table 3. Li and Henry's metrics

Metric	Definition	Properties
Message passing coupling (MPC)	MPC= the number of method invocations in a clas.s	Coupling/ Messaging
Data abstraction coupling (DAC)	The number of attributes in a class that have as their type another class.	Coupling/ Abstraction
SIZE1	It is a variation of traditional LOC (Lines of Code) defined specifically for the Ada language. We obviate its definition.	Design size
SIZE2	SIZE2 = number of attributes + number of local methods.	Design size

Table 4. Bansiya and Davis metric model

Metric	Definition	Properties
Design size of classes (DSC)	Total number of classes in the design	Design size
Number of hierarchies (NOH)	Number of class	Hierarchies
Average number of ancestors (ANA)	Average number of ancestors	Abstraction
Data access metric (DAM)	Ratio of the number of private (protected) attributes to the total number of attributes declared in the class	Encapsulation
Direct class coupling (DCC)	Count of different number of classes that a class is directly related to. The metric includes classes that are directly related by attribute declarations and message passing (parameters) in methods	Coupling
Cohesion among methods of class (CAM)	This metric computes the relatedness methods of a class based upon the parameter list of the methods. The metric is computed using the summation of the intersection of parameters of a method with the maximum independent set of all parameter types in the class.	Cohesion
Measure of aggregation (MOA)	This metric measures the extent of the part-whole relationship, realised by using attributes. The metric is a count of the number of data declarations whose types are user de?ned classes.	Composition
Measure of functional abstraction (MFA)	Ratio of the number of methods inherited by a class to the total number of methods accessible by member methods of the class	Inheritance
Number of polymorphic methods (NPM)	Number of methods that can exhibit polymorphic behaviour (virtual in C++ and non ?nal in Java)	Polymorphism
Class interface size (CIS)	Count of the number of public methods in a class	Messaging
Number of methods (NOM)	Count of methods de?ned in a class.	Complexity

inheritance depth of a class) was an Inheritance measure. AID was defined as zero, for a class without ancestors and the average AID of its parent classes increased by one.

Conclusion on Metrics

In Purao and Vaishnavi (2003) and Briand et al. (2000), a detailed listing of metrics is presented. An important conclusion drawn after reviewing these metrics is that, although they claim, in many cases, to be OO design metrics they are not since they need source code to be analysed or measure code size. Another important conclusion is that most metrics suites focus just in a very constrained set of properties, namely, coupling, cohesion and inheritance. There are some exceptions like Briand et al. (2000), which gives a set of metrics taken partly from previous suites that cover all properties considered in their assessment model.

Current State of the Art in Design Quality Assessment Models

Review Questions

The objective behind this review is to find out if there is any solid research to relate software design high level indicators with OO design knowledge (patterns, heuristics, bad smells, best practices, rules, and principles). The future trend of research, on the one hand, is to relate current (or new) OO metrics with ISO 9126 internal characteristics, or establish a new set if necessary, and see if they can be measured through them. On the other hand, we are after the relation between the application of OO knowledge and the impact of those metrics, and therefore, the quality characteristics.

The review tries to determine if this gap exists or not in the OO area of knowledge. We are constrained exclusively to the design phase and more specifically to OO micro architecture.[2] We are not interested in metrics or models for process quality, effort, estimation, or project tracking metrics. The area of research is always focused on metrics intended for design improvement.

The primary question of research is:

Research Question 1: *Are there object-oriented design quality assessment models that use a set of metrics, based only in design entities,[3] to measure levels of accomplishment in internal product quality attributes (as those in ISO 9126)? And what are those attributes or high level indicators?*

Needless to say, we are interested in quantified models, so that those metrics are numerically related to the characteristics, directly or through other numerical relations with intermediate elements, such as OO properties, which, on the other hand, is what is found in all cases as we have advanced in the Background section.

The secondary question of research is:

Research Question 2: *Do those models use any of the OO knowledge elements in Garzás & Piattini (2005) as part of that assessment model and how?*

This secondary question leads necessarily to models where there is a detection of those elements in the design by using speciûc metrics. Since the future work will establish a way to improve the design through the application of design transformations based on those knowledge elements, it is very useful to know in advance how much that will impact the desired quality attributes and if those transformations are already present in the design.

Review Methods

A systematic review protocol following Kitchenham (2004) was used. The sources consulted were all digital, and the intention was to cover as many periodicals and conference proceedings related with metrics, software quality, OO knowledge, and software maintenance as possible. The sources chosen were IEEE Digital Library, ACM Digital Library, Journal of Systems and Software (Elsevier), Journal of Software Maintenance and Evolution (Wiley) and Software Practice and experience (Wiley).

Our search strategy was to compose queries that included in different Boolean expressions the following terms:

- Object-oriented design
- Metrics
- Quality
- High level indicators
- Assessment
- Method
- Patterns
- Heuristics
- Bad smells
- Principles
- Rules
- Refactoring
- Lessons learned
- Best practice

Different synonyms were chosen for some of the above terms like assessment for which we chose "assess," "assessing," "evaluation," "evaluate," and "evaluating"; also, "method" had different synonyms. The singular was chosen as in "pattern" instead of "patterns" in order to obtain expressions that included both variations, since the first is a substring of the second. Different queries were created with these terms and executed in the search engines. However, some of them had to be expanded, like in the case of the Journal of Systems and Software given to obtain a decent set of results and afterwards the selection had to be manually reviewed to exclude publications that were completely out of the scope. Several different queries were tried in both engines and the search was broaden more than initially thought given the initial low number of results, for instance in IEEE Digital Library the following query was executed:

"(metrics<in>metadata)<and>(object-oriented design<in>metadata)." Surprisingly enough, this query threw only 62 results (in IEEE Digital Library) which was less than other more restrictive ones. One first conclusion of the first round of searches was that, although there are many metrics suites for OO systems there are very few centered exclusively in the design phase and using only design entities as the measurable elements.

Repetitions were taken out since there were references to the same study from different sources (i.e., from IEEE and ACM Digital Libraries), the same can be said about those studies that were different publications of the same work, where we always took the most recent one, as Kitchenham (2004) advises. Once repetitions were taken out 481 studies remained. After obtaining this initial list of results we did a quick review of abstracts when available or the introduction of the paper and directly discarded those elements not having to do with object-oriented metrics. After that initial review we did a more thorough review by reading one by one the publications and using the exclusion criteria explained in section "Included and excluded studies" to discard those not interesting to us. We recorded the reason for each discard whether it was in the first quick review or in the thorough one.

For the ones not discarded, that is, the primary sources object of our review, we recorded its type according to a set quality assessment levels suggested by Kitchenham (2004) according to the experimental data they included. The set of quality levels is given in Table 5.

Table 5. Quality levels for primary sources, as in Kitchenham (2004)

Level	Name	Description
1	Randomised trial	Evidence obtained from at least one properly-designed randomised controlled trial
2	Pseudo-randomised trial	Evidence obtained from well-designed pseudo-randomised controlled trials
3	Concurrent cohort	Evidence obtained from comparative studies with concurrent controls and allocation not randomised, cohort studies, case-control studies or interrupted time series with a control group.
4	Historical control	Evidence obtained from comparative studies with historical control, two or more single arm studies, or interrupted time series without a parallel control group
5	Randomised experiment	Evidence obtained from a randomised experiment performed in an artificial setting
6	Case series	Evidence obtained from case series, either post-test or pre-test/post-test
7	Pseudo-randomised experiment	Evidence obtained from a quasi-random experiment performed in an artificial setting
8	Expert opinion	Evidence obtained from expert opinion based on theory or consensus

Table 6. Summary of data collected

	Number of Studies			Accepted Studies		Primary Sources	
Total	Accepted	Discarded	Primary Sources	Secondary Sources	Full Model		Basic
481	58	423	23	35	4		19

After the review we could verify that all primary sources were below three (concurrent cohort). We decided not to establish a quality threshold and take into account all studies that passed the exclusion criteria regardless of their experimental (quality) level.

Included and Excluded Studies

The exclusion criteria used in the more thorough review were:

Exclusion criterion 1: *Study not focused on metrics for design improvement, like those too general and including effort and quality assurance.*

Exclusion criterion 2: *It does not propose an assessment model with quality attributes as target of the metrics*

Given the low number of studies (only 23) that passed the exclusion criteria we decided to record as well those studies that, not proposing a general assessment model, were focused on prediction of one or two quality attributes, recording those attributes as well.

Data Extraction

We were interested primarily in obtaining the high level indicators or internal quality attributes that could be utilised in a design improvement methodology, so we recorded all those indicators in the primary studies. We also recorded which of these studies, or "primary sources," were proposing an explicit model of assessment with a full mapping of metrics to intermediate properties and from there to high level indicators or attributes. Although the selected studies proposed a method for quality evaluation based on high level indicators and their associated metrics, only four of them proposed formally a complete mapping with explicit mappings or relations to the high level indicators, we called them "full models" (see Table 6). Later on we also recorded attributes for those discarded studies that were focused only on the prediction of one or two attributes, that we have indicated in Table 7 as "secondary sources"; in that table we can see all the indicators or attributes collected from both sources.

Table 7. Collected high level indicators

Property Name	Full Model	Primary Sources	Secondary Sources
Adaptability	0	1	0
Analysability	1	1	0
Change proneness	0	0	1
Changeability	1	2	3
Completeness	0	2	0
Complexity	0	3	0
Comprehensibility	1	1	0
Consistency	0	2	0
Correctness	0	2	0
Effectiveness	1	1	0
Efficiency	0	0	1
Extensibility	1	4	3
Flexibility	1	1	2
Functionality	1	1	0
Maintainability	1	10	10
Performance	1	2	0
Realisability	0	1	0
Reliability	0	4	9
Reusability	2	5	5
Security	0	1	0
Stability	1	1	2
Testability	1	5	2
Traceability	0	1	0
Unambiguity	0	1	0
Understandability	1	4	3
Usability	0	1	0
Verifiability	0	0	1

It can be observed that there are many attributes that are really synonyms, as for example analysability, comprehensibility, and understand ability. As we expected, maintainability is the most referred in both kinds of studies by itself or adding their subcharacteristics, analysability, comprehensibility, changeability, stability, and testability. On the other hand, it must be taken into account that all these attributes refer to design and that, for instance, "understandability" means in this context that the design is easily understandable by a software developer other than its author; therefore it must not be taken as the sub-characteristic beneath "usability" in ISO 9126.

Results: Description of Primary Studies and Findings

From the data obtained in Table 7 we can conclude that, for the so called *full models*, maintainability, counting its subcharacteristics, was the highest scoring quality attribute with a total of eight appearances. Maintainability is comprised of analysability, changeability, stability, and testability, and, in this context, an

Table 8. Use of OO knowledge in the four full models

	Principles	Patterns	Heuristics	Bad smells
Bansiya & Davis	No	No	No	No
Miller, Hsia & Kung	Yes	No	No	No
Barber & Graser	No	Indirectly	Yes	No
Marinescu & Ratiu	No	Partially	No	Yes

analysability, comprehensibility, and understandability are synonyms, or at least that was the semantic behind the word in the selected studies, and the same can be said about changeability, flexibility, and extensibility. Another important attribute or high level indicator is reusability.

In primary studies, those not stating explicit relation between OO properties and quality attributes, maintainability and reusability were the two most important indicators and reliability appears as the next one. In the secondary studies, reliability outperforms reusability. Apparently reliability and, in decreasing importance, performance and efficiency (and effectiveness as its synonym) take more importance as the studies try to predict a specific quality attribute instead of evaluating the overall quality.

Apparently, when trying to establish a quality evaluation method, reliability, defect proneness, and functional correctness and consistency are way less important than maintainability. On the other hand, there are many studies that try to predict and decrease defects early in the design phases. One possible interpretation is that quality evaluation methods, as we said before, are not seen as a replacement for software quality assurance and try to establish a way to measure and compare different designs that are semantically equivalent, that is, built for the same functional requirements, and mostly correct (defect-free).

Given the resulting figures, a statistical analysis was not considered relevant. Only four studies were considered relevant to our study and they will be summarised. In Table 8, a brief summary is shown about the use these studies make of the OO micro architecture knowledge; only those elements that have appeared in at least one of the studies is listed.

Bansiya and Davis's QMOOD

Bansiya and Davis (2002) propose a model for the assessment of high level design quality attributes in object-oriented designs called *quality model for object-oriented design* (QMOOD). It is decomposed in four levels, OO design components (level 4 or L_4), OO design metrics (level 3 or L_3), OO design properties (level 2 or L_2) and finally design quality attributes (level 1 or L_1), and links between adjacent levels, L_{34} (from L_3 to L_4), L_{23} (from L_3 to L_2) and L_{12} (from L_2 to L_1). This model is very similar to that depicted in Figure 1 and the quality attributes are taken partly from the ISO 9126 quality attributes: reusability, flexibility, understandability, functionality, extendability, and effectiveness.

In each of the links, Bansiya and Davis identify explicit relation between components of both levels, for L_{23} the mapping is exactly one to one, one metric for each of the properties (design size, hierarchies, abstraction, encapsulation, coupling, cohesion, composition, inheritance, polymorphism, messaging, and complexity), and in L_{12} the mapping is even more explicit because each quality attribute (from ISO 9126) is the result of the sum of each of the calculated metrics multiplied by its weight, for instance, Reusability equals 0.25*Coupling +0.25*Cohesion+ 0.5*Messaging +0.5*Design Size.

The weights can be positive or negative and were calculated somehow intuitively; in fact, the study states that the weights, as well as other mappings, can be changed to reflect the goals of the organisation.

On the other hand, relative importance of each quality attribute is not stated and is left to the designer's decision.

Finally, there is no use in the model of OO knowledge such as design patterns, principles, refactorings, or other such elements.

Miller, Hsia and Kung OO Architecture Measures

Miller, Hsia, and Kung (1999) define an OO architecture quality measurement method that fills, in a way, the gap that Bansiya and Davis had. They use quantitatively OO architecture knowledge, in the form of well known principles. Again there are defined design components, metrics (they call them measurements) and OO principles; they substitute the OO properties for these latter. Unfortunately, they stop there, not quantifying the impact of those principles in general quality attributes; in fact, they do not identify quality attributes or refer to ISO 9126, although they give high importance to the extendability, flexibility, and maintainability of the architecture.

The design components they use are hierarchies, relationship, classes, methods, and attributes (they call the operations) but in defining how to obtain the measures, they give a high importance to operations, and the impact on all of the measures. Their measurements are class abstractness, hierarchy chain brittleness, class abstraction cohesion, pure inheritance index, and relationship abstraction index. As for the principles used: open-closed, Liskov substitution, dependency inversion, interface segregation, reuse/release equivalency, common closure, common reuse, stable abstractions, least astonishment, deep abstract hierarchies, and Demeter (see Miller et al., 1999 for references).

In summary, this study is not really a quality evaluation model since it does not calculate (explicitly) internal or external software quality attributes. It does not use general OO properties either but it is interesting because it uses some OO knowledge in a quantitative way.

Barber and Graser's RARE

Barber and Graser's (2000) study is not, strictly speaking, a quality evaluation model or method but a tool for creating evaluation models by specifying which quality attributes are the target for the designer. This tool is called RARE (Reference Architecture Representation Environment). Barber and Graser state that quality attributes have an impact on each other and that not all of them can be maximised at the same time and, therefore, the designer must explicitly solve the conflicts that arise. The idea behind this study is that no single quality model can be established given that, for instance, flexibility or extensibility will negatively impact on performance and there are application domains where one or the other can be more important. As a matter of example, the study mentions reusability, extensibility, comprehensibility, and performance as the main quality attributes to work with, although it does not imply that others cannot be added.

As in the other models there are mappings that drive calculations from OO design metrics to quality attributes, but in this case the intermediate elements are OO knowledge elements: *heuristics* and *strategies* (as refactorings and design transformations that guide the application of heuristics). Thus, Barber and Graser incorporate OO knowledge not as a goal, as in Miller et al. (1999), but rather as a tool to achieve quality attribute enhancement. The quality attributes chosen by the designer and their associated importance weights are quality goals; the metrics calculate the degree of achievement of the heuristics, which are used to calculate the level of achievement of the goals. This tool uses strategies to help the designer to change design in order to increase certain heuristics, and the order in which they are suggested to the designer is driven by the goals.

Unfortunately the study talks about a tool still under construction and, in our searches, we have not seen further notice of it. No quantitative measures are given in the paper about the calculation of each heuristic, nor a list of heuristics and strategies is given for it; although promising, we must discard this study as incomplete.

Marinescu and Ratiu's Factor Strategy Model

In Marinescu and Ratiu (2004),yet another perspective is given, this time an indirect measurement of the quality is proposed, instead of measuring the quality of the design, Marinescu and Ratiu measure the lack of quality by detecting common design flaws. The model is comprised of OO metrics, design flaws and, finally, quality factors and goals. The first two set of elements are tied together through principles, rules, and heuristics and with them design flaws are quantified through *detection strategies*. Each quality factor has an associated formula for calculating its level from the set of design flaws (quantified from metrics through detection strategies) and the total quality is given by the quality goals chosen (ISO 9126 quality attributes such as maintainability or reliability) and the weight given to each one. Quality goals are divided into factors exactly as in ISO 9126, and the study refers to it and gives two example formulae for maintainability from its sub-factors (changeability, testability, analysability, and stability) exemplifying that different weights could be used for each subfactor according to experience. There are similar formulae to associate factors and detection strategies and the relative weights must be provided by the designers.

This is probably the most promising of all the selected studies since it takes into account OO knowledge as a tool for improvement and measurement of the design quality and establishes that quality is decomposed in general software quality attributes that can be derived from those knowledge elements. OO properties are not quantitatively present in the model, although there is a table identifying which design flaws impact on what properties (only coupling, cohesion, complexity, and encapsulation are listed).

We see that, on the one hand, quantification of the different mappings must be provided by the developer and, on the other hand, the design flaws (and detection strategies) are categorised according to the design component they are tied to; however, we see that OO knowledge is not properly classified and there are missing elements (only "bad smells" and some "patterns" are used). Probably a better ontology could be used as rules used instead of detection strategies, for that Garzás and Piattini (2005) could be used.

Conclusion and Future Work

With all the sources, primary, secondary, and discarded ones, we can conclude that studies dealing with OO quality evaluation and metrics can be classified as follows:

- True quality evaluation models based on quality attributes quantification
- Prediction models for a single or few OO properties or quality factors
- Design flaw detection methods and their associated refactorings or design transformations
- OO metrics suites

The first set is the one that interests us and can be further subdivided in models that favor specific quality indicators or those that propose a flexible model in which the user (i.e., designer or other stakeholder) must set the quality factors and their weights.

One important conclusion of our review is that maintainability is the most used high-level quality indicator, which is logical given that Object Orientation has been seen as a paradigm that favors flexibility and reuse. Other quality indicators or attributes, such as efficiency or portability are missing in the full models, which can be due to the fact that all the studies are biased by the fact that different application domains are not considered.

Surprisingly reliability is also very important in those studies that are just prediction models.

Only four studies establish a full quality evaluation model and, of them, no one establishes an explicit hierarchy between the high-level indicators. Two of the four studies are flexible models and three of the four use, partially, OO micro architecture knowledge.

In future works two main objective can be targeted, on the one hand, by trying to establish hierarchies between quality attributes, which may be according to different hierarchy sets corresponding to application domains, and on the other hand a better application of OO micro architecture knowledge in the construction of the evaluation methods through the use of ontologies.

References

Abran, A., James, W. M., Bourque, P., & Dupuis, R. (2004). *Guide to the software engineering body of knowledge. 2004 version.* SWEBOK: IEEE Press.

ACM Digital Library. (2005). Retrieved from http://portal.acm.org

Bansiya, J., & Davis, C. G. (2002). A hierarchical model for object-oriented design quality assessment. *IEEE Transaction on Software Engineering, 28*(1), 4.

Barber, K. S., & Graser, T. J. (2000). *Tool support for systematic class identification in object-oriented software architectures.* Paper presented at the 37th International Conference on Technology of Object-Oriented Languages and Systems, Sydney, NSW, Australia.

Basili, V. R., Briand, L. C., & Melo, W. L. (1996). A validation of object-oriented design metrics as quality indicators. *IEEE Transactions on Software Engineering, 22*(10), 751.

Briand, L. C., Wust, J., Daly, J. W., & Porter, D. (2000). Exploring the relationships between design measures and software quality in object-oriented systems. *Journal of Systems and Software, 51*(3), 245.

Brito e Abreu, F., & Melo, W. (1996). *Evaluating the impact of object-oriented design on software quality.* Paper presented at the Software Metrics Symposium, Berlin, Germany.

Brown, W. J., Malveau, R. C., Brown, W. H., McCormick, H. W., & Mowbray, T. J. (1998). *Antipatterns: Refactoring software, architectures and projects in crisis.* NY: John Wiley & Sons.

Chidamber, S. R., & Kemerer, C. F. (1991). *Towards a metrics suite for object-oriented design.* Paper presented at the OOPSLA '91, Conference Proceedings on Object-orientedProgramming Systems, Languages, and Applications, New York.

Deligiannis, I., Shepperd, M., Roumeliotis, M., & Stamelos, I. (2003). An empirical investigation of an object-oriented design heuristic for maintainability. *Journal of Systems and Software, 65*(2), 127.

Dumke, R. R., & Kuhrau, I. (1994). *Tool-based quality management in object-oriented software development.* Paper presented at the Symposium Assessment of Quality Software Development Tools, Washington, DC.

Fenton, N. E., & Pfleeger, S. L. (1998). *Software metrics: A rigorous and practical approach.* Boston: PWS Publishing Co.

Fowler, M. (2000). *Refactoring: Improving the design of existing code:* Addison-Wesley.

Gamma, E., Helm, R., Johnson, R., & Vlissides, J. (1995). *Design patterns: Elements of reusable object-oriented software.* Boston: Addison-Wesley Longman Publishing.

Garzás, J., & Piattini, M. (2005). An ontology for microarchitectural design knowledge. *IEEE Software, 22*(2), 28.

Henderson-Sellers, B., Constantine, L. L., & Graham, I. M. (1996). Coupling and cohesion (towards a valid metrics suite for object-oriented analysis and design). *Object-oriented Systems, 3,* 142-158.

Humphrey, W. S. (1989). *Managing the software process.* Boston: Addison-Wesley Longman Publishing.

Humphrey, W. S., Snyder, T. R., & Willis, R. R. (1991). Software process improvement at hughes aircraft. *IEEE Software, 8*(4), 11-23.

IEEE Digital Library. (2005). Retrieved from http://ieeexplore.ieee.org

ISO/IEC. (1999). *Information technology — software product evaluatiom — part 1: General overview.* Geneva, Switzerland: ISO/IEC.

ISO/IEC. (2001). *Software engineering — product quality — part 1: Quality model.* Geneva, Switzerland: ISO/IEC.

Journal of Systems and Software. (2005). Retrieved from http://ees.elsevier.com/jss/

Journal of Software Maintenance and Evolution. (2005). Retrieved from http://www3.interscience.wiley.com/cgi-bin/jhome/77004487

Kitchenham, B. (2004). *Procedures for performing systematic reviews* (Joint Tech. Rep. No. 0400011T.1): Keele University and Empirical Software Engineering National ICT Australia, Software Engineering Group, Department of Computer Science.

Li, W., & Henry, S. (1993). *Maintenance metrics for the object-oriented paradigm.* Paper presented at the Software Metrics Symposium, Baltimore, MD.

Marinescu, R., & Ratiu, D. (2004). *Quantifying the quality of object-oriented design: The factor-strategy model.* Paper presented at the 11th Working Conference on Reverse Engineering.

McCabe, T. J. (1976). A software complexity measure. *IEEE Transactions on Software Engineering, 2,* 308-320.

Miller, B. K., Hsia, P., & Kung, C. (1999). *Object-oriented architecture measures.* Paper presented at the Hawaii International Conference on System Sciences.

Oakland, J. S. (1990). *Statistical process control: A practical guide.* Oxford: Butterworth-Heineman.

Paulk, M., Curtis, B., Chrissis, M., & Weber, C. (1993). *Capability maturity model for software (version 1.1)* (Tech. Rep. No. CMU/SEI-93-TR-024). Carnegie Mellon University, Software Engineering Institute.

Purao, S., & Vaishnavi, V. (2003). Product metrics for object-oriented systems. *ACM Computer Survey, 35*(2), 191-221.

Riel, A. J. (1996). *Object-oriented design heuristics.* Reading, MA: Addison-Wesley.

Software design, part 2. (2004) *IEEE Software, 21*(6), c3.

Software: Practice and Experience. (2005). Retrieved from http://www3.intersci ence.wiley.com/cgi-bin/jhome/1752

Subramanyam, R., & Krishnan, M. S. (2003). Empirical analysis of ck metrics for object-oriented design complexity: Implications for software defects. *IEEE Transactions on Software Engineering, 29*(4), 297.

Chapter X

A Catalog of Design Rules for OO Micro-Architecture

Javier Garzás, Oficina de Cooperación Universitaria (OCU) S.A., Spain

Mario Piattini, University of Castilla - La Mancha, Spain

Abstract

This chapter presents a catalog of different rules for help to design object-oriented micro-architectures. These rules form an important part of the object-oriented design knowledge. Rules, like patterns, or accumulated knowledge, are discovered, not invented.

Introduction

This catalog unifies, completes, and formats under the term "rule": principles, bad smells, best practices, and so on. These rules are applicable to object-oriented (OO) micro-architectural design, according to the OO design knowledge ontology presented in Chapter II.

For the description of a rule, the catalog takes as a base the sections which Gamma, Helm, Johnson & Vlissides (1995) use to describe a pattern, generalizing and detailing these sections (see Chapter II).

The relationships of rules with patterns and refactorings come under the following categories:

- **Implies the use of [patterns]:** Patterns that are necessary in a design resulting from the application of a rule. These patterns solve design problems of the new micro-architecture.

- **Is introduced by [refactorings]:** Refactorings or operations, which place the rule on the micro- architecture.

On the other hand, another important issue is that each rule is identified by a meaningful name. We have been careful in the choice of these names, in order to help the designer to identify speedily where and when a rule is violated. So, we have avoided names which may be attention-catching but which are not very meaningful (as happens, for instance with bad smells (Fowler, Beck, Brant, Opdyke, & Roberts, 2000) with names such as Lazy Class or Shotgun Surgery. Therefore, the rules are named according to their antecedent.

If There are Dependencies on Concrete Classes

Intent

Depends on interfaces or abstract classes rather than on concrete elements.

Also Known As

Dependency inversion principle (DIP) (Martin, 1996)

Program to an interface, not an implementation (Gamma, Helm, Johnson, & Vlissides, 1995).

Figure 1. Procedural architecture

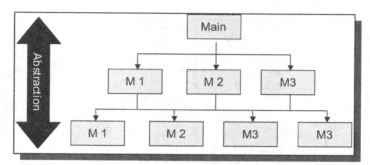

Motivation

This rule is set out by Martin (1996), and in a shorter version by Gamma et al. (1995).

It recommends the strategy of depending on interfaces or abstract classes more than on concrete elements.

The structured design shows a particular type of dependency. As Figure 1 shows, the structures go from a high level of detail down to a low level of detail. The high-level modules depend on those of a lower level, and these in turn depend on others even lower, and so on. This type of dependence makes the structures weak. The high-level modules deal with policies with a low level of application. In general, these policies have little to do with details of how they are implemented. Therefore, why do modules at a high level depend directly on implementation modules?

An OO architecture shows a structure in which the greater part of dependencies point to abstractions. Moreover, the modules that contain implementation details depend on abstractions and these are not depended on themselves. The dependency has been inverted (see Figure 2).

This rule implies that each dependency should have an interface or an abstract class as its objective, avoiding dependencies on concrete classes. Concrete elements change a lot, while abstract elements change to a much lesser degree. Therefore, abstractions are "hinges," and they represent places where the design may curve or extend without being modified.

Even though, sometimes the use of this rule may be excessive; for example, the class Array is very concrete and not volatile, and we do not need to apply this rule.

Figure 2. Dependency in OO micro-architecture

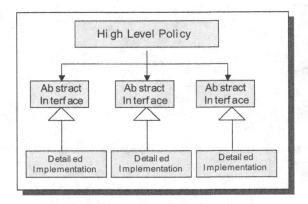

Recommendation

IF there are dependencies on concrete classes
THEN these dependencies should be on abstractions.

Applicability

Use this rule when:

* You find dependencies (associations) on concrete classes, which could change.

Do not use this rule when:

* Even if there is a dependency on a concrete class, this class could seldom change (for example, class libraries from the programming environment, such as Array or Integer)

Structure

See Figure 3.

Figure 3. Structures of if there are dependencies on concrete classes

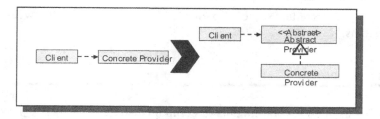

Participants

Client class, initially associated with the concrete provider class, dependent on the abstract provider class.

Abstract provider, an abstract entity with the interface of the concrete provider class.

Concrete provider, a concrete class with the services and methods that the client uses.

Collaborations

The client class depends on the abstract entity and the provider class has the task of implementing the services of the abstract provider class.

Consequences

This rule has the following consequences:

- The introduction of abstractions by which the design may be extended without being modified.
- The limiting of the impact of the variations in the design.
- All the subclasses can thus respond to the requests from the interface, making all of these subtypes of the abstract class.
- Clients are not aware of the specific types of the objects they use, as long as the objects are in line with the interface that the clients expect.

- Clients are not aware of the classes that these objects implement, they only know about the abstract classes that define the interface.

- This greatly reduces the implementation dependencies between sub-systems.

Known Uses

This rule is used on several models of components (COM, CORBA, EJB, and so on). It may also be observed in many design patterns and frameworks.

Implies the Use of Patterns

One of the most common places where design depends on concrete classes is when instances are created. By definition, instances cannot be made from abstract classes. Creating instances, therefore, means depending on concrete classes. The concrete classes have to be instantiated (that is, a particular implementation must be specified) in some part of the system and the creational patterns (such as *abstract factory, builder, factory method, prototype, and Singleton* [Gamma et al., 1995]) allow just this. The creational patterns ensure that the system is designed according to interfaces and not according to implementations.

Introduced by Refactorings

As seen in the Fowler et al. (2000) catalog, this rule can be introduced with the following refactoring: Extract Interface.

If an Object Has Different Behavior According to Its Internal State

Intent

To avoid classes with behavior depending on the internal state of the class.

Also Known As

No other names have been found for this rule, although there is a "bad smell" known as "switch statements" (Fowler et al., 2000) with a similar objective.

Motivation

Riel (1996) talks about it in one of his heuristics: be sure that the abstractions that you model are classes and not simply the roles; the objects may change their role in run-time, and the state may indicate the role.

Sometimes, a class has different behavior (methods) according to its internal state (attribute values). In this situation it is characteristic to see a complex conditional logic, a lot of "if" or "switch" sentences, complex state diagrams, and so on. Therefore, to add new states and their transitions is complex, the transitions are not explicit, states are not localized, and so on. It is tedious to read and harder to maintain

A preferable option for dealing with these behaviors dependent on internal state is to place each one of these in a class, create an abstraction for these new classes, and make an association form the original class to the new abstract class. Hence, through polymorphism and in run-time the necessary behavior will be chosen.

Recommendation

> **If** an object has different behavior according to its internal state
> **Then** Place each one of these behaviors in a separate class.

Applicability

Use this rule when:

- A class has different behavior according to its internal state.

Structure

Does not apply.

Participants

Does not apply.

Collaborations

Does not apply.

Consequences

This rule has the following consequences:

* Adding a new state and their transitions is easy.
* The transitions between states are explicit.
* The states can be shared.
* It increases the maintainability as it increases the analyzability and stability.
* The class population is increased.

Known Uses

This rule can be seen in many patterns, frameworks, and software systems.

Implies the Use of [Patterns]

The patterns state and strategy (Gamma et al., 1995) are ideal for solving the violation of this rule.

Is Introduced by [Refactorings]

Does not apply.

If a Hierarchy of Classes
Has Too Many Levels

Intent

To avoid large hierarchies which are difficult to maintain.

Also Known As

No other names for this rule were found.

Motivation

Riel (1996) comments that inheritance hierarchies should not have a depth that is greater than the number of classes that a person can hold in his or her short-term memory, where a typical value is around six. Gamma et al. (1995) recommend using solutions based on composition as opposed to inheritance.

The two most common techniques for re-using functionality in OO systems are the inheritance of classes and the composition of objects. Re-use through inheritance (it is also known as "white box" reuse) is characterized by visibility, since many internal aspects of parent classes are visible to the subclasses. The composition of objects is an alternative to the inheritance of classes, where new functionalities are obtained by composing objects. This other style of re-use is also known as "black box," since no internal aspects are visible.

Inheritance of classes is defined at compilation time, and it has the following disadvantages:

- The inheritance relationships cannot be changed in run time, since this relationship is static and it is defined at compilation time.

- The inheritance can break the encapsulation. Many languages provide a protected level of visibility (in addition to public and private). Attributes and methods that are marked as protected are hidden from a client class but, however, are available from sub classes, and these sub classes have access to implementation details. This is another kind of hard dependency.

If inheritance is over used, flexibility and reusability can be reduced (this is one of the reasons because it is recommended only to inherit from abstract classes or interfaces, since these give little, or never, implementation details).

The composition of objects is defined in run-time; if an object implements a specific interface, it can be replaced in run-time by any compatible type. Any compatible type can be replaced in run-time. Adding new responsibilities to an object dynamically is an alternative to creating too many subclasses by inheritance.

Recommendation

>**If** a hierarchy of classes has too many levels
>**Then**
>>Reduce the level of inheritance using composition or redesign

Applicability

Use this rule when:

- An overuse of inheritance is observed.
- There are hierarchies with too many levels.

Structure

Does not apply.

Participants

Does not apply.

Collaborations

Does not apply.

Consequences

This rule has the following consequences:

- Using composition as opposed to inheritance increases the number of objects, thereby reducing the number of classes.
- It avoids rigidity in design.

Known Uses

This practice is common in any quality software system.

Implies the Use of [Patterns]

Composite and decorator (Gamma et al., 1995) are typical patterns for reducing and controlling inheritance hierarchies. Both patterns have similar structure diagrams based on composition, in order to organize an open and recurring number of objects.

Is Introduced by [Refactorings]

According to Fowler et al.'s (2000) catalog, this rule can be introduced, mainly, with the following refactoring: Collapse Hierarchy.

If There are Unused or Little Used Items

Intent

To avoid the existence of elements neither use nor usefulness.

Also Known As

No other names are known for this rule.

Motivation

The main reference to this rule is by Fowler et al. (2000); it is commented in a few lines in several of his bad smells ("lazy class," "middle man," and "speculative generality").

On many occasions, designs contain unused elements (such as attributes, classes, and so on). An example are the hierarchies with unused classes, these has been inserted for the future, classes that do nothing. These elements often appear subsequent to a process of refactoring or reengineering. On other occasions, it may also happen that there are elements in the design of low-level usability, such as classes which work as intermediaries.

These elements make it hard to maintain and understand the design. These elements make the design more complicated to understand, less easy to analyze, and thus less maintainable. We should not forget that every class has its development cost and its maintenance cost.

Recommendation

> **If** there are unused or little used items
> **Then**
> > Eliminate them.

Applicability

Use this rule when:

- A design contains unused elements.

Structure

Does not apply.

Participants

Does not apply.

Collaborations

Does not apply.

Consequences

This rule has the following consequences:

- Elements with no usability in the design disappear.
- The class population decreases.
- The design becomes easier to analyze and to understand —
- The design is more maintainable.

Known Uses

This practice is common in several software systems.

Implies the Use of [Patterns]

Does not apply.

Is Introduced by [Refactorings]

This rule can be introduced with any of the refactorings whose goal it is to eliminate elements. Fowler et al.'s (2000) catalog shows one of the refactorings most widely used to keep this rule: remove middle man.

If a Superclass Knows
Any of Its Subclasses

Intent

To avoid that a superclass knows any of its subclasses.

Also Known As

No other names are known for this rule.

Motivation

In this sense, (Riel, 1996) comments on his heuristic 5.2: *Derived classes must have knowledge about their base class by definition, but base classes should not know anything about their derived classes.*

This is a basic rule for a good application of OO, since if it is broken it has a direct impact on the polymorphism, and thus on the flexibility of the system.

By definition, a child class knows its parent class by the inheritance type association, and the subclass has access to the public or protected services defined in the superclass. When we have this structure, we have the basic scheme for the application of polymorphism, that is, clients on the superclass will be able to obtain the behavior of its subclasses without knowing any of these subclasses. For that reason, these subclasses may be easily substituted freely, even in run-time, without affecting to the client class of the superclass. This allows the behavior of the system to be changed in a flexible way. However, if a superclass knows its subclass the aforementioned advantages disappear, since these child class could not be substituted.

Recommendation

If a Superclass knows any of its subclasses
Then Eliminate it.

Applicability

Use this rule when:

- An association exists from a parent class to a child class.

Structure

Does not apply.

Participants

Does not apply.

Collaborations

Does not apply.

Consequences

This rule has the following consequences:

- It permits a flexible and scalable design.
- It allows the behavior of the services to be changed easily, by associating any subclass to the client class that requires the services.
- It increases the maintainability by increasing the ability of the system to change.

Known Uses

This rule can be observed in many design patterns, frameworks, and software systems.

Implies the Use of [Patterns]

If a class parent needs the services of a child class this can be done through strategies such as those presented by the state andstrategy patterns (Gamma et al., 1995). These introduce a level of indirection and apply delegation.

Is Introduced by [Refactorings]

Does not apply.

If a Class Collaborates with Too Many Others

Intent

To avoid classes with a high level of collaboration.

Also Known As

No other names are known for this rule.

Motivation

This is a typical rule, described by several authors and applied to various different levels of abstraction.

When a class has associations with many others, the maintenance of it in a change has a high cost. Any change will affect the associated class, which will need to be compiled again. A common solution to this problem is to put in an intermediary class.

Recommendation

If a class collaborates with too many others

Then reduce the number of collaborations.

Applicability

Use this rule when:

*   A class has associations with a large number of others class.

Structure

Does not apply.

Participants

Does not apply.

Collaborations

Does not apply.

Consequences

This rule has the following consequences:

*   It limits the impact caused when changes occur.
*   Coupling and collaborations are reduced.

Known Uses

This practice is common in any quality software system.

Implies the Use of [Patterns]

The facade pattern is a typical solution to this problem.

Is Introduced by [Refactorings]

Does not apply.

If a Change in an Interface
Has an Impact on Many Clients

Intent

To avoid using interfaces which provide support for many clients with different needs.

Also Known As

Interface segregation principle (ISP) (Martin, 1996).

Motivation

Some pieces of work refer to this rule, such as of those of Meyer (1997) and Martin (1996).

The general picture of the rule is the following: if there is an interface with various clients then make specific interfaces for each client. It is better to have many specific interfaces than to have a single general-purpose one.

Figure 4. Many dependencies in a single interface

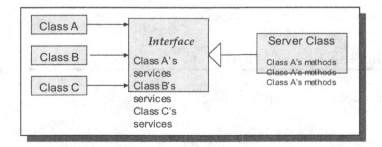

Figure 5. Application of ISP

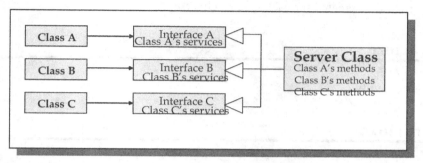

Figure 4 shows a class with many clients and a large interface to serve them. If a change is produced in one of the methods called up by client A, clients B and client C will be affected. This will mean the inevitable recompilation.

One technique for improving this situation is as shown in Figure 5. The methods that each client needs are placed in interfaces specific to that client. If client A's interfaces change, there is no need to touch client B and client C.

When the OO applications are maintained, the interfaces frequently change. When the modification of an interface may have a great impact, new interfaces should be added.

Recommendation

If a change in an interface has an impact on many clients
Then create specific interfaces for each client.

Applicability

Use this rule when:

• There is an interface with various clients, then, create specific interfaces for each client.

Do not use this rule when:

• This rule is not recommended for the purpose that each service have its own interface. Low cohesion might be detected if this principle had to be used widely. In the case that clients should be categorized by type the interfaces should be created for each type of client.

Structure

Does not apply.

Participants

Does not apply.

Collaborations

Does not apply.

Consequences

This rule has the following consequences:

* This rule allows classes and components to be more portable and useful.
* This rule reduces the impact of changes, by increasing quality due to the higher level of maintainability by the increasing of system stability.

Known Uses

This rule can be observed in many patterns, frameworks and software systems.

Implies the Use of [Patterns]

Does not apply.

Is Introduced by [Refactorings]

According to Fowler et al. (2000) catalog, this rule may be introduced with the following refactorings: extract interface.

If There is Not an Abstract Class Between an Interface and Its Implementation

Intent

To use implementations by default.

Also Known As

No other names are known for this rule.

Motivation

No references to this rule were found.

Interfaces contain a subset of operations without implementation. The difference between an interface and an abstract class is that the first one has no any operations with implementation or method.

If there is not an abstract class between an interface and its implementation classes, then it will occur that each one of the implementation classes will make the implementation of the services defined in the interface. In addition, if two or more implementation classes need the same implementation both will make duplicate code. This is usually solved by placing an abstract class, which implements by default the majority of the operations of the interface.

We could think about eliminating the interface and leaving only the abstract class. However, if future concrete subclasses not to want a default behavior, then it overwriting the abstract class's methods and it is not a good solution (see IF a Class Rejects Something that it Inherited).

Recommendation

If there is not an Abstract class between an interface and its implementation, Then create an abstract class with an implementation by default between the interface and the class that implements it.

Figure 6. Structure of abstraction by default

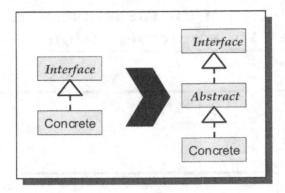

Applicability

Use this rule when:

Between an Interface and its implementation there is not an abstraction by default.

Participants

Does not apply.

Collaborations

Does not apply.

Consequences

This rule has the following consequences:

*   It eliminates the possibility of a duplicate code: all subclasses have a default implementation, such that each class does not need to create one.
*   It avoids concrete classes implementing services that are not their whole responsibility.

Known Uses

This rule can be observed in many patterns, frameworks, and software systems.

Implies the Use of [Patterns]

Does not apply.

Is Introduced by [Refactorings]

According to (Fowler et al., 2000)'s catalog states this rule can be introduced, mainly, with the following refactorings: extract interface, extract subclass, extract superclass, pull up field, pull up method, push down field, and push down method.

If a Superclass is a Concrete Class

Intent

To avoid the existence of concrete superclasses.

Also Known As

No other names are known for this rule.

Motivation

This rule is described briefly in Riel (1996) and in a somewhat broader form by Priestley (2001).

Let us look at an example to show the outworking and advantages of this rule. We take as our supposition the diagram of classes in Figure 7. In this Figure both classes are concrete (all their services have implementation or method) and the class "savings account" inherits and uses the operation "account maintenance charge."

Figure 7. Example of the " IF a superclass is a concrete class"

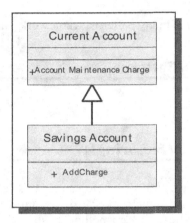

However, let us imagine that we need to make a change in the functionality that the "current account" class is giving and this implies a change in "account maintenance charge." The following solutions could be envisaged.

"Account maintenance charge" could be modified directly, but this is inherited by "savings account" and the savings account should not possess the new functionality.

We could overwrite the "account maintenance charge" operation, in "savings account" but this would be an artificial solution. It would result in a code replication and such a phenomenon is usually seen as a symptom of a failure in design (the "IF a class rejects something that it inherited" would be broken).

 "Account maintenance charge" could be designed to perform in different ways (in one way for the objects of "current account" and in another for those of "savings account"). But this would make explicit reference to a subclass, so that, when adding or eliminating subclasses, the code of "current account" should be modified [the class is not closed (open - closed) property (Meyer, 1997), and the violations of "IF a superclass" and "if an object has different behavior according to its internal state"].

The problem is that the superclass is performing two roles:

•   It is a superclass and is, therefore, defining an interface that all classes have to fulfill.
•   It is providing an interface implementation by default.

This conflict of roles happens when functionality (a method or behavior) is associated with objects of the superclass. The solution is to apply the "IF a superclass is a concrete class," thereby obtaining the following scheme, (to which a default abstraction should be added for it to be complete).

As Gamma et al. (1995) say, the inheritance of class is only a mechanism for extending the functionality of an application, re using the functionality of the parent classes. It allows the rapid defining of a new type of object, using a previous one. It permits us to achieve new applications. Nevertheless, the reuse of implementation is just a part. The ability of inheritance to define families of objects with identical interfaces (usually inheriting from an abstract class), is also important. Why? Because polymorphism is based on it.

When the inheritance is used appropriately, all classes derived from an abstract class share its interface. This implies that a subclass does not hide operations from a superclass.

Recommendation

> **If** a superclass is a concrete class
> **Then** re-structure to eliminate it.

Applicability

Use this rule when:

Figure 8. Solution to the conflict of roles

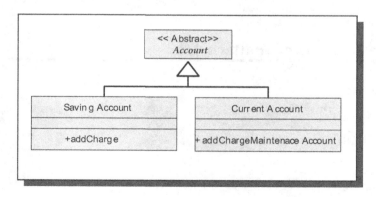

- You find concrete superclasses or (see consequences) an abstract class that is a child of a concrete one.

Structure

Does not apply.

Participants

Does not apply.

Collaborations

Does not apply.

Consequences

This rule has the following consequences:

- An abstract class can never be a child of a concrete one.
- The scalability of the system is not limited.

Known Uses

This rule can be observed in many patterns, frameworks and software systems, in essence in any design of quality.

Implies the Use of [Patterns]

Does not apply.

Is Introduced by [Refactorings]

According to Fowler et al.'s (2000) catalog this rule can be introduced, mainly, with the following refactorings: extract interface, extract subclass, extract superclass, pull up field, pull up method, push down field, and push down method.

IF a Service Has Many Parameters

Intent

To avoid services that have a large number of parameters which are not easy to understand and which increase the coupling.

Also Known As

Long parameter list (bad smell) (Fowler et al., 2000).

Minimize the number of messages in the protocol of a class (heuristic) (Riel, 1996).

Principle of Small Interfaces (Meyer, 1997).

Motivation

Regarding this area of problems, Fowler et al. (2000) give some brief remarks on how long lists of parameters are not necessary when working in OO.

This type of violation is frequently observed. It occurs when a set of data has to be passed to a class and it is decided to get a single method.

The main problem with these long lists of parameters is that they increase re-coupling and that they are hard to understand.

The solution to the problem is usually:

- Instead of having just a few services with lot of parameters, the tendency should be to have many services with few parameters.
- If it is not possible to separate this data, it is preferable to get a class with all of these.

Recommendation

If a service has many parameters

Then create various methods, reducing the list or put these into an object.

Applicability

Use this rule when:

- You come across a long list of parameters. There should not be more than four parameters in one service.

Structure

Does not apply.

Participants

Does not apply.

Collaborations

Does not apply.

Consequences

This rule has the following consequences:

- A reduction of the coupling of the client class with the provider class.
- A reduction of the lists of parameters and calls to methods.
- It increases quality because it raises maintainability, in the sense that it makes the system more stable when it faces changes.

Known Uses

The use of this rule can be seen in the library classes of popular platforms such as Java.

Implies the Use of [Patterns]

Does not apply.

Is Introduced by [Refactorings]

According to Fowler et al.'s (2000) catalog, this rule can be introduced with the following refactorings: replace parameter with method, introduce parameter object, and preserve whole object.

IF a Class is Too Large

Intent

To avoid large classes which have little cohesion.

Also Known As

Large class (bad smell) (Fowler et al., 2000).

The single responsibility principle (Martin, 1996)

Motivation

This rule is one of the earliest. It was described a long time ago by DeMarco (1979) and Page-Jones (1998) and more recently by Fowler et al. (2000), Riel (1996), and Martin (1996).

The non-fulfilling of this rule may be detected when classes with many services and which have a low level of cohesion are observed, or ones which have a lot of instance variables.

It also tends to be a product of functional design, in which a main class with an important responsibility appears.

The problem with this is the complicated maintainability. Martin (1996) highlights how a class should change for just one single reason. If a change of business or domain makes a class change, then changes in the BBDD scheme, the user interface, and so on, should not imply a change for the class. Each responsibility should be in a separate class, since each responsibility can be a change.

Recommendation

If a class is too large
Then reduce its size by sharing out functionality over other classes.

Applicability

Use this rule when:

- Others use a class with a large number of services.
- There are services with little cohesion.

Structure

Does not apply.

Participants

Does not apply.

Collaborations

Does not apply.

Consequences

This rule has the following consequences:

- The number of system classes increases.
- The classes have greater cohesion.
- The system is more maintainable, since changes are localized. The system is more stable.

Known Uses

This practice is common in any quality software system.

Implies the Use of [Patterns]

Does not apply.

Is Introduced by [Refactorings]

According to Fowler et al.'s (2000) catalog, this rule can be introduced with the following refactorings: extract class, extract subclass, extract superclass, extractinterface, and replace data value with object.

If Any Element of the User Interface are in Domain Entities

Intent

To avoid that domain classes having elements whose objective is how the information is represented.

Also Known As

No other names are known for this rule.

Motivation

There are many reference works that discuss this rule; the brevity of these texts have encouraged us to produce a description of this rule.

This is a rule that was formulated quite some time ago and is well known. It is, moreover, one of the most important. It is usually dealt with in nearly all the levels of abstraction in the design; it is even at the heart of technologies such as XML (which aims to separate content from presentation).

The business elements belong to a different domain from that of the elements of the user interface. Both domains work together but they should be as independent of each other as possible, to such an extent that they are at times even developed as paradigms and technologies that are very different. Thus, for example, the business domain can be based on OO and the presentation or interface of the user of the same can be developed with html type technology or by voice recognition. In general, in an information system, the most important part of the design and development is the one that models the business rules, that is, how a system works and how it behaves. If we fuse the presentation domain with business, we create a high level of dependency in both. Thus, if a change in the presentation should affect the business logic, it would be complicated to include another way of presentation, and so forth. Any design-code that works with a user interface should only involve the code of the user interface. The user interface could take an input from the user space and show the information, but it ought not to handle more information than is necessary for making the transformations in the information.

The point is that business rules have nothing to do with how the results are shown or how data is given to them.

When the domain presentation is separated, you have to ensure that no part of the domain refers to the presentation code. If an application is being written with a graphical user interface (GUI), you should be able to write an interface in character mode.

Recommendation

If any element of the user interface are in domain entities
Then place these elements in a separate entity.

Applicability

Use this rule when:

- Elements (services, attributes, etc.) which correspond to the user interface (views or presentation) are in domain elements.

Structure

Does not apply.

Participants

User interface elements whose main responsibility must be the interaction with the users.

New class or modules, which take up the responsibility of everything that has to do with the user interface.

Collaborations

When removing elements from the class that contains them and passing them to another, collaboration between these two should be established. This collaboration should be done with as little re-coupling as possible since a domain class should never possess knowledge about the layer of the user interface. To ensure this, the strategies described in the section "implies the use of patterns" will be employed.

Consequences

This rule has the following consequences:

- Introduction of specific modules which save, and are responsible for, whatever relates to user interface.

- Separation of design into various areas of complexity. A large amount of presentations mean complex programming, a set of particular libraries, and so forth. The changes demanded for presentation normally happen at a rate that is different from that occurring in the domain.

- Availability of a number of presentations for the same domain. The domain is usually more platform-portable while the presentation tends to depend more on the operative system or on the hardware.

- Avoiding of code duplication, since, for example, different screens require a similar validation logic which should not be duplicated.

- Maintainability is increased.

Known Uses

This rule can be seen in many patterns, frameworks and software systems.

Implies the Use of [Patterns]

The application of this rule will require the use of design patterns, which make a decoupling between the class that did contain user interface elements and the class that now contains elements of the user interface. The patterns that are normally used are the observer, command, mediator, and chain of responsibility (Gamma et al., 1995).

Is Introduced by [Refactorings]

According to Fowler et al.'s (2000) catalog, this rule can be introduced, mainly, with the following refactorings: move method, extract method, and duplicate observer data. Fowler et al.'s (2000) catalog shows a refactorings known as "separate domain from presentation," which is also applicable in this rule, and the refactoring "hide presentation tier-specific details from business tier" by Alur, Malks & Crupi (2003).

If a Class Uses More Things from Another Class Than from Itself

Intent

To avoid that the intelligence of one class is distributed.

Also Known As

Feature envy (bad smell) (Fowler et al., 2000).

Motivation

This rule is described in part and briefly in (Fowler et al., 2000).

It sometimes happens that a method in a class uses a greater quantity of things from another than from itself. This increases the number of calls and the impact of the changes. The violation of this rule indicates that the method is not correctly placed. When this occurs, the solution is to pass the method to the class from which it takes the greatest part of the things that it needs to work.

Intent

> **If** a class uses more things from another class than from itself
> **Then** pass these things to the class that uses them most.

Applicability

Use this rule when:

> You see a method that uses or needs more things from another class than from the one to which it belongs.

Structure

Does not apply.

Participants

Does not apply.

Collaborations

Does not apply.

Consequences (Consequences)

This rule has the following consequences:

> It raises the quality of maintenance, increasing the stability of the system, since the impact of the changes will be less.
>
> Increasing the cohesion.

Known Uses

This practice is common in any quality software system and can be observed in design patterns.

(Implies the Use of Patterns)

Does not apply.

Is Introduced by [Refactorings]

According to Fowler et al.'s (2000) catalog, this rule can be introduced with the following refactorings: move method and extract method.

If a Class Rejects Something That It Inherited

Intent

To avoid rejecting what the classes inherit from the superclasses.

Also Known As

Refused bequest (bad smell) (Fowler et al., 2000).

Motivation

No explicit reference to this rule has been found in the literature. Riel (1996) in one of his heuristics says: "it should be illegal for a derived class to invalidate the method of a base class, for example, with a method that doesn't do anything"; and the brief description given by Fowler et al. (2000) in their "bad smell" "refused bequest"; and the mention of Liskov and Zilles (1974).

This rule can be observed in subclasses which only use a little of what their parent classes offer them, or even have to reject it. Generally, this means that the inheritance is badly applied. The violation of this rule produces an overload in the classes, designs that are hard to understand (maintenance costs), and classes that present services with no concrete answer.

Recommendation

> **If** a class rejects something that it inherited
> **Then** avoid it, generally for delegation.

Applicability

Use this rule when:

> A subclass inherits a service for which it cannot give an answer, and it has to annul it or rewrite it.

Structure

Does not apply.

Participants

Does not apply.

Collaborations

Does not apply.

Consequences

This rule has the following consequences:

* A more compressible design.
* Smaller classes.

Known Uses

This practice is common in any quality software system.

Implies the Use of [Patterns]

Does not apply.

Is Introduced by [Refactorings]

Fowler et al.'s (2000) catalog says that this rule can be introduced with any of
the refactorings whose objective is to restructure inheritance relationship:
extract interface, extract class, extract superclass, replace inheritance with
delegation, pull up method, and so on.

If the Attributes of a Class are Public or Protected

Intent

To avoid access to the attributes of an object.

Also Known As

No other concrete names are known for this rule.

Motivation

Many authors have quoted this rule, but the justification is not always clearly described. Riel (1996) gives some brief comments in his heuristic 2.1 "all data should be hidden within its class", heuristic 5.3 "all data in a base class should be private, i.e. do not use protected data", and heuristic 9.2 "do not change the state of an object without going through its public interface."

Why should there be no access to the attributes of an object? The attributes should not know the attributes for various reasons:

If a client class accedes to the internal data structure of a provider class, this last one will never be able to change this data structure. For example, if age is stored in a simple structure (for example, an integer) and if in the future we wish to store the last 10 ages, with an array being the best option, we will have to change and look for all the clients, who in addition will have to change the way they access the piece of data.

The way to obtain information is known only by the provider class. An object can give us out the age and yet not have it calculated. If there is an age attribute and we read it, nobody takes responsibility for its being updated. For example, only the date of birth might be stored. Not using methods of access to attributes implies knowing what information the object stores. There is information stored by the object and there is other information that it calculates when it is required.

Making attributes private also avoids the appearance of centralized structures of data from which everything depends. This is one of the problems of structured programming.

We cannot forget that one thing is object attributes and another is the information that objects may give:

Information that the object may provide = attributes and calculations with the attributes.

Recommendation

If the attributes of a vlass are public or protected
Then make them private and access to them through services.

Applicability

Use this rule when:

* There are public or protected attributes.

Structure

Does not apply.

Participants

Does not apply.

Collaborations

Does not apply.

Consequences

This rule has the following consequences:

* Dependencies on attributes are eliminated.
* All access should be done through services.
* Maintainability is increased as the system stability becomes greater.

Known Uses

This practice is common in any quality software system.

Implies the Use of [Patterns]

Does not apply.

Is Introduced by [Refactorings]

This rule can be introduced by restructuring how attributes are accessed. Besides, according to Fowler et al.'s (2000) catalog, the following refactorings could be applied: hide method, encapsulate field, encapsulate collection, move method, move field, change bi-directional association to unidirectional, replace inheritance with delegation, and hide delegate.

References

Alur, D., Malks, D., & Crupi, J. (2003). *Core J2EE™ patterns: Best practices and design strategies* (2nd ed.). Saddle River, NJ: Prentice Hall.

DeMarco, T. (1979). *Structured analysis and system specification.* Englewood Cliffs, NJ: Yourdon Press.

Fowler, M., Beck, K., Brant, J., Opdyke, W., & Roberts, D. (2000). *Refactoring: Improving the design of existing code.* Boston: Addison-Wesley Professional.

Gamma, E., Helm, R., Johnson, R., & Vlissides, J. (1995). *Design patterns.* Addison-Wesley Professional.

Liskov, B. H., & Zilles, S. N. (1974). Programming with abstract data types. *SIGPLAN Notices, 9*(4), 50-59.

Martin, R. C. (1996). The dependency inversion principle. *C++ Report, 8*(6), 61-66.

Meyer, B. (1997). *Object-oriented software construction* (2nd ed.). NJ: Prentice Hall.

Page-Jones, M. (1998). *The practical guide to structured systems design* (2nd ed.). Englewood Cliffs, NJ: Yourdon Press.

Priestley, M. (2001). *Practical object-oriented design with UML*. London: McGraw-Hill.

Riel, A. J. (1996). *Object-oriented design heuristic*. Boston: Addison-Wesley Professional.

About the Authors

Javier Garzás (javierg@ocu.es * or jgarzas@gmail.com) is the chief technology officer (CTO) at Oficina de Cooperación Universitaria (OCU) S.A., Madrid, Spain. Additionally, he is a lecturer at Rey Juan Carlos University. Due to his experiences at several important companies, his research and software engineering skills cover areas such as OO design, CMM, software process, and project management. He earned his MSc and PhD degrees in computer science from the University of Castilla - La Mancha, Spain. He also has a master's degree in enterprise application integration.

Mario Piattini (Mario.Piattini@uclm.es) is a full professor at the University of Castilla - La Mancha, Spain, where he leads the Alarcos Research Group. His research interests include advanced database design, database quality, software metrics, object-oriented metrics, and software maintenance. He earned his MSc and the PhD degrees in computer science from the Polytechnic University of Madrid, an MSc in psychology at UNED, and CISA and CISM by the ISACA.

* * *

Deepak Advani earned a master's degree in advanced information systems from Birkbeck, London, UK (2004). He is currently an independent researcher attached to the School of Computer Science and Information Systems at Birkbeck. Advani has previously worked as a developer in the software industry. His research interests are in the Java programming language, refactoring, and software tools.

Manoli Albert is a PhD student in the Department of Information Systems and Computation (DISC) at the Valencia University of Technology, Spain, where she is also an assistant professor of advanced software design. She is a member of the OO-Method Research Group (http:\\oomethod.dsic.upv.es). Her main research subject is the study of the association abstraction in analysis and design levels. She has published several works on this topic in different conferences and workshops. Other research interests are model-driven development, design patterns and Web engineering.

Alejandra Cechich is an adjunct professor and head of the Research Group on Software Engineering (GIISCO: http://giisco.uncoma.edu.ar) at the University of Comahue, Argentina. Her interests are centered on object and component technology and their use in the systematic development of software systems. She received an MSc in computer science from the University of South Argentina, and a PhD in informatics from the University of Castilla - La Mancha, Spain.

Steve Counsell is a lecturer in the School of Computing, Information Systems, and Mathematics at Brunel University, UK, which he joined in November 2004. Dr. Counsell earned a PhD in software engineering from Birkbeck, London (2002) where he was a lecturer. Between 1996 and 1998, Dr. Counsell worked as a research fellow at Southampton University. Dr. Counsell's research interests focus on metrics, refactoring, and empirical studies.

Yania Crespo is a lecturer at the Universidad de Valladolid, Spain. She received a BS and an MSc in computer science at the University of Havana (Cuba) in 1995 and a PhD at University of Valladolid in 2000. She is currently leading the GIRO (software reuse and object-orientation) research group at this university. Her research interest is focused on software refactoring, refactoring opportunities detection, refactoring inference, refactoring operation definition, formal and tool support for refactoring, and language independency. She is the author and co-author of works published in the *Journal of Object-Oriented Programming, LNCS,* as well as presented at conferences such as TOOLS, OOIS, and so forth.

Isabel Díaz is an associate professor of the Central University of Venezuela, Venezuela. She earned an MSc degree in computer science and a specialist degree in information systems from this university. Her research interests include requirements engineering, natural language processing, knowledge management, ontology engineering, information systems, and software automatic production. She is a candidate for a PhD in computer science at the Technical University of Valencia, Spain. She is a member of the Logic Programming & Software Engineering Research Group of this university and of the TOOLS Research Laboratory of the Central University of Venezuela.

Andrés Flores is an assistant professor and a member of the GIISCO Group at the University of Comahue, Argentina. His interests are centered on verification, component-based system, software architectures, and object-oriented applications. He received an MSc in computer science from the University of South, Argentina, and he is currently a PhD candidate at the University of Castilla - La Mancha, Spain.

Yann-Gaël Guéhéneuc is an assistant professor with the Department of Computer Science and Operations Research (software engineering group) of the University of Montreal, Canada. He holds a PhD in software engineering from the University of Nantes, France (under Professor Pierre Cointe's supervision) since 2003 and an Engineering Diploma from Ecole des Mines of Nantes since 1998. His PhD thesis was funded by Object Technology International, Inc. (now IBM OTI Labs), where he worked in 1999 and 2000. His research interests are program understanding and program quality during development and maintenance, in particular through the use and the identification of recurring patterns. He is interested also in empirical software engineering and in software laws and theories. He has published many papers at international conferences and leads the Ptidej project, a tool suite to evaluate and enhance the quality of object-oriented programs by promoting the use of patterns.

Jean-Yves Guyomarc'h graduated from the EPUNSA (École Polytechnique de l'Université de Nice Sophia-Antipolis, France) in 2004, where he received an engineer degree in computer science. He is currently a master's student in software engineering at the Department of Informatics and Operations Research, University of Montreal, Canada. His research focuses on aspect-oriented programming and quality.

Youssef Hassoun earned a PhD from Birkbeck, London (2005) investigating the reflection model in Java. He is currently a researcher in the School of

Computer Science and Information Systems at Birkbeck. Previously, Dr. Hassoun has worked in the software industry as a developer and project manager. His research interests are Java and programming paradigms. Dr. Hassoun also holds a PhD in mathematical physics from King's College, London, UK.

Khashayar Khosravi received his bachelor's degree and is currently a a master's student in software engineering in the Department of Informatics and Operations Research of the University of Montreal, Canada. His research focuses on the quality of object-oriented programs and the use of patterns to assess the architectural quality of programs. He has published articles on the use of design patterns and metrics to assess the quality of program architectures.

Carlos López received his BS from Universidad de Valladolid, Spain, in 2000. He has been a lecturer at the Universidad de Burgos, Spain, since 1999. He is a PhD student and has been a member of the GIRO Research Group (Universidad de Valladolid) since 2003. This group is focused on systematic reuse in software system development. His research is focused on defining a refactoring engine and repository which executes refactoring by transforming instances of a metamodel. He is validating UML as a metamodel to store the programming language characteristics.

Raúl Marticorena received his BS degree from the Universidad de Valladolid, Spain, in 2000. He has been a lecturer at the Universidad de Burgos, Spain, since 2002. He is a PhD student and has been a member of the GIRO Research Group (University of Valladolid) since 2003. This group is focused on systematic reuse in software system development. His research is focused on refactoring, language independence, and refactoring inference. Currently, he is working on the relations between metrics and bad smells to infer refactoring opportunities.

María Esperanza Manso Martínez is TEU professor with the Department of Computer Language and Systems Universidad de Valladolid, Spain. She has a major in mathematics from the Universidad de Valladolid. She is currently working toward her PhD. She is especially interested in the software maintenance and reuse experimentation. Her works have been accepted in several international congresses (OOIS, CAISE, METRICS,ISESE).

Alfredo Matteo is a full professor in the School of Computer Science, Faculty of Science, Central University of Venezuela (UCV), Venezuela. He received his PhD in computer science from the Paul Sabatier University (Toulouse, France).

He coordinates the TOOLS Research Laboratory of the Science Faculty of the UCV. His research includes software engineering environments and architectures, methodologies and standards for software development, requirements specification, and model driven development. Dr. Matteo has participated in numerous international and national research projects and he has been included in scientific committees of several journals, conferences, and workshops.

Lidia Moreno is an associate professor of the Department of Information Systems and Computation of the Technical University of Valencia, Spain. She holds a PhD in computer science of this university (1993) and an MSc in computer science of the Deusto University, Bilbao-Spain (1982). She is the leader of the Natural Language Processing Group of the Technical University of Valencia, and of several research projects of the Spanish Research Funding Agency, and other European foundations. Research activities include question answering, information retrieval, semantic-syntactic-lexical ambiguity, and the application of natural language processing (NLP) to the information systems. She has published numerous papers in international conference proceedings, books, and international journals including *Computational Linguistics Journal, Machine Translation, Recent Advances in Natural Language Processing,* and *Proceedings of ACL*, Colling and of the others international events. She has been secretary of SEPLN, the Spain association of NLP (2005-2006).

Javier Muñoz is a PhD student in the Department of Informations Systems and Computation (DSIC) at the Valencia University of Technology, Spain. His research interests are model driven development, pervasive systems, model transformations, and software factories. He is a member of the OO-Method Research Group, and he has published contributions to international events like CAiSE and MOMPES. His PhD presents a method based on the MDA and the Software Factories proposals for the development of pervasive systems.

Juan José Olmedilla received an MSc in computer science from the Polytechnic University of Madrid, Spain, and is working toward a PhD. He is currently a technical director with Almira Labs (Spain). He has been working for nine years developing software for the telecommunications sector of different companies (Spain and UK), using object oriented languages and patterns. Among his current interests are CMMi and distributed systems programming.

Oscar Pastor is the head of the Department of Information Systems and Computation of the Technical University of Valencia, Spain. He obtained a PhD in computer science from this university (1992). He is the author of over 100 research papers in conference proceedings, journals, and books, and he has received numerous research grants from public institutions and private industry. His research activities focus on Web engineering, object-oriented conceptual modeling, requirements engineering, information systems and model-based software production. Dr. Pastor is leader of the project, undertaken since 1996 by the Valencia University of Technology and CONSOFT S.A., that has originated the Oliva Nova Model Execution, an advanced MDA-based tool that produces a final software product starting from a conceptual schema where the system requirements are captured. Within this tool scope, he is responsible for the research team working from the university on the improvement of the underlying framework. He is a member of over 50 scientific committees of well-known international conferences and workshops, a member of several editorial boards of journals and book series, and he has been a participant researcher in national and international research projects and has been invited to give conferences in different universities and research centers.

Vicente Pelechano is an associate professor in the Department of Information Systems and Computation (DISC) at the Valencia University of Technology, Spain. His research interests are Web engineering, conceptual modeling, requirements engineering, software patterns, Web services, pervasive systems and model driven development. He received his PhD from the Valencia University of Technology in 2001. He is currently teaching software engineering, design and implementation of Web services, component-based software development, and design patterns at the Valencia University of Technology. He is a member of the OO-Method Research Group at the DISC. He has published in several well-known scientific journals (*Information Systems, Data & Knowledge Engineering, Information and Software Technology,* etc.), and international conferences (ER, CAiSE, WWW, ICWE, DEXA, etc.). He is a member of scientific committees of well-known international conferences and workshops such as as CAiSE, ICWE, ICEIS, ACM MT and IADIS.

Marta Ruiz is a PhD student in the Department of Information Systems and Computation (DISC) at the Valencia University of Technology, Spain. Her research interests are Web engineering, Web services, conceptual modeling and model-driven development. She is a member of the OO-Method Research group, and she has published several contributions to international conferences. Her PhD is presenting a methodological guide to design Web services from conceptual models.

Rodrigo Ruiz is an assistant professor and a member of the GIISCO group at the University of Comahue, Argentina. His interests are centered on object and component development. He is currently a postgraduate student at University of Comahue, Argentina.

Houari Sahraoui has been a professor of software engineering at DIRO, University of Montreal, Canada, since 1999. Previously, he worked as principal researcher and team leader of the software engineering group at CRIM, Montreal. His interests are the use of AI techniques to software engineering, metrics and software quality, and reengineering. He wrote more than 60 conference and workshop papers and published two books. He was on the program committees of many prestigious conferences (ASE, ECOOP, METRICS), a member of the reading committee of two journals, and the organizers of many workshops, including the annual Quantitative Approches in Object-Oriented Software Engineering" workshop since 1998. He was general chair of the IEEE Automated Software Engineering Conference, 2003.

Index

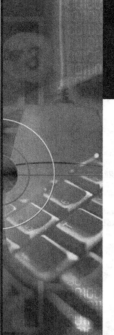

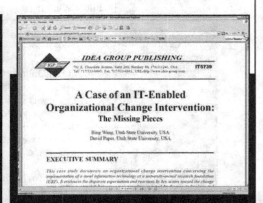